AF352281

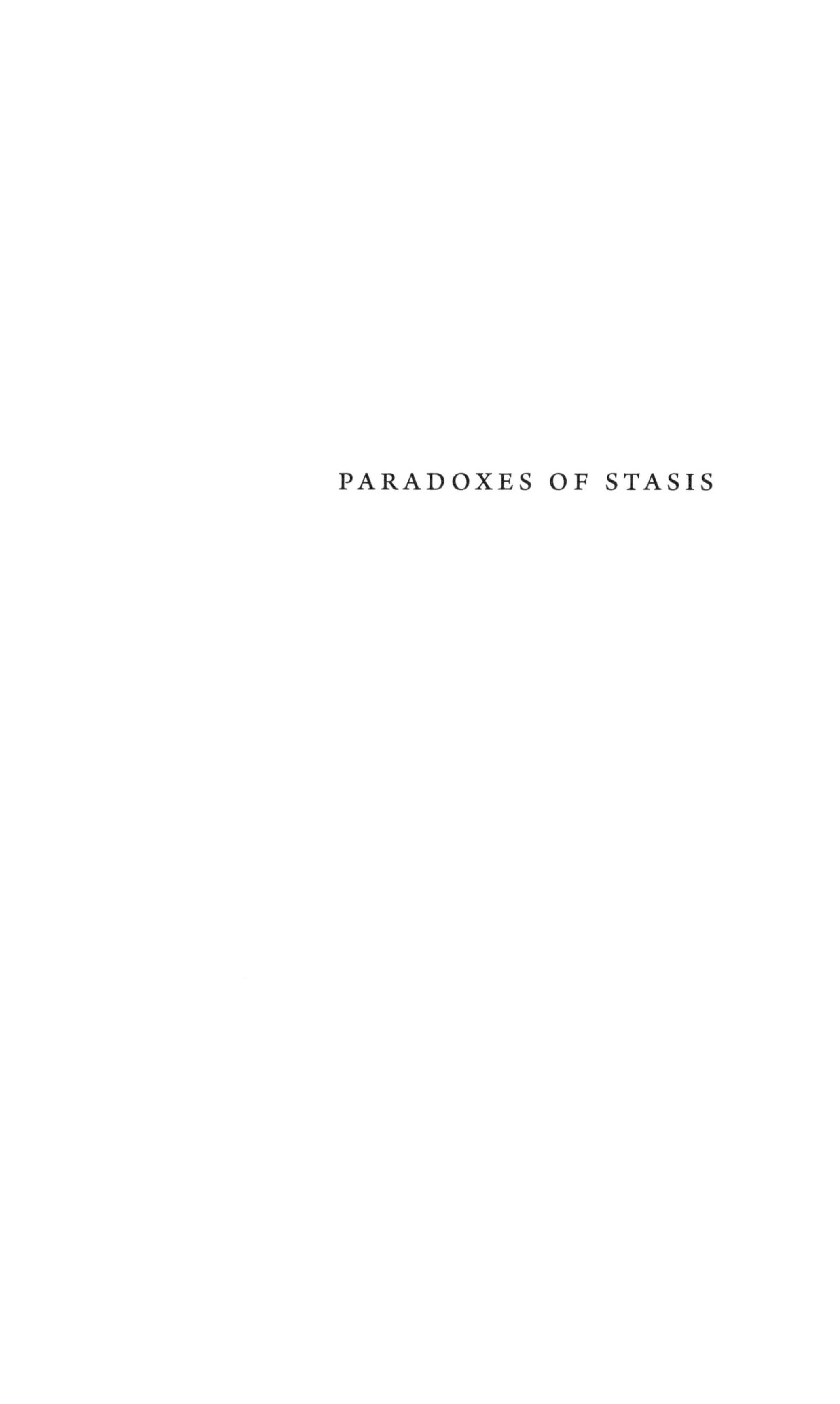

PARADOXES OF STASIS

PARADOXES OF STASIS

Literature, Politics, and
Thought in Francoist Spain

TATJANA GAJIĆ

UNIVERSITY OF NEBRASKA PRESS   *Lincoln and London*

A portion of chapter 1 was originally published as
"Francoist Legality: Crisis of Authority and the
Limits of Liberalism in Jesus Fueyo and Jose Ortega
y Gasset" in *The European Legacy* 13, no. 2 (2008):
161–74. © International Society for the Study of
European Ideas, reprinted by permission of Taylor
& Francis Ltd, www.tandfonline.com on behalf of
International Society for the Study of European Ideas.

A portion of chapter 2 was originally published
as "Dionisio Ridruejo's Anabasis: Politics and the
Double Movement of the Sea in 'Elegia ante la mar'"
in *Journal of Spanish Cultural Studies* 13, no. 3 (2012):
217–33. https://www.tandfonline.com/loi/cjsc20.

Library of Congress Cataloging-in-Publication Data
Names: Gajić, Tatjana, 1964– author.
Title: Paradoxes of stasis: literature, politics, and
thought in Francoist Spain / Tatjana Gajić.
Description: Lincoln: University of Nebraska
Press, 2019. | Series: New Hispanisms | Includes
bibliographical references and index.
Identifiers: LCCN 2018022543
ISBN 9781496208422 (cloth: alk. paper)
ISBN 9781496212993 (epub)
ISBN 9781496213006 (mobi)
ISBN 9781496213013 (pdf)
Subjects: LCSH: Spanish literature—20th
century—History and criticism. | Politics
in literature. | Francoism in literature. |
Fascism and literature—Spain.
Classification: LCC PQ6073.P6 G35 2019 |
DDC 860.9/358—dc23 LC record available
at https://lccn.loc.gov/2018022543

Set in Arno by E. Cuddy.
Designed by N. Putens.

CONTENTS

ACKNOWLEDGMENTS

I am thankful for the generosity and goodwill of colleagues and mentors who supported me on my "long march through the institutions": John Beverley at University of Pittsburgh; Hazel Gold, Karen Stolley, Hernán Feldman, María Mercedes Carrión, and José Quiroga at Emory. At decisive moments, my colleagues from the University of Illinois at Chicago gave me the space and encouragement to round off this project. Without Rosilie Hernández, Margarita Saona, Luis López, Imke Meyer, and Stephen Engelmann's dedication and unwavering support for my work, I might not have arrived or stayed at UIC. The personal and institutional support I received at the UIC Institute for Humanities furthered my thinking and created intellectual synergies.

In large part, this book exists thanks to the friends who knew and understood my intellectual and personal struggle. Long conversations with Fabricio Forastelli are embedded in the first chapter. Roxani Margariti was a constant interlocutor and the first one with whom I discussed *stasis*, the term which would become an anchor for the whole project. With brilliance and generosity, Jaime Rodríguez Matos read and commented on the third chapter. In addition to editing the entire manuscript, Carl Good was and is the kind of reader I trust and aspire to be. My friendship with Carmen Pereira Muro is much older than this book, and so is my debt to Jasmina Čubrilo and Filip Mladenović, two guiding lights in the chaotic times of our common post-Yugoslavian history.

For all the years it took to write this book, my parents, Marija and Branko, and my sister, Branka Gajić, were with me through thick and thin. Along the way, Jana Beltrán Janés and Katarina Emma Linton, two shining beauties, entered my life and continue to grow, day by day. Miraculously, Steven Marsh stuck with me and allowed me to love him the best I can.

PARADOXES OF STASIS

Introduction

Unstable Stasis

Two quotes, separated by more than a century, frame this introduction and the book that follows. The first one appears in Miguel de Unamuno's 1905 *Vida de Don Quijote y Sancho*, in a chapter that glosses the episode of the "yelmo de Mambrino," the barber's basin that Don Quixote claims is Mambrino's golden helmet, purveyor of immortality for the one who wears it. The controversy provoked by Don Quixote's insistence on the object's supernatural properties stands in contrast to the aversion to conflict and debate that Unamuno considers a feature of his era:

> Se proclama que hay principios indiscutibles, y cuando se trata de ponerlos en tela de juicio no falta quien ponga el grito en el cielo. . . . ¡Inoportuno! Estoy harto de oír llamar inoportunas las cosas más oportunas. . . . ¿Qué se teme? ¿Que se trabe pendencia y que se encienda la guerra civil de nuevo? Mejor que mejor. Es lo que necesitamos. Sí, es lo que necesitamos: una nueva guerra civil.

> It is proclaimed that there are indisputable principles, and any attempt to examine them creates outrage. . . . Inconvenient! I am tired of hearing how the most convenient things are proclaimed inconvenient. . . . What do we fear? To start a fight that would unleash another civil war? So much the better. That is what we need. Yes, that is what we need: another civil war.[1]

The cruelty of the civil wars that ensued, in both Spain and a myriad of other places, since the time Unamuno wrote these words, makes them chilling when they are read today. Yet, in order to grasp the true nature of the provocation in Unamuno's defense of the civic virtues of civil war, a reader should remember what Unamuno taught at the University of Salamanca: ancient Greek. The Greek term for civil strife was *stasis*, a word whose multiple meanings include but are by no means limited to what today we call civil war, namely, armed conflict between the citizens of the same political community. I will return to the problem of stasis in greater detail later in this introduction and throughout the book, but for now it is important to observe that the civil war Unamuno invokes is a battle of ideas, not armies: a dispute among those who hold different positions regarding the principles that govern a political community. While advocating for civil war in the Greek sense of stasis—as a battle of contrary interpretations—Unamuno opposes stasis in the habitual, Latin, sense: a state of stagnation or immobility that excludes the possibility of discord.

The author of the second quote is Juan Carlos Monedero, a founder of Podemos, a political party that emerged from the 15-M movement, named after May 15, 2011, a date marking the rise of a wave of popular protests against the political establishment and the economic policies of the European Union throughout Spain.

> ¿Cómo repetir sin sonrojo "no pasarán"? No sólo pasaron en el 36 sino que se quedaron los cuarenta años de la dictadura y una buena parte de los decenios posteriores. Mucho tiene que ver con este impasse que vivimos esa celebración falangista del "¡Pasamos!". . . . Cuando un pueblo se gana a pulso la democracia y su relato—también su relato—, no le pasa un Rajoy y su estela de corrupción e ineficiencia con esta impunidad. Tenía razón aquella pancarta del 15-M: "Qué largo se me está haciendo el franquismo". ¿Por qué la izquierda y sus aires de familia ampliada no se enteran?

> How can one repeat "no pasarán" without blushing? Not only did they pass in 1936, but they remained during the forty years of the dictatorship

and a good part of the following decades. The impasse we are living today has much to do with the falangist celebration of "¡Pasamos!" [We did pass]. . . . When after a hard battle a people wins democracy and its narrative—its narrative as well—then someone like Rajoy and his trail of corruption and inefficiency do not come to pass with this level of impunity. The 15-M banner that read "Francoism's been going on so long" was right. Why is it that the left and its extended family do not get it?[2]

Monedero is reflecting on the political impasse in Spain following the June 2016 general elections that resulted in the victory of the incumbent prime minister, Mariano Rajoy, leader of the Partido Popular (PP), while deepening the split on the left between PSOE, the previously hegemonic Socialist Party, and Podemos. The inability of either of the two main parties—PP and PSOE—to secure a parliamentary majority left the country without a government for the second time in a row, ushering in the prospect of another round of elections, which were likely to strengthen support for the Right. While bemoaning the likelihood of another Rajoy government and critiquing the incapacity of the Left and its "extended family" to construct a viable alternative to the neoliberal ideology of the Partido Popular and its European allies, the quote from Monedero strikes another, more dramatic chord. His references to a long string of defeats of the Left—Francisco Franco's victory in the Civil War, forty years of dictatorship, and the usurped story of Spain's democratic transition—transform the latest electoral victory of the Right into another episode in a longer historical narrative that started with the Civil War and has not yet reached a clear political closure. The shame Monedero associates with "No pasarán" originates in the inability to utter the slogan of Republican resistance without recalling the self-congratulatory, mocking tone of "We did pass!" that sealed the victory of Franco's forces. These two kinds of violence—the physical defeat of resistance and the verbal appropriation and parody of the defeated Republican cause—reflect what came to pass in 1939 and continued throughout the Francoist dictatorship.

Moreover, claims Monedero, the official narrative of Spain's transition to democracy and the political culture it established have been based on a similar kind of disregard for the Spanish people's willingness to wage and win the hard battle for a democratic future. Instead of celebrating victory in the struggle against the dictatorship, the official narrative of the democratic transition favored continuity over confrontation. That cry, "¡Pasamos!," which marked the beginning of Francoism, echoes in the narrative of the peaceful and orderly passage to the democratic era, championed by the King Juan Carlos I, Franco's appointed successor. It comes as no surprise, complains Monedero, that Rajoy might receive another mandate. The likelihood of that outcome is not primarily a sign of popular support for his policies but is more a reflection of the fragmentation of the Left that, once again, might allow the Right to pass and stay.

But what to make of that 15-M banner—"¡Qué largo se me está haciendo el franquismo!" (Francoism's been going on so long!)—which Monedero reads as an accurate comment on the current Spanish political context? The message on the banner might seem puzzling, not only because the Francoist regime ended decades ago but also because a significant number of the *indignados* who occupied public squares in 2011 were born or came of age after it. By speaking of Francoism in the continuous present tense, the message disputes both that the regime ended and that, for those gathered on the square, it is only an historical reference. Could it be that our very distance from Francoism makes its duration seem even longer than it was? Could Francoism's "going on so long" be a reflection not of its actual duration but of its influence, which is becoming heavier, more burdensome, and more evident with time? The end of Francoism is not a fact but a promise whose fulfillment is contingent on another promise: the arrival of a democracy able to put a real end to the Francoist era. In 2011 both promises seemed distant, so that the banner could be read as saying that Francoism ended but did not pass, did not become past.

Like Unamuno, who questions a conventional understanding of civil war, Monedero seeks to reframe the historical meaning of both "No pasarán" and "Pasamos." In the current crisis of democracy, Monedero advocates for a civic engagement necessary to insure that entrenched attitudes and modes of doing politics do not continue to pass. At the same time, he calls for resistance to the temporal non-passing, an interruption of the numbing continuity *with* and *of* the past.

I wish to consider the elements that link these quotes to this book's broader theme and to my interpretative focus, grounded in the multiple meanings of the Greek notion of stasis. A claim that runs throughout this book is that the Greek approach to stasis allows us to confront the issue of the unique, even paradoxical, nature of the Francoist regime, which is related to its long duration. The importance of stasis for politics more broadly, and for Francoism more specifically, rests on the polysemy of the term, which designates phenomena characterized by the presence or excess of movement but also describes those conditions in which movement is halted or absent. While designating the internal fractioning of the polis that leads to sedition or civil war, *stasis* also forms the root of terms such as *state, status*, and even *constitution*, all of which connote stability as a principal feature of a political order. How does this fundamental ambiguity in the term *stasis* contribute to our understanding of Francoism?

Instead of calling on the established categories of historical periodization that identify different phases in the regime's evolution, I claim that the key to Francoism's endurance lies in its necessarily limited success in carrying out the task of achieving its lasting institutional stability while grappling with the always present uncertainty regarding its end. The lingering and ultimately unsolvable question of Spain's political future after Franco's demise generated a need for the regime to change and adapt, which was inseparable from its will to halt or control its demise, to the extent that— and as long as—it was possible. The sense that Francoism is becoming or feeling a bit too long-lived, which Spain's current political and economic crisis has exacerbated, was not born with the 15-M movement. This book's broader point is that the uncertainty about the dictatorship's ending was a feature of the Francoist era that persists today, albeit in an inverted form: not so much as an attempt to avert that ending, but as a critique of the regime's continued persistence within Spanish democracy. The underlying paradox of Francoism consists in the irreducible tension between its two seemingly opposed aspects, which nevertheless complement and inform each other: the restlessness and instability generated by the regime's lack of permanence—its finitude—and its capacity to endure and linger on, in defiance of its impermanence.

Greek *stasis* names a co-presence of movement and immobility that manifests itself in different areas: from politics to legal rhetoric, from medicine to navigation. While illuminating the internal contradictions of the Francoist regime and their impact on the culture of the era, the notion of stasis provides a new and fruitful way of advancing understandings of Francoism and its relation to the democratic Spanish state. My engagement with the tensions of the Francoist period responds to the challenge of thinking political conflict outside the paralyzing logic of civil war, while seeing inner restlessness and conflict not as an obstacle to democracy but as a key to its dynamic potential.

Unending Francoism

Longevity may have been one of Francoism's main achievements, but it was also one of the regime's fundamental problems. Rather than designating a historical period with a beginning and end, Francoism's duration depended on two related, and to some extent incompatible, tasks: consolidating the regime born out of the ashes of the Civil War and securing its future. The process of dismantling the liberal democracy of the Second Republic and building the new state entailed the creation of an alternative political system whose nature, at the end of the war, was yet to be determined. The ideologically heterogeneous coalition of right-wing groups that emerged victorious in 1939 faced a difficult balancing act. It had to surmount its internal differences in order to secure the existence of the regime for which all of its factions had fought and on which their political survival and material privileges depended. This balancing act points to a larger paradox that characterized the history of the Francoist regime. In order to last, the regime had to establish political, legal, and economic principles that would give it stability, and yet the very task of defining those principles brought to the fore—and even exacerbated—differences and disagreements between the factions, thereby making the process of the regime's consolidation open ended at best and interminable at worst.

The task of redistributing power among different factions fell to Franco, who sought to ensure that no single faction would continuously dominate others or become identified with the regime as a whole. In other words, the regime's unity and permanence depended on the different amount of power granted to each "family," as the factions were known at the time. While fostering rivalry within the regime, these periodic changes also limited the aspirations of each group. In the absence of ideological homogeneity, the regime's future depended on Franco's dual role as a moderator of power and the embodiment of the dictatorship's historical mission of securing the Civil War victory.

As different chapters in this book show, both the regime's insiders and its opponents were acutely aware that, without a clear idea of the future following Franco's demise, these strategies of adaptation were a way of buying time, of postponing the inevitable. However, the regime's capacity to survive for four decades acquired a new meaning in the context of post-Franco Spain. As Monedero's quote suggests, rather than spelling the regime's conclusive end, the era that began in the aftermath of Franco's death inherited a problem that can indeed be seen as the flip side of Francoism's obsession with its future. While the regime was haunted by the prospect of its ending, the post-Franco era is haunted by the dictatorship's non-ending. I would suggest that the same nonbinary relationship that characterized the interplay between unity and internal division within Francoism also characterizes the relation between the regime's end and its non-ending. When it comes to the protracted life of Francoism itself, we can say that the end of the regime was a condition for its non-ending but also vice versa: Its non-ending was a condition for its ending. The end of Francoism—the demise of the dictator followed by the gradual dismantling of the regime and the establishment of democratic institutions—did not impede its continuing presence within democracy. This phenomenon applies not just to individual figures but also to some important features of the post-1978 political system: the monarchy of Juan Carlos I, the amnesty applied to the dictatorship era, and a particular conception of the unity of the Spanish nation.

As many critics observed in the aftermath of 15-M, the defense of the political system of the Transition rests on the assumption that the continuity of the democratic system whose foundations were established between 1975 and 1978 is the only thing standing between political stability and the threat of disorder. What Iñigo Errejón refers to as "the regime of 1978" was based on the pacts that made the Transition possible without a clear rupture with the Francoist past. Errejón argues that instead of invalidating the entire process of Transition, the relationship between Francoism and democracy facilitates an analysis of the complex dynamic of political change, which entails "la reordenación de los equilibrios rotos, en este caso *un cambio sustancial necesario para que no cambiase todo* con la muerte del dictador" (the reordering of the broken equilibriums, in this case *a substantial change that was necessary so that not everything would change* with the dictator's death).[3]

It is this necessary tension between change and stagnation, order and disturbance, movement and immobility, which the ancient Greek language refers to as *stasis*, a term and a concept that is crucial for elucidating Greek ideas about politics and conflicts. As the following brief overview of contemporary theoretical accounts of stasis shows, what makes this term an important interpretative tool for the study of the politics and culture of the Francoist era is not so much its multiplicity of meanings but the possibility it affords for thinking movement and immobility outside a binary logic that would limit our understanding of both Francoism and democracy.

Greek *Stasis* and Its Forgetting

> Terminology is "the poetic," hence productive moment of thought.
> —GIORGIO AGAMBEN, "Movement"

Recent political theory has seen a resurgence of interest in the term *stasis*. While Nicole Loraux's *Divided City*, a collection of essays written in the 1980s and 1990s, remains a definitive work on stasis in the Greek context, the term holds theoretical relevance for thinkers whose focus is by no means limited to ancient Greece, ranging from the Nazi jurist Carl Schmitt's *Political Theology II* (1970)—a lesser-known companion to his famous 1922 *Political Theology I*—to Giorgio Agamben's 2015 *Stasis: Civil War as a Political Paradigm* and Dimitris Vardoulakis's *Stasis before the State* (2018), which examines the relevance of stasis for democratic theory. At the same time, the global spread of popular anti-establishment uprisings against neoliberal governance has brought the notions of civil war and revolt—both of them included in the semantic field of stasis—to the forefront of contemporary political debates.

For Loraux, stasis offers a point of entry for examining the Greek conception of politics in general and Athenian democracy in particular. Some of the complexities of Greek ideas about political conflict are inscribed in the semantics of the word *stasis*, which has an etymological origin in the verb *istamai* or *istemi*—"to stand up," "to be standing," or "to be waiting." The connection between this primary meaning and its derivations in the political sphere is not always apparent. In politics, stasis designates a party or faction, a group constituted in opposition to rival ones, and is therefore associated with sedition and civil war. The bifurcation of meaning between a body in upright position and a group of bodies that rise up in opposition to another segment within the polis captures the fundamental ambiguity of stasis that is, as Loraux puts it, "endlessly caught between rest and motion."[4] Vardoulakis makes the same point: "*Stasis* branches out into two clusters of meaning derived from the literal and figurative image of movement or lack thereof. In the first cluster, stasis refers to a lack of movement, in the second, excessive movement."[5]

The fact that the Greeks saw stasis, or internal strife, as a supreme political danger, a misfortune capable of endangering the existence of the polity, illustrates, as it were, by rebound the importance Greek political thought placed on ideas of unity and familial bond among fellow citizens. In that sense, stasis emerges as a borderline term that imperfectly mediates, binds, and unbinds two competing visions of the polis. First, there is the mythical notion of the polis as One, a family unit held together by a common origin—autochthony—by virtue of which all male Athenian citizens are brothers, children of the same mother. At the same time, this myth of a unified polis runs into the reality of the democratic process, which inevitably splits citizens into rival camps. The polysemy of stasis reveals an inherent tension in the Greek approach to two radically different forms of political conflict: the turmoil of internecine war and the practice of democracy, which transforms the division among citizens into the very condition of politics. "Civil war," argues Loraux, "is precisely what the invention of the political is supposed to avert, since the city would have introduced voting as a 'preventive remedy' for bloody division."[6] This is why, in 403 BC, following a civil war between democratic and oligarchic forces in Athens, the victorious democrats granted amnesty to the citizens who had sided with the regime of Thirty Tyrants. The institution of amnesty exemplifies how the officially sanctioned forgetting of the civil war functions as a present/absent foundation of the democratic polis.

Loraux argues that, by suppressing stasis and seeking to forget past divisions, the foundation of the democratic polis is constituted on *the forgetting of the political as such.*[7] The forgetting of the political goes hand in hand with subordinating those aspects of stasis that are associated with internal division and excess of movement to those associated with unity and immobility. Although the story Loraux tells about the convergence of movement and immobility in the term stasis draws on ancient Greek language and culture, it is not an exclusively Greek story. Latin derivations of stasis in Western European political vocabulary further consolidate the forgetting of those components of stasis that refer to movement, while designating phenomena whose primary features are stability and absence of movement or change. That is why Loraux affirms that "we need to invent a language that is not Roman in order to speak of *stasis*."[8] While the Latin term *bellum civile* thinks the city within the paradigm of war, stasis "is something completely different—movement at rest, a front that does not yield and introduces into the city the paradoxical unity that characterizes the simultaneous insurrection of two halves of a whole."[9]

Vardoulakis locates the main shortcoming of Loraux's analysis of stasis in the latter's reluctance "to bring the political import of the Greek polis—and of stasis—to bear upon contemporary notions of the political."[10] Since the establishment of the polis takes place prior to the advent of Christianity and the invention of a metaphysics of presence, stasis can destabilize the relationship between politics and religion, which informs modern debates about sovereignty, political theology, and democracy. It would be impossible to elucidate here all ramifications of such a far-reaching and complex argument concerning stasis. I will tease out just one dimension of Vardoulakis's argument that, while linking his work to Loraux, is also relevant for this project. In an important way, Vardoulakis stands Loraux's argument on its head. If the forgetting of stasis has played a crucial role in shaping Greek and Western ideas about politics, then, in Vardoulakis's view, it is possible to reverse that forgetting by reintroducing the fundamental ambiguity of stasis into our understanding of notions such as democracy and sovereignty. In other words, the ambiguity of stasis can undermine the binary exclusionary logic that informs many crucial political concepts. I argue that the tension between immobility and movement inscribed in stasis allows us to capture the internal dynamic of the Francoist regime while problematizing the idea of a lineal progress from dictatorship to democracy. The exclusion of stasis as internal conflict represents a condition sine qua non for the existence of a sovereign state, which Schmitt described as "an organized political entity, internally peaceful, territorially enclosed, and impenetrable to aliens."[11] As is well known, the fundamental political distinction for Schmitt is that between friend and enemy. Sovereignty therefore entails identifying an external enemy and eliminating internal discord. From the standpoint of Schmitt's conception of the political, civil war is a self-laceration, "a self-inflicted disease that should be expunged from the state."[12] In *Political Theology II*, written decades after the first volume established an analogy between the sovereign and God, Schmitt brings up the notion of stasis in order to argue that only the Christian God, and not the sovereign, can withstand internal conflict without therefore jeopardizing integrity of its power.

Recalling fourth-century theologian Gregory of Nazianzus's doctrine of the Trinity—"The One is always in revolt [stasis] against itself"—Schmitt seeks to consolidate the analogy between politics and religion, which is one of the trademarks of his thought.[13] Analogy, in this particular case, does not entail only similarity but also a fundamental difference. Only God can split into three while remaining One. Sovereignty, on the other hand, reasserts itself by mobilizing against an external enemy and crumbles under internal threats. If, for Schmitt, the existence of internal enemies jeopardizes sovereignty, and if there is no politics without sovereignty, then civil war triggers the collapse of politics. That is why Schmitt critiqued the tendency toward the weakening of state sovereignty and the establishment of a unified global order, which he saw as an expression of utopian humanism, at best, or as a dangerous process that would spell the end of the political and the beginning of the era of generalized civil war. Without proving Schmitt right, the current erosion of state sovereignty and the proliferation of armed conflicts that do not resemble a conventional war between states do give a new meaning to the notion of "global civil war."

In contrast to Schmitt, Vardoulakis underscores the democratic potential of stasis. He discusses the fifth-century-BC Solon's law, which prohibited neutrality during civil war, in order to argue that the fundamental political distinction for radical democracy is not between friend and enemy, "us" and "them," but between active and passive citizenship. Solon's law, which punished with loss of citizenship those citizens who remained neutral during an outbreak of civil war, might seem counterintuitive and even shocking today. For Vardoulakis, instead of promoting violence and animosity among citizens, the law declares that during an acute political crisis neutrality is politically, ethically, and legally unacceptable: "Solon's law describes not only the state in which one is—active or inactive—but also indicates that one *ought to be active* at the cost of losing their citizenship."[14] When the polis is in turmoil, only the state of generalized unrest holds the potential of future peace. The law of stasis, specifies Vardoulakis, "positions the citizens to make judgments."[15] This does not amount to passing a judgment *about* a particular conflict but to assuming a position *in* a conflict from which no one is excluded and from which one cannot opt out except by risking exclusion. Solon's law of stasis establishes a limit at which engagement in conflict becomes a condition of political co-existence. Hence, the democratic potential of stasis lies in the conception of "being" as "being with," which, while constituting a condition of democratic citizenship, is not limited to politics but also has ethical and ontological underpinnings.

As this overview of Loraux's and Vardoulakis's arguments shows, stasis is much more than a synonym for civil war. It is a privileged example of the "agonistic mode of being" that permeated different spheres of Greek culture: politics, war, justice, rhetoric, and philosophy. The semantics of stasis indicates that conflict and peace, division and unity, and, more broadly, movement and immobility are indissociable. In this book, stasis designates the irreducible tension between movement and immobility in the Francoist era and illuminates how that tension operates in different fields, texts, and genres (legal treatises, poetry, novels, essays). This study argues that, while putting an end to one kind of stasis, the regime that resulted from the Spanish Civil War transformed the conflict between movement and immobility—internal division and unity, change and stagnation—into the very principle of its survival. A peculiar combination of development and paralysis was necessary in order for the regime to last, all the while anticipating, trying to postpone and control, its end. In that sense, the dynamic of stasis connects the problem of the long life of Francoism to the question of its afterlife, its legacy.

The authors studied in this book, both the regime's supporters and opponents, were similarly preoccupied with finding a way out of the political, intellectual, and aesthetic impasse associated with Francoism's ability to change and endure. Without analyzing that impasse and the different responses it generated it is impossible to grasp the internal tensions of the era and its broader significance. By ignoring Francoist stasis, we subscribe to a tamed and sanitized idea of the dictatorship period as a simple dead-end or parenthesis that a return to democratic normalcy has corrected. By throwing away the stale water of a long dictatorship, we get rid of the inner unrest and turbulence that the regime sought to suppress but that democracy must acknowledge if it is not to confuse stability with immobility. Different chapters in this book delve into the paradox of the restless immobility or "hectic inertia" that permeated politics, thought, and literature of the Francoist era.[16] Before describing the chapters, however, I here outline the basic historical parameters for speaking about the internal contradictions of the regime.

The Consolidation of Francoism

Unity and disunity are embedded in the founding moment of the Francoist regime, the 1937 "Decree of Unification," which officially brought different factions making up the amalgam of the Nationalist camp together under Franco's military and political leadership. The long and cumbersome name given to the political organization that emerged from the unification process—FET de las JONS (Falange Española Tradicionalista de las Juntas de Ofensiva Nacional Sindicalista)—testified to an unnatural ideological coupling. The nucleus of the organization, the Falange Española Tradicionalista (FET), consolidated in one body two diverging sets of political ideas and goals: on the one hand, the overtly fascist Falange and on the other, those groups committed to defending their version of an autochthonous—that is, Catholic, monarchical, or, sometimes, regionalist—tradition. This ideological rift established the template of the new regime following the Nationalist victory in 1939. The history of the Francoist regime, in the form in which it endured well into the 1960s, speaks to an ongoing struggle between two conceptions of politics and society, represented by the Falange and its right-wing rivals. Falange saw itself as a party-movement whose project of building a new society rested on two pillars: the defense of its ideological principles and its position as a lynchpin in the regime's structure entrusted with binding together the providential figure of *el caudillo* (Franco) and the people. Suspicious of the Falange's revolutionary rhetoric and its attempts to concentrate a large portion of political power in its hands, the traditionalists affirmed their trust in the institutions (church, army, and the corporatist parliament, or

Cortes) rather than in ideologies and movements, and in this way sought to defend the values of family, religion, and social harmony. At stake in the rift and rivalry between the Falange and the traditionalists was not just the regime's internal dynamic, which conditioned its practices and policies, but also the self-definition of Francoism, its foundational purpose, goal, or mission. While the Falange associated the foundational purpose with the realization of its own political project, the traditionalists—adhering to an idea of the historical constitution and permanence of the Spanish nation—viewed the Falange's attempts to determine the course of the new regime as a usurpation of the role of the institutions that embodied the continuity of the nation through time.

After the defeat of the Axis Powers in 1945, and especially during the Cold War, this ideological friction was reframed according to the vocabulary of the era. As charges of totalitarianism were hurled against the Falange, the group denounced its rivals as not just conservative antirevolutionaries but as closeted supporters of liberalism who advocated the return of the old liberal monarchy. While the presence of this internal friction could have debilitated the regime, it somewhat paradoxically contributed to strengthening it. On the one hand, the friction consolidated Franco's role as a figure able to navigate these internal tensions and prevent them from escalating into a full-scale crisis. Franco, a seasoned soldier whose unrealized youthful ambition had been to become a naval officer, maintained control of the ship of state. He kept in check opposing ideological aspirations whose confrontations were a crucial element in periodical changes and crises that marked the stages of the regime's history. As the historian Ismael Saz put it, the history of Francoism is the history of its crises.[17]

On the other hand, Franco's art of balancing the tensions between the different factions—or "families"—of the regime by allotting parcels of power to each one according to the calculus of the moment allowed for a certain amount of pluralism within the regime. Limited pluralism was a feature that, in accordance with Juan Linz's famous 1964 essay,[18] defined Francoism as an authoritarian, rather than totalitarian, regime. In one sense, this limited pluralism was accidental, a product of historical circumstances and the concrete interests of different political actors. In another sense, though, it was necessary because it allowed the regime to move forward. It contributed to the evolution of Francoism through time without altering its undemocratic nature. While some (particularly the convinced Falangists) argued that the existence of pluralism revealed the ideological hollowness of the regime and its lack of political coherence, that pluralism also contributed to the idea of Francoism's uniqueness, its peculiar ability to combine unity and plurality, stability and change, and thereby secure its persistence through time.

Uncertainty about the future was part of Francoism's authoritarian DNA. As Ramón Serrano Suñer, Franco's brother-in-law and a Nazi supporter who was removed from the government in 1942, once remarked: "What [the regime] would have been without the World War only God knows. What it will finally be is still to be seen."[19] The mixture of "would have been" and "will be" that structures Serrano Suñer's sentence situates Francoism in the temporal fissure between a retrospective and a prospective vision. Pulled between a hypothetical past and an equally hypothetical future, the regime existed in the uncertainty of an interregnum, a moment before something happens or while it still hasn't happened.

The pressing issue of the future direction of the regime, the uncertainty about "what it will finally be"—a question mirrored by its antonym, "what it would have been, if it hadn't been for . . ."—both revealed an already existing discord and generated still more discord within the regime. Not only did the existing ideological fractures center on the question of the regime's future—the issue of its legal and institutional shape, the role of different actors both during Franco's life and after—but those fractures were exacerbated by the anxieties and struggles that this issue provoked. The regime's strategy for dealing with internal discord was essentially the same as that for dealing with its future. On the one hand, Francoism continued on the path of institutionalization while keeping open—that is, postponing or deferring—a final resolution regarding its future, its definite shape. On the other, the balance between opposing ideas about its nature provided a key (however precarious) to the regime's continuity.

The question of the historical continuity or, alternatively, the rupture between the Francoist regime and post-Franco democratic Spain, which still haunts Spanish society and politics, was not born with democracy but has its origins in the regime's preoccupation with its own future. The importance of legislation for the legitimation and self-constitution of Francoism is a case in point. A key to Francoist legislation was the concept of an "open constitution," a series of laws that regulated the regime's politics from its beginnings in the Civil War to its final years. "Open constitution" means that each law represents a stage in the regime's development, so that legislative action becomes an instrument of its transformation, allowing it to stay abreast—or at least keep in step—with societal changes. This instrumental approach to legality as a link in the joint evolution of the regime and Spanish society reflected the philosophy of the less intransigent, more reformist members of the regime, like Manuel Fraga, a reputable legal scholar and the minister who spearheaded Spain's 1960s tourist boom. Fraga's philosophy of government is encapsulated in a sentence that Justin Crumbaugh quotes in his insightful analysis of Fraga's career as minister of tourism. In his 1962 book, *El nuevo anti-Maquiavelo*, Fraga writes: "The state only serves a purpose if it fulfills the ends that justify it."[20] This deceptively simple sentence does not specify if the purpose of the state is given by the intrinsic value of its ends, or if the state designs the ends that justify its purpose a posteriori (in the end, as it were). The ambiguity of the sentence leaves space for multiple interpretations of the relationship between the means—the form of the state (democratic, authoritarian, and so on)—and the ends (social stability, peace, and prosperity) that justify the means. However one interprets it, the sentence leaves one wondering if Fraga views the state as an instrument for achieving specific ends or, rather, as an accidental form leading to the fulfillment of ends that can be achieved by different types of states (Francoist *or* democratic).

Chapter 1. Legislating Francoism

In the first chapter of this book I analyze the chasm between legality and legitimacy revealed in the debates surrounding the creation of the Law of

Fundamental Principles of the Movimiento Nacional (1958). Examining memoirs, political treatises, and periodicals, I identify three approaches to legality under Francoism, typified, respectively, by José Luis Arrese, leader of the Falange; Manuel Fraga, a legal scholar and influential government minister in the 1960s; and Jesús Fueyo, a follower of Carl Schmitt and a theorist of the idea of authority. I show that the difficulties in defining the nature and direction of Francoism had to do not only with the role of the Falange and Movimiento Nacional within it but also with the precarious balance between change and immobility that characterized the regime as a whole.

Chapter 2. The Movement of Divergence:
Dionisio Ridruejo from Totalitarianism to Liberalism

In the second chapter I examine the poetry, prose, and political writings of Dionisio Ridruejo (1913–75), who is remembered in Spain less for his literature than as a paradigmatic example of a "fascist turned liberal." The chapter questions the existing interpretations of Ridruejo's political trajectory from fascism to liberal democracy, which tend to view this change either as a debatable ideological "conversion" or as a result of a personal evolution leading to political maturity. In contrast to these approaches, I argue that a more nuanced understanding of the changes in Ridruejo's politics requires the consideration of different accounts of nonlinear movement in his literature and political writings.

The first part of the chapter underscores the importance of Ridruejo's elegiac poetry in understanding his disillusionment with Francoism and his search for an existential and political alternative. I argue that the figure of *anabasis*, which names the experience of being adrift and finding a path of return through wandering, holds a key to his change of direction. In the second part, I analyze Ridruejo's collection of poetic prose, entitled *Diario de una tregua*. I examine his vision of the Catalonian landscape as an example of rootedness, laboriousness, and the "love of limits," qualities that he views as an antidote to the metaphysical longing and striving for the infinite that he associates with the landscape of his native Castile. In the chapter's final section I analyze the figure of the swimming instructor, which Ridruejo posits, both in *Diario* and in his explicitly political writings, as an alternative model of movement and political action, one where the emphasis is not on a common goal but on reaching the other shore, even though there are no fixed paths leading to it.

Chapter 3. Paradoxes of Francoist Stasis:
Miguel Espinosa and the Art of Protest

The third chapter engages with Miguel Espinosa's novel *Escuela de mandarines*, which stands out as the most probing literary examination of the nature of the Francoist regime. Written over a period of two decades and published in 1974, *Escuela* is a monumental text, with close to 600 pages, 488 characters, and a lengthy apparatus of footnotes. Its loose narrative thread incorporates different genres (poetry, drama, scholarly treatise) as it chronicles the voyage of the protagonist, Eremita, through Happy Governance, an oppressive, unjust, and seemingly eternal fictional polity. The starting point for my analysis is the parallelism between the critique of Francoism in the novel and the lengthy process of its creation. I argue that the author's twenty-year-long commitment to writing three complete versions of the text remains inscribed in the multifaceted nature of the novel, which is at once a testimony to the endurance of Francoism, a fierce critique and rebuttal of the regime's principles, and a vehicle for generating protest against it. Persevering with the project was not only Espinosa's statement on—and response to—the regime's refusal to come to an end but also the author's way of making good on his protagonist's claim to be the regime's most constant enemy.

The concept of stasis operates at different levels in my analysis of Espinosa's novel. Loraux's notion of stasis as a "bond of division" allows me to approach *Escuela de mandarines* as a testimony to the unbreakable bond of hostility tying Espinosa's life and literature to Francoism. That bond of hostility propels Eremita on his voyage, in the course of which he meets members of the regime as well as its enemies. The chapter shows how different meanings of stasis inform both Espinosa's critique of the regime—the history of civil wars, its rule over a passive and pacified society—and his concept of dissidence. In opposition to the regime's world of fixity and isolation, an itinerant and transitory community of dissidents emerges out of the movement that generates encounters, lively debates, and exchange of knowledge. The sense of stasis as standing up with and against others informs my interpretation of Eremita's protest as a way of being, or "being with" in tense proximity with others.

Chapter 4. Standstills of History: Nothingness, Tragedy,
and Exile in María Zambrano's Thought

The fourth chapter focuses on the thought of María Zambrano, who, with the possible exception of her teacher, José Ortega y Gasset, was Spain's foremost twentieth-century philosopher. The chapter opens with a reading of specific sections of *El hombre y lo divino* (1955), a work that represents a culmination of Zambrano's exploration of the philosophical and religious roots of European violence as a problem brought to the fore by her experience of the Spanish Civil War and the onset of World War II. Zambrano examines different forms of violence embedded in the Western project of the humanization of history, whose bases are found in the philosophical conception of Being as logos and the Christian idea of shared human-divine essence. She sees Nietzsche's proclamation of the death of God as an appropriate culmination of the violent process of humanization, after which only one resistance remains on the path to absolute human freedom. That last resistance is Nothingness, *la nada*. For Zambrano, I argue in the chapter, the main feature of Nothingness—as a concept and as a state or experience—is the way in which it combines and confounds movement and immobility, activity and passivity, dynamic resistance and enveloping void. Following a discussion of Nothingness in *El hombre y lo divino*, I examine other instances in Zambrano's thought in which movement and immobility are conjoined, notably, exile and tragedy. Through the figure of Antigone, Zambrano links the genre of tragedy to exile: her own, that of the Second Republic, and exile more broadly. Therefore, different philosophical configurations of stasis in Zambrano's thought conjure up, but also disperse, the ghost of the Spanish Civil War.

CHAPTER 1

Legislating Francoism

Although the Franco regime came to power as a result of the victory of the Nationalist forces in the Spanish Civil War, it was the process of building and consolidating the new state that determined the nature and the consequences of that victory. As I stated in the introduction, the consolidation of power was already underway in 1937, through the unification of the fascist Falange and traditionalist monarchical forces grouped under Franco's leadership, and it continued throughout the war and after the nationalist victory. The unification of force and law at the moment of the foundation of the regime was noted by Manuel Fraga, who would later become Franco's minister for tourism and information and one of the regime's most influential ideologues. Fraga wrote: "With July 18, 1936 [the day the Civil War began], a constituent period opened for Spain."[1] That is, not a war, but a constituent period; not a violation of the existing constitution, but the clearing of the way for a new one.

Declaring that the beginning of the Civil War was simultaneous with the commencement of a "constituent period" suggests that the legality of Francoism was based on the understanding of the "Alzamiento Glorioso" (Glorious Uprising) as an originary moment that gave retrospective legitimacy to the regime and its legal creations. In other words, the "Glorious Uprising" legitimized Francoism, which then proceeded to constitute its own legality. In another text dealing with the legal evolution of Franco's regime, Fraga argues that the failure of previous Spanish constitutions explains the reluctance of the regime to create a new one of its own (Francoism never produced a constitution as such). He recalls the bitter words of nineteenth-century historian Macías Picavea: "There are seven Spanish constitutions, like seven deadly sins."[2] In Fraga's view, what had characterized Spanish constitutional history between 1808 and 1936 was a vicious circle of crisis and reinstitution: A political crisis (crisis of the state) usually came to an end through the use of force, and a new government was established. It proclaimed a new constitution, but, invariably, continuing governmental instability created conditions for the outbreak of yet another crisis, which functioned as a prelude to a new constitution. This tension between legislating and governing, between law and politics, is what had made the rule of law (*estado de derecho*) impossible in Spain, even under de facto constitutional governments. Alluding to the double sense of the word *pronunciamiento*, which means "pronouncement" but since the middle of the nineteenth century had become a synonym for coup d'état, Fraga declares: "A coup [*pronunciamiento*] is not an act of force but an act of logic."[3] A logic of tragedy, one might add: The coup was not inescapable because it was logical, but vice versa; it was logical because it was inescapable.

It would seem that Franco's coup against the Republic was located both inside and outside that logic. The new regime suspended the Republican Constitution without proclaiming a new one.[4] It responded with violence to the crisis of the constitutional regime but refused to "fix" the crisis by building a new constitutional government. It used a situation of social and political crisis as a trigger for the use of force; however, this use of force was not portrayed as an instrument but as a foundational act. It went against the liberal regime not only by force of arms but by virtue of situating itself outside the logic of reinstitution that had ruled every previous pronunciamiento. We might say that Francoism substantially altered the instrumental role that force had played in those pronunciamientos. Whereas force had previously served as a tool for instituting law during regime changes, under Francoism the law itself assumed the instrumental role for constituting the regime and establishing its legality.

In the legal evolution of Francoism, the emphasis was placed not on *law* as an abstract concept, but on *laws* and *legislation*. By legislation I mean a process that defined and established the place that each individual law occupied in relation to both past and future laws; that is to say, in relation to the totality of Francoist legislation. Such a totality was an open one, since the body of Francoist legislation was under continuous construction and expansion through the addition of new laws that reincorporated existing ones. The specificity of this legislation, as Francoist legal experts repeated tirelessly, was constituted by the fact that it did not rest on a set of fixed norms but on the permanence of a small number of fundamental principles. It was a constitution that affirmed and constituted itself through time; hence, one that was permanently in the making and, thereby, through that very process of making, asserted its permanence. As Francoist legal scholar Carlos Iglesias Selgas states, quoting Rodrigo Fernández Carvajal, this was a legislation, "whose final horizon [*término final*] cannot be predetermined whether with regard to the time-period or its substance."[5]

The permanence of the Francoist constituent period manifested itself in two ways. First, in the sense that Francoist legislation, which aspired to be a total and organic body of laws, saw each law as only a piece of a totality that a single law could not contain and could only insinuate. Each law invoked those that preceded it, and some of them even referred to other laws that would follow, even if they had not yet been written and even if a law that followed was logically prior to and "more fundamental" than the one preceding it. For example, in 1947 the regime proclaimed the Law of Succession, which, as its name indicates, regulated the single most important issue that preoccupied the regime: What would happen after Franco? The law established that after Franco's death, or in the event that he should become incapacitated, Spain would return to the political system that its tradition dictated: social, Catholic, representative monarchy. The return of the monarchy, however, was not to be seen as a simple restoration after a decades-long hiatus but as an *instauración* (establishment), meaning that the future monarch would be required to abide by the fundamental principles of the Movimiento Nacional and would be obliged to take an oath to uphold those principles before being allowed to assume the throne. The fundamental principles cited as succession criteria in the 1947 law did not themselves become law until 1958, at which point the Law of Fundamental Principles of the Movimiento Nacional had to abide by the principle of monarchic succession, despite the fact that the Movimiento itself was the basis for the reestablishment of the monarchy.

In its necessarily general and repetitive nature, each law legislated a piece of legality and could do so because the legality of all of the laws was rooted in the outcome of the Glorious Uprising. Therefore, Francoist legislation perpetuated the split between law and legality that, as we have already seen, was characteristic of pre–Civil War liberal regimes, although it did so in exactly the opposite direction. Since in Francoism legislation and legality were meant to be one and the same, and since legality was given and prior to any laws, then the laws served to prescribe the legality of what was beyond the law (the Glorious Uprising and, by extension, Francoism). As demonstrated by Juan Ferrando Badia, among others, this division between law and legality was filled by the role of *el caudillo*, Franco, and by *caudillaje,* as a form of rule: "The role that '*el caudillaje*' has—or pretends to have—is the establishment of a new order. For that reason, . . . the leader embodies the constituent power; he is called [*se llama*] the *founder*. He is not bound by any positive norms. He is the *negation of the state. He is a-legal.*"[6]

The second sense in which we might speak of the permanent constituent period points to the link between the legal structure of Francoism and the question of the regime's continuity and permanence. There was an inherent paradox in the nature of Francoism. While, on the one hand, the consolidation of the regime was the criterion that fully determined the shape of its legislation, in the long run the question that haunted the regime pertained to what it could not legislate: its own continuity. As time passed, it became increasingly clear to everyone inside and outside the regime that the question of the nature of Francoism and the question of its succession was one and the same. This resulted in a dramatic quest in which Francoism was forced to look for a key to its permanence not in what was presumably eternal—its fundamental principles—but in what was historical and bound to change: the embodiment of those principles in the institutional shape that was to be given to the succession. Theoretically, Francoism claimed that it had achieved a synthesis between revolution and tradition, between the eternal and unquestionable principles of Christian humanism and the historical conditions of Cold War Europe (in which Spain stood out like a sore thumb, an anomalous residue of fascism). That synthesis, which was essential for the self-definition of the regime because it was meant to differentiate it from both liberalism and totalitarianism, in fact played out as a battle within the regime over the fundamental question of its continuity as well as over the practical matter of who would inherit Francoism after the death of el caudillo. Instead of fusing two facets of Francoism (the political and the legal), instead of fulfilling the design of victory through the creation of a lasting body of laws, the constituent period revealed and deepened the gap between law and politics. The regime, obsessed by the question of its permanence, could never fully constitute itself.

In what follows, I analyze three different approaches to consolidating the Francoist regime or, at the very least, to prolonging its existence. A common element in all of them is the attempt to situate the debate over the regime's future in the sphere of legal and political theory. Although the very idea that the Francoist regime produced a legal and political theory worthy of its name might sound suspicious, the issue at stake is not the theoretical soundness of the authors' ideas. Rather, the texts analyzed here reveal a chronic concern within the regime about its future and show how important it was to align the problem of futurity with the issue of legality. One must recall the importance that, during Spain's transition to democracy, was placed on the regime's orderly, that is, fully *legal* character. In 1976, Adolfo Suárez, then the prime minister, clearly stated: "There cannot exist, nor will there ever exist, a constitutional vacuum, much less a vacuum of legality. . . . Legality is precisely the foundation [*el asidero*] we have for guaranteeing political freedoms."[7] For the authors studied in this chapter, the notion of "Francoist legality" was not an oxymoron but a vital element for securing the regime's past, present, and future. Each of them collaborated in the consolidation of Francoism at some level: José Luis Arrese by trying to legally regulate the status of the Movimiento Nacional, Manuel Fraga and Carlos Ruíz de Castillo by elaborating on the notion of a Francoist material constitution, and Jesus Fueyo through a critique of liberalism based on the notion of authority (*auctoritas*). In different ways they were all concerned with solving the ultimately unsolvable problem of the gap between legality and legitimacy, which dated back to the regime's violent origins. They also sought to address legal and political problems emerging from a lack of ideological unity within Francoism. Most important, however, they saw the legal consolidation of the regime as a way of averting or postponing the return of liberal democracy.

Falange, Movimiento Nacional, and the Rule of Law

The Movimiento Nacional was the only political organization allowed to exist during Franco's regime, aside from those associations considered natural and nonideological, such as family, corporatist unions (*sindicatos verticales*), and municipalities.[8] The initiative to formalize the role of the Movimiento within the regime came from José Luis Arrese, a leader of the Falange who in 1956 assumed the position of the Movimiento's secretary general for the second time.[9] Arrese attempted to secure the future of the Francoist regime by promulgating a series of laws aimed at sanctioning the Movimiento Nacional's role in dictating and overseeing the regime's succession. Different reasons, both systemic and circumstantial, compelled Arrese to undertake the project of defining the legal status of the Movimiento Nacional at that time. The systemic reasons concern the 1947 Fundamental Law, which stipulated that in the event of Franco's death the title of head of state would pass on to a king. This law did not address the other two posts held by el caudillo: president of the government and leader of the Movimiento Nacional. Without giving the Movimiento the legal power to oversee and, if necessary, override the decisions of the future head of state, the Francoist regime curtailed its power to prevent monarchic support for a return of parliamentary democracy. Arrese's preoccupation with the issue of the regime's future was exacerbated by a series of events that accentuated the fissures within the Movimiento and testified to the Falange's declining power. In the early months of 1956, tensions surrounding the election of the leader of the SEU, a student union that used to be one of the bastions of the Falange, escalated into a full-fledged protest at Madrid University, the first one under Francoism. Within an already tense atmosphere, the Falange's commemoration of the death of one of its "martyrs," Mateo Moral, evolved into a public scuffle on the streets of Madrid between students and members of the Falange, during which an eighteen-year-old Falangist was shot. In response, Franco forced the resignation of Minister of Education Joaquín Ruíz Giménez, a Christian democrat, and the leader of the Movimiento, the Falangist Raimundo Fernández Cuesta, who was replaced by Arrese. Moreover, the country's unfavorable economic situation was further aggravated by a 20 percent raise in workers' salaries, championed by the minister of labor, José Antonio Girón, who privileged the Falange's idea of social justice over the parameters of economic rationality. These accumulated political and economic tensions foreboded a kind of turning point for the regime. Within that atmosphere of crisis, Arrese's proposals for reform served as a catalyst that exacerbated existing disagreements within the regime. By the same token, the failure of his initiative and the composition of a new government, in which "technocrats" from Opus Dei took charge of economic development, were the signs of a new era, one dominated by an overtly anti-Falangist doctrine that Arrese characterized as "capitalist, monarchic and liberal."[10]

Given the futility of Arrese's efforts, and the absurdity of his attempt to legislate the future, his frustrated legal reform could be seen as a minor affair, a nonevent. Why would anyone pay attention to doctrinal disagreements among Francoist factions, especially given that, in the aftermath of Arrese's failure, things didn't take a dramatic turn for him, the Falange, or the regime itself? Following the proclamation of the new cabinet in

1957, Arrese went on to occupy a ministerial post in the Department of Housing (Ministerio de Vivienda) created especially for him; another, watered-down version of the Law of Principles of Movimiento Nacional was approved in 1958; and, if anything, the regime and Spanish society benefitted from the era of economic growth that resulted from the reforms championed by Opus Dei ministers. I engage here with *Una etapa constituyente*, Arrese's lengthy (and often tedious) chronicle of the events that transpired between the beginning of his work on the new legislation and the failure of his project. Arrese's text is unique in that it provides an insider's account of the regime's inability to find a solution to the problem of its transitoriness. Moreover, it is precisely his compulsively detailed report of day-to-day interactions between Franco and his collaborators that illuminates the nature of stasis, restlessness within immobility, which was not only an external feature of Francoism—possibly a reflection of the calculatedness and the stalling that characterized el caudillo's style of leadership—but an inherent trait that was necessary for the regime's survival. As we shall see, Arrese's initiative, which sought to establish the continuity of the Movimiento's fundamental principles by constituting them into law, evolved into a typically liberal exercise of endless debate among different factions of the regime. The intensity of that debate diverted attention from the principles themselves and undermined the purpose of securing them.

In retrospect, we can see the failure of Arrese's initiative as proof that the goal of ensuring the persistence of Francoism after Franco could not be achieved purely through legal means and without popular participation. Even so, one emerges from reading his chronicle struck by the intensity of Arrese's preoccupation with the future, which mirrors the regime's attempts to foresee things it might control and influence those it could not. Much to Arrese's dismay, the hostile reactions his proposals met among the representatives of different factions (another meaning of the term *stasis*), illustrated what the regime did best: change while remaining the same, move forward by equivocating and reshuffling portions of power among ideologically disparate groups. Rather than seeing that equivocation as a flaw—which Arrese did—many of Franco's supporters portrayed it as a necessity dictated by the existence of internal pluralism. The regime moved on by placing obstacles to the very notion of a determinate goal that would necessitate concerted political movement; most of its members understood that movement in politics generates—and is generated by—opposition and resistance. Arrese's account of his failed reforms demonstrates that Franco and the conservative forces gathered around his leadership secured their power by subduing the Falange's ambitions so as to avoid stasis (civil war) among its factions. Additionally, the neutralization of (what Arrese's rivals qualified as) the totalitarian features of his reforms benefitted the regime's efforts to normalize its relationship with liberal democracies, which had already yielded significant results: trade and military alliance with the United States (1953) and the reinstatement of Spain's membership in the UN (1955).

One final remark is in order before engaging with specific elements of Arrese's text. While today, four decades after the dissolution of the Francoist regime, it is impossible to muster any sympathy for Arrese's lamentations about the regime's liberal turn and its disregard for the Movimiento Nacional, it is equally difficult to suppress revulsion at the defense of depoliticized conformism that his enemies presented as their— and, in fact, *the only*—alternative to totalitarianism. The important thing is not that monarchist, Catholic, and Opus Dei factions won and Arrese lost but that the attitude of the forces that emerged victorious in that battle—a mixture of pragmatism, economic efficiency, and suppression of conflict—not only survived Francoism but represent a blueprint for the neoliberal ideology espoused by the current Spanish government and the leadership of the European Union. Arrese's battle against the liberalization of Francoism, which strangely enough was grounded in his praise for the liberal respect for legality, showed that in some important aspects Francoism and (neo)liberalism were not at odds. Moreover, irony of ironies, it was Arrese himself who, as the minister of housing, called for building "un país de propietarios, no de proletarios" (a nation of property owners, not of proletarians).[11] Arrese's position, which Isidro López and Emmanuel Rodríguez have qualified as "Thacherism *avant la lettre*," indicates how easily he embraced the ideology of his "liberal" enemies.[12]

Let us retrace our steps and turn to Arrese's efforts to complete the structure of Francoist legislation with a series of laws aimed at disassociating the question of the regime's future from the ever-present eventuality of Franco's passing. Arrese often used the example of the liberal state to prove that the only thing that could give permanence to the regime beyond the lifespan of its founder was legal consolidation and enforcement of the fundamental principles. The liberal state, he asserted, survived for an extended period of time precisely because it had a legal structure that ensured continuity despite frequent changes of government. Without legally established political criteria of succession dictated and controlled by the Movimiento, he argued, Francoism would be nothing but an historical parenthesis closed by el caudillo's demise, and the Movimiento would constitute no more than a political fiction necessary for the regime's survival, while it lasted.

Unlike other European fascist or authoritarian regimes of the first half of the twentieth century, which had risen from crises of the liberal state but had failed to establish themselves in the long run, the Franco regime had managed to successfully create a new and lasting state out of the ashes of liberalism. But Arrese and others who had come to Francoism from the Falange feared for the future of that victory. What if the triumph of Francoism was a poisoned gift, and its very duration, combined with its lack of definite legal structure, inevitably risked reversing its trajectory through a return journey back to liberalism? It is not necessary to share Arrese's ideological perspective to grasp his anxiety. The possibility of a return to liberalism gave Francoism an interim character. The fact that the inconclusive Francoist legal structure not only enabled but actually invited a certain amount of ideological pluralism—the regime's historically necessary post-1945 repudiation of totalitarianism required some limited pluralism for its survival—meant that the only constant in the life of the regime was the uncertainty over its future. In a sense, what was originally devised to provide Francoism with stability (its rootedness in purportedly unchanging principles) ended up constituting its most ephemeral aspect. Institutionally speaking, the regime was like a shipwreck survivor clinging to the plank of Franco's life, to cite Arrese's own metaphor (in which one can almost hear his distress): "Necesitábamos su vida con angustia de futuros náufragos" (we needed his life with the anguish of future shipwrecks).[13] If that is so, then what about all those who had fallen in the Civil War; and who was to guide the living?

Arrese's defense of the path of legality rested on a double function that the proposed laws were to fulfill. In the first place, they would secure the foundations of the regime by consecrating its victory as the legitimate outcome of a struggle between two distinct and irreconcilable systems (liberalism and National Catholicism) and not merely as a contingent outcome of the Civil War. Second, by securing the legitimacy of the victory through the formation of a new legality, the laws would prevent the possibility of a future reversal. This could happen only by closing the gap between the regime's proclaimed loyalty to the values of the Movimiento Nacional and its actual policies. Various examples support Arrese's claim that many far-reaching decisions about the future of the regime were made without consulting the Movimiento's leadership. Among them was the 1947 Law of Succession, which Franco promulgated without even requesting collaboration from the Movimiento before convoking referendum. Moreover, all Francoist governments were *gobiernos de concentración*, composed of representatives of different ideological groups that privileged their own ideological positions over the Movimiento's interests. Arrese's proposal aimed to reverse the existing hierarchy, postulating that it was the task of the Consejo Nacional, the Movimiento's governing body, to select three candidates from whom the head of state would appoint a prime minister. Alas, in 1956, when Arrese assumed his position, the Consejo Nacional had not met for a period of eleven years!

Chronologically speaking, Arrese's second term as the Movimiento's secretary general marked the regime's midpoint, two decades after 1936 and nineteen years before Franco's death. Clearly, it is only in retrospect that we can see 1956 as the year that marked the chronological midpoint in the life of the regime. However, not only for Arrese but for other figures studied in this book—particularly Dionisio Ridruejo and Miguel Espinosa—that date marked a political and personal turning point that was by no means unrelated to the changes undergone by the regime.[14] Arrese's initiative delineated a stage in the development of a regime that was becoming fully aware of its condition as an interregnum. At this charged and conflictive point, the failure of the *etapa constituyente* (constitutive period), centered on the role of the Movimiento, inaugurated another phase in the regime's development, one best known for the entry of Opus Dei ministers into the government in 1958. The significance of Arrese's failure lies in its complex and contradictory nature. Not only did his attempt to legislate the continuity of Francoism fail due to its own shortcomings but also, and more important, those shortcomings provided the opportunity for the different factions of Francoism to air out their ideological differences in ways that would otherwise have remained secret: disagreements dressed up as agreements. Arrese, despite himself, brought to the surface (and had to endure the consequences of) the paradox of Francoist pluralism. In that sense, Arrese's initiative allowed for legally unsanctioned but effectively tolerated differences within the regime to be expressed in a strictly legal context: a discussion about the legality of the initiative itself. His project became a catalyst for a debate that he had to initiate but could not win—at least not within the realm of legality, which was the only path available to him for asserting the role of the Movimiento. Other, more direct, methods had already become untenable for the leader of an organization that many Francoists saw as little more than a barely disguised effort to reconquer for the Falange the position it had already lost. Ideologically speaking, the Movimiento Nacional, seen as a stand-in for the Falange, was subject to accusations of totalitarianism, while its legitimacy had been weakened by the role that the 1947 Law of Succession assigned to the monarchy.

The proposals provoked virulent opposition, which targeted virtually every one of the measures. The monarchists reacted against turning Franco's successor, king or regent, into a mere figurehead who would have to answer to the Consejo Nacional. Some Catholic members of the government, such as Minister of Foreign Affairs Martín Artajo, claimed that the proposals contained many totalitarian components, which made them incompatible with Spain's Catholic identity. More moderate opposition came from others, like Carrero Blanco or Franco himself, who criticized the legal, and not the ideological, aspects of the proposals, such as the decision to turn the Consejo Nacional into an autonomous legislative or overseeing body in addition to the already existing ones, the Parliament (Cortes) and the Council of the Realm (Consejo de Reino). Arrese quickly realized that it was impossible to mediate between those who rejected the project as a whole and those who demanded changes. While there was no possible dialogue with the former, even the less radical disagreements revealed a deeply ingrained misunderstanding of the nature and role of the Movimiento. For example, a large number of those who sent their comments still used the terms Falange and Movimiento interchangeably, as if they were one and the same thing.[15] Others, who criticized the proposals for introducing a dual sovereignty—a split between the future monarch and the Consejo Nacional—saw the Movimiento as an additional element in the system that would represent an obstacle to establishing full sovereignty. For Arrese, on the other hand, the Movimiento was not an additional element but the central component of the system. The Movimiento was, as he puts it, "the real society, because it was identified with its [society's] mission, distant from the barbarous and amorphous conception of the collectivity based on a number."[16]

Arrese's attempts to legislate the role of the Movimiento within the state had the undesired effect of revealing the irreconcilable conflict of interests within the regime. In their attacks on the legislation, different forces within Francoism began to *behave* like political parties without actually *being* parties. These different groups, often further divided into still more factions, coalesced around their respective irreconcilable positions, which, rather than articulating true ideological pluralism, merely expressed the sense of confusion and division beneath the surface of the Movimiento's unity. The Movimiento's overseeing role, which depended on its institutional ability to channel the existing pluralism and to secure the ideological basis of the state, was rendered illusory by growing disagreement, which reflected not only differences between the groups but their fundamental disagreement over the Movimiento's role in the regime.

Arrese's laws fell prey to accusations of totalitarianism, something he had sought to avoid precisely through the recourse to legality; that is, by consolidating the Movimiento as a statutory body that would function as the intermediary between state and society, channel the political participation of the citizens, and oversee the policies of the government. The only alternative to this recourse was the complete domination of the Movimiento by the state or by the government. In practice, the pivotal political role that should have belonged to the Movimiento had been neutralized and toned down by the predominance of the merely administrative approach to politics that resulted from the ideologically heterogeneous nature of Francoist governments. So, while the pragmatically minded Franco made balancing the composition of the government into an art form, Arrese (who was an architect by profession) argued that the regime's edifice should have basic principles for its foundations, laws for its pillars, and popular consent for its roof. Clearly, he was inverting the parliamentary edifice of liberalism, making societal will the safety lid of the system instead of its basis.

Embattled from many different directions, Arrese aspired to find an ideologically coherent solution to the problem of succession, which, given the lasting nature of Francoism, was both a political problem that became a legal one and a legal problem that became political. Far from achieving his goals, Arrese's laws fell prey to the game of politics that his own appeal to legality had sought to limit or, to use his favorite word, to channel (*encauzar*). Instead of breaking the vicious circle that tied Francoist legality to politics in a way that left room for indeterminacy and change, Arrese's attempt to firmly bind legality and ideology by putting the Movimiento in control of the future reached its limit in the legislation he wanted to promote. What he sought to impede in the future—the return of liberalism through the back door of Francoist legality—seeped in, under the guise of controlled pluralism, through the cracks of Arrese's project and slowly sank it. By virtue of its failure, Arrese's proposal had the unwanted effect of legitimizing precisely what it sought to legislate—Francoism's limited pluralism—and encouraging what it sought to avoid: the possibility of liberalism's gradual return.

In *Una etapa constituyente* Arrese acknowledges that his initiative fell short on multiple levels. It failed to produce an ideologically coherent answer to the question of the future of the regime by being unable to reach a consensus through open discussion among its different sectors. It also represented his personal failure to achieve the two main goals he had announced for the Movimiento in his first speech after assuming the position of secretary general for the second time: "Ganar la calle y estructurar el Régimen" (win the streets and structure the Regime).[17] The most significant conclusion that Arrese drew from his frustrated legislative initiative was that the very attempt to secure the future of Francoism through the constituent process was an impossible undertaking. During one of his conversations with Franco, at a point when disagreements and objections to the proposed laws had begun to pile up, Arrese brought up the question of how one could account for the radical change that had taken place between the early years of the regime, when its unity was unquestionable, and 1956, when it seemed no one in the regime could agree with anyone else. His own answer to this question is categorical: "In my opinion . . . [what changed] is the regime's political unity, which has fractured irremediably, and that might be our fault."[18]

What Arrese failed to take into consideration was that the resistance to his project not only testified to a loss of the regime's unity but also represented a decisive step away from Francoism's original vision. The very thing he had conceived as the solution to the problem of the regime's continuity (strengthening the Movimiento's position), ended up spawning new questions and disagreements that led the regime in a direction entirely beyond what Arrese had envisaged. To put it somewhat differently, although his legislative initiative aimed to put the Movimiento in control of the future by giving it legal self-sufficiency in relation to both el caudillo and the amalgam of different ideological tendencies within the regime and the government, the result of that effort was the rapid consignment of Arrese and his conception of the Movimiento to the past. So much so that Arrese's successor as secretary general, José Solís Ruiz, is considered, in the words of Juan Linz, "the first real head of the Movimiento" rather than of "the *old provisional*" nationalist coalition party.[19] What Arrese conceived as the culmination of the National-Catholic revolution through its legal consummation ended up constituting a key episode in the long process of the dual restoration of monarchy and liberalism.

I would argue that the fundamental flaw of Arrese's project lay in its attempt to reestablish the power of the Falange and the Movimiento as the only real sources of the regime's legitimacy, while at the same time siding with a formal or positivistic notion of legality that dictates that anything that is written into law is legal.[20] The initiative's totalitarian aspects consisted in aspiring to legalize and transform into norms the principles of the Movimiento that were purportedly unquestionable and therefore outside the realm of positive legality. On the other hand, its legalism consisted in the attempt to reestablish by pure force of law, *de iure*, the power that the Falange, as the historical foundation of the Movimiento, had de facto lost once the constitutive violence of the war gave way to the consolidation of the new state.

Arrese took it upon himself to reverse the gradual supplantation and progressive depoliticization of the Movimiento. The Francoist-limited pluralism that, according to Juan Linz's famous thesis, "made the regime authoritarian rather than totalitarian," also turned the Movimiento into an organization that stood midway between a totalitarian single party and an ideologically heterogeneous and depoliticized organization.[21] What ostensibly held this precarious balance together was the need to prevent the regime from slipping toward either of the extremes of totalitarianism or overt pluralism. This delicate equilibrium haunted Arrese's project and yielded the predicament whereby excluding one of the extremes would inevitably mean sliding toward the other, thereby undermining the regime while simultaneously attempting to construct it. How to admit the existence of pluralism within Francoism without also admitting (the risks) of a full expression of pluralism—that is, liberalism—which would mean negating the very specificity of Franco's regime and the meaning of the victory? How to endorse legally the fundamental role of the Movimiento without it actually becoming a single party in the style of totalitarianism?

Arrese was keenly aware of this dilemma. While he knew that the circumstances surrounding discussions of his proposals would be difficult, he quickly discovered that they verged on the impossible, given that those looking for an opportunity to attack Arrese's conception of the Movimiento could do so indirectly by attacking the laws. Ostensibly, it was the laws themselves, and not the Movimiento, nor the Falange, nor the future of Francoism, that motivated the attacks coming from virtually all sectors of the regime: the monarchists, the traditionalists, the Christian Democrats, all the way to the hierarchy of the Catholic Church, which would end up delivering the final blow. In its response to the proposals, the Church issued a warning against the threat of totalitarianism while shrewdly reminding el caudillo of the importance of the regime's international standing, which in the mid-1950s was better than ever: "[Está] hoy en su feliz coyuntura" (is at this auspicious juncture).[22] Powerless before the authority of the Church and fearing a virulently anticlerical response from the radical sector of the Falange, Arrese deemed that the withdrawal of his proposal was preferable to assuming the burden of responsibility for an outbreak of violence that would reawaken the ghost of civil war.

The course of the discussion that led to the collapse of Arrese's initiative made it clear that the problem resided not only in the laws but also within the regime itself. As is evident from his chronicle, Arrese found the magnitude of his failure insignificant compared to the burden of responsibility that lay with the regime as a whole for not reversing the process that had diverted it from its original path. At the same time, he was well aware that there was no jumping off the train of Francoism for him or anyone else who claimed a stake in the Civil War victory. The Movimiento Nacional, an artificial combination of different "families" of the regime, was trapped in its own victory. The only alternative to the legislation that Arrese could envision was an impossible one: either continue with self-deception or prepare for a false repentance in the future. "If the cause of my enemies turned triumphant, there probably would be no laws. What is certain, though, is that we would continue living the farce of this political carnival, waiting for the *Caudillo*'s death to shamelessly strip off the mask of our adherence to the Movimiento."[23]

Almost against the will of those engaged in the debate, the ideological battles over the principles and the purpose of the laws brought to light the question of parallelisms—similarities and differences—between Francoism and liberalism. These correlations concerned questions of the relationship between violence and power as well as between the exercise of power and the enforcement of legality. The debate and the lack of agreement about the regime's ideological foundations meant, quite simply, that Francoist power did not rest on respect for the regime's fundamental principles but was exercised *in spite* of them.[24] Whereas in the liberal state, legality and legitimacy are inextricably bound together, in Francoism they did not go hand in hand.[25]

The ever-growing gap between the realm of ideology and the exercise of political power in Francoism—the former based on undisputed principles and latter on the political dictates of the moment as interpreted by el caudillo—directly influenced the impossibility of regulating legally the relationship between the Movimiento and the state. Simply put, twenty years after the war, the Movimiento had a legality that derived from the legitimacy of the victory, but not a legitimacy that derived from legality. (I return to the problem of legality and legitimacy in my discussion of Jesús Fueyo's writings on the issue.)

It is crucial to realize that Arrese framed this dilemma in terms of legality precisely in order to *avoid* framing it in other terms, whether political or ideological. Framing it in ideological terms, as a question of power held by different currents of the regime, would have undermined Arrese's initiative from the outset. Admitting that the proclamation of the laws depended on the political contingencies of the moment, which indeed was the case, would have exposed the illusory nature of Arrese's claim that the Movimiento's task was to regulate that contingency. The result of Arrese's initiative was that the principles of the Movimiento and previously of the Falange, which by 1956 were outdated, became even more obsolete by virtue of Arrese's attempt to enforce them. At the time of Arrese's initiative, it was impossible to stage an open battle for the future of Francoism. Objectively, it was both too late to assert the regime's ideological unity and too early to stage the definite battle for the succession. In light of the regime's awareness of its intrinsic finitude, it was only logical that Franco would leave the decision about the future of Francoism to his successor. However, doing so meant keeping the door open for the unpredictable.

The Francoist Material Constitution

When it was proclaimed on May 18, 1958, the Law of Fundamental Principles of the Movimiento Nacional was hailed by Francoist legal scholars as a major achievement both for the regime and the Movimiento. As we shall see, Manuel Fraga, a legal expert and the regime's rising political star, and Carlos Ruíz de Castillo, Fraga's mentor from the University of Santiago de Compostela, saw this law as a reflection of the "material constitution" of Franco's Spain, prior to and more important than any formal or written one.[26] The law's proclamation consecrated the Movimiento's fundamental principles as a loyal reflection of the inner nature of the regime whose concrete necessities would determine positive legal norms. However problematic, this assertion contained an element of pragmatism. As Fraga, who would later become one of the authors of the 1978 Spanish Constitution, observed in *La crisis del estado* (1955), only time can tell whether a certain constitutional form "had created, improved, or destroyed some or many institutions."[27] Therefore, rather than extolling the value of a constitution as such, it is the material constitution (i.e., the regime) that determines the legal and institutional framework of the state.

Following the proclamation of the Law of Fundamental Principles, scholarly journals such as *Arbor* and *Revista de Estudios Politicos* published comments about various aspects of the law, from more technical issues (theory of representation, ordering of the articles) to others dealing with practical matters (the regime's social policy, or industrial and scientific development). Reading these comments today from the historical distance of several decades allows us to grasp something about the character of the event. The law's proclamation provided provisional closure to the political struggles that had accompanied its creation. Having survived endless debates about the future of the Movimiento and the regime, the law could finally shine with its legal symbolism in order to better fulfill its function: advancing the process of the regime's legal consolidation.

The content of the new law was inseparable from its larger meaning, which was related to the fact that it represented a new component of Francoism's open constitution. It possessed two main features that characterized the basic legislation of the regime: Its formulations were sufficiently general and repetitive to reaffirm the regime's unquestionable principles, while at the same time its statements left no room for doubt about the specific form of the regime—a system inspired in the values of Catholic universalism and organized as an organic democracy that would eventually adopt a form of monarchy. However, the law did not only summarize or spell out the principles that characterized the regime. Rather, it reflected the nature of its legality. In other words, its importance resided not only in restating the principles of Francoism but also in asserting the bases of Francoist legality. Several commentators duly noted how decisively different Francoist legality-in-the-making was from the closed and formalistic liberal process: how strong the link was between the doctrine and the institutional development of Francoism and how diluted that same link was in the liberal system, where the proclamation of universal values, such as freedom, is not so much supported as potentially undermined by the atomized, individualistic nature of procedures like the voting system.

In a speech commemorating the proclamation of the new law, Franco emphasized the compatibility between the political component of the regime, embodied by the Movimiento Nacional, and its legal system. That compatibility gave the 1958 law a truly foundational or, rather, re-foundational character. In this case, it was not the regime that derived its legitimacy from the law, but instead it was the law that accompanied the development of the regime, projecting its future against a background of the foundational realities to which Francoism owed its existence. One could certainly apply to Francoist legislation a sentence by British political scientist Samuel E. Finer that Manuel Fraga quotes in *La crisis del estado*: "A Constitution is an autobiography of a relationship of power."[28] And what a strange "constitution" it was: one that purposefully defied the idea of a written and stable supreme legal document and instead transformed into a norm the principle that what exists in reality—that is, the regime and its institutions—is itself the norm. Those commenting on the law observed, more or less explicitly, that its importance resided not just in what it stated but in what it was: a foundational document containing the constitution, which was, in turn, conspicuously absent.

When Francoist legal scholars, whether of a traditionalist, monarchist, or Falangist current, write about the Law of Fundamental Principles they do not offer a professional commentary on it as a law but instead analyze it as analogous with a constitution. The distinction "law vs. constitution" is an important one here. Succinctly stated, the function of laws is to regulate social relationships and forms of behavior, while constitutions represent a juridical ordering of the political system as a whole. This is how Carlos Ruíz de Castillo, a traditionalist and a representative of the Catholic natural law tradition, spells out the constitutional character of the Law of Fundamental Principles: "The Principles situate themselves above the legal texts of highest rank and, like the latter, they are endowed with a constituent value . . . more than a super-law, they are a Super-Constitution: like a living breath, they float above a constitution, or inspire it like a spirit that gives it potentiality."[29] As a (super) constitution, the law does not so much prescribe or sanction; it orders juridical reality and functions as an ideal mirror in which political reality acquires higher meaning. Rather than a positive document, the Francoist Constitution is, for Ruíz de Castillo, a reality of the regime reflected (and elevated) in the mirror of the law.

What does the character of the 1958 law, one of seven Fundamental Laws, tell us about Francoist legality, including the laws that preceded and followed it? As some of the brightest stars of Francoist jurisprudence, such as Manuel Fraga, Luis Sánchez Agesta, and Jesús Fueyo, argued, the law's relevance was that it juridically consecrated certain unchangeable principles rather than establishing new principles or dictating rules. This means that the Francoist legal system corrected (or defied) liberal jurisprudence on two fronts: first, in the sense that the validity of Francoist principles is historical in nature; and second, insofar as the law draws its legitimacy from principles instead of claiming, as liberals do, that law itself is the highest principle. While the basis of the liberal regime resides in the modern system of parliamentary democracy and its highest legal instrument is the constitution, the basis of the Francoist system was to be found in its historically inherited basic principles (Catholicism, monarchic form of state, equality before law, organic democracy, respect for the dignity of the person and for the shared forms of existence), all of which are spelled out and preserved in the Fundamental Laws. In the same way in which the regime linked its legitimacy—a product of the Civil War victory—to its historical role of defending authentic Spanish values, it also linked its own legality to the defense of certain principles. Pushing this line of reasoning further, we can argue that if we accept Fraga's rather Hobbesian assertion that the state is what puts an end to civil war—a point to which I return later, in relation to Agamben's reading of Hobbes—then we would also have to agree that the law, as the instrument of further legitimation of the state, is what makes victory endure. That, at least, is what the Francoist legal scholars hoped.

In that sense, Ruíz de Castillo and Fraga are right on the mark in characterizing the 1958 Fundamental Law as truly a metaconstitution. It did not merely determine what was legal, as a law would, nor did it represent an act of self-constitution on the part of a political community, in the manner of a constitution. (As I have argued throughout this chapter, it was the Civil War that functioned as a proto-constitution for Francoism.) Instead, it instituted the legal form of the regime as the necessary form of the political ordering of the Spanish national community. This is how Fraga explains the link between the Fundamental Law and the ordering of the

Spanish political community. The 1958 law, he argues, was in many ways a summary of the most important aspects of existing Francoist legislation. It functioned as a compendium of the regime's legality, a law of laws. As such, it derived its legitimacy from the nature of the principles themselves and not from some external act of legitimation, such as parliamentary vote, social contract, or popular will. "Legitimacy means that which is the opposite of political voluntarism, or arbitrary decision. . . . That is why there has to exist an area that is not open for debate, which cannot be revoked without a struggle. Designating *what is not debatable* means, by the very game of logic [*por el juego mismo de la lógica*], relegating *everything else* to the realm of what can be amended."[30] Fraga's words contain a warning and a promise; a warning for those who consider Francoist laws as nothing but *papel mojado* (a dead letter) and a promise for the pragmatists both within and outside the regime, who know that, in the future, they will have to play the game of logic and engage in a debate about what is debatable. Fraga makes patently clear that the future will situate the regime and its enemies before the same alternative: either risking another civil war by attempting to preserve or demolish the entirety of the Francoist system or agreeing to revise those aspects of it that are bound to change. Even in 1958 it was clear what option he would choose. With an alarming astuteness and circular logic Fraga claims that a tout court opposition to the principles consecrated in the Law of the Principles of the Movimiento Nacional does not simply position a person against the regime but places him or her on the side of revolution: "The principles are the *basis of legitimacy* and *the foundation of the continuity of the political order*. For that reason, they cannot be modified without substantially altering the *regime* itself. What remains outside the Principles is revolution."[31] For Fraga, the real dilemma is not "Francoism or democracy" but "legality or revolution." This amounts to asserting that it was impossible to oppose the regime while remaining *outside* the logic of the evolving Francoist constitution, which he was laying out.

Paraphrasing the title of one of Carl Schmitt's books, we could say that Fraga assumed the position of a "guardian of the [Francoist] Constitution," except that, in this case, what was being guarded was not a classical constitution but a constitution considered identical to, and identified with, the regime: "It is not, then, the formal constitution but the *material* constitution of the *regime*; that is to say, the *concrete ordering of the political institutions* at the service of the realization of the Movimiento Nacional."[32] This is a crucial statement, which declares that, unlike a classical, liberal constitution—a constitution in a formal sense—the Francoist one is a constitution in a material sense.

The distinction between a material and a formal constitution can be used in a way that associates the former with the unwritten and the latter with the written, or by defining a material constitution as the expression of the authentic nature of the community that conditions its political will. Fraga draws the notion of "material constitution" from French Catholic jurist Maurice Hauriou.[33] For Hauriou and Fraga, the material constitution means quite simply the "regime," a term they associate with the *true order* of the political community, one that exists independently from the form of government the regime may adopt—independently, therefore, of the classical Aristotelian division of the forms of government into democracy, aristocracy, and monarchy. While the classification of the forms of government presupposes a distinction between the state and society, the concept of regime designates a relationship between those who are governed and those who govern. To comprehend this latter relationship, argues Fraga—again following Hauriou—the most important concept is not that of state or society but that of the institution.[34] Political thought in both France and Spain, he observes, has become increasingly aware of the centrality of the concept of the institution (the family, the union, or the political party) for understanding contemporary politics, in contrast to the predominance in the nineteenth century of the dualism "individual vs. society." The state itself, according to the institutionalist theory of law, is nothing more than the largest and most general institution. Given this link between the notions of material constitution, regime, and institution, it is not surprising that Fraga then proceeds to declare that the tendency to establish a typology of constitutions—and one might imagine that this extends to a typology of states—is an unsatisfactory way of explaining contemporary social and political reality, which should instead be seen as consisting of a plurality of *regimes*.

I would argue that by insisting on the plurality of regimes, which are defined by their material, rather than formal or written, constitutions, Fraga also indirectly affirms the existence of a certain amount of pluralism *within* each regime. What, if not a certain degree of *internal* pluralism and difference within regimes, could account for their plurality? One way of accounting for differences between regimes would, obviously, be historical and empirical, given that each regime—and Fraga is primarily concerned with Francoism—constitutes a unique historical reality, a category of its own. That uniqueness is evident in its relation to law. Whereas regimes with written or formal constitutions follow the principle of self-limitation, a regime in Fraga's sense is not limited by a legal text but is instead defined by the way in which its own legality reflects and frames the political reality.[35] Fraga spells this out when he states that Francoism's fundamental laws confirm the "existence of certain *norms that are superior to the fundamental laws themselves*, [norms] from which the latter derive their *legitimacy* and that are by their very nature *permanent and unchangeable*, serving at the same time as a measure of validity for all other juridical norms."[36] By ordering its own legality, the regime automatically sets the standard for the status of the norms it proclaims: that is, it not only sets its own norms but determines the rules and the criteria by which they are to be interpreted and, if need be, contested.

Jesús Fueyo: Legality and Legitimacy

I now turn to Jesús Fueyo, an exemplary figure for examining the theory of authority and the tension between legality and legitimacy under Francoism. A follower of Carl Schmitt and an admirer of Tocqueville, Fueyo was a legal theorist, prolific journalist, and, on two occasions, director of the Francoist (more specifically, Falangist) think tank Instituto de Estudios Politícos. Today his work has been largely forgotten, except within quite narrow academic circles in Spain, although, interestingly,

Giorgio Agamben quotes Fueyo's essay on the concept of authority in *State of Exception.* In addition to examining Fueyo's account of the tension between legality and legitimacy and his theory of authority, I also focus on his intellectual relationship with José Ortega y Gasset, Spain's liberal philosopher par excellence. Enlisting Ortega's intellectual prestige for his own project illustrates Fueyo's attempts to develop his theory of Francoism as a unique political system that does not comply with either a liberal or a totalitarian model.

As I have previously shown, the paradox of Francoist legality was that, in order to secure the regime's continuity, it was necessary to give it a legal form. At the same time, the legal form to be adopted depended almost entirely on the demands of its continuity. Through the years, the regime had constantly built and rebuilt the structure of its legality, but it was clear to everyone inside and outside the Francoist establishment that what gave legitimacy to that structure was nothing but the permanence of the regime itself. This double-edged nature of the Francoist legal structure resulted in an uneasy relationship between the regime's legality and its legitimacy.

The distinction between legality and legitimacy is a classical one in legal theory. In the 1930s Carl Schmitt offered an elaboration of it that was well known to Spanish jurists.[37] Schmitt argues that in modern political systems based on the rule of law, the question of the legitimacy of power, that is, the question of who is entitled to hold power and why, is irrelevant. Power is based on the universal, general, and autonomous principle of the legal norm: "In that state 'the laws prevail,' not the authorities. More precisely, the laws do not prevail, but limit themselves to rule as norms."[38] The principle of legality is based on the norm and its application. Nothing stands, or at least nothing should stand, between the two. That empty space between the norm and the application is filled by the very structure of legality, which is based on the separation of powers: legislative, juridical, and executive. The validity of the legal norm depends on that separation because the norm itself prescribes and requires noninterference between different powers.

An anecdote from Franco's life, recounted by Jesús Fueyo in his book *La época insegura,* is useful for contrasting the principle of legality with that of legitimacy. In 1936, the Republican government, concerned about a possible military conspiracy, decided to send Franco to a military post in Morocco in order to keep him away from the peninsula. At a meeting prior to the general's departure, President Nicolás Alcalá Zamora, a lawyer by profession, attempted to assuage Franco's qualms about the situation in Spain. Referring to the governmental crackdown on the 1934 revolutionary uprising in Asturias, the president reportedly told his general: "You can go in peace. . . . The Revolution was defeated in Asturias. There will be no communism in Spain." To which Franco replied, "Whatever has to happen will happen [*sucederá lo que tenga que ocurrir*], Mr. President. But wherever I am, there will be no communism."[39] Whether or not Franco actually made this statement is unimportant: It serves to express his real intention to intervene in the empty space between Republican legality and the communist menace, a space the legitimate government was unable to secure. In his response to the president, Franco defines his role as that of eliminating communism wherever he is and under any circumstances, independently of the Republic's power to defend its own legality. His response constitutes a vow to both supplement and invalidate Republican legality. He renders Republican legality unnecessary by declaring his intention to defend the state while wresting from it the force of law, which is the only legitimate instrument the state possesses for its own defense. In fact, by asserting that the application of the norm depends on him alone and not on the relationship between the norm and the offense established by law, Franco situates the offense outside the purview of the law, thereby collapsing the very structure of legality. By founding the exception (communism can exist everywhere except where he is), he also founds the rule: that communism is the total—one could say, ontological—enemy of Spain and Franco.

The communist menace, for Franco, is something different and much more serious than a political problem. The mere possibility of the communist threat, whatever its origin or nature—whether real or potential, whether posed by domestic or foreign agencies, and whether or not it can be dealt with using legal means—puts Republican legality in question.

While it is completely irrelevant if the threat of communism is real or potential, what is certain, from Franco's point of view, is the effect it will have on Republican legality. The communist threat has the effect of turning Republican legality inside out and splitting it from within. It renders Republican legality *mere* legality and thereby calls for the creation of a new and different constitution, to be based not on a formal and self-enclosed set of norms but on an *organic and living set of principles* that will found new rules. In the face of that crisis, Franco's prophetic comment suggests two possibilities. In the best case the collapse, or short circuit, of Republican legality calls for a military defense of the defenseless state ("defenseless" in the legal sense outlined here). In the worst case—which ended up happening in 1936—the crisis of legality reveals itself in the collapse, signified by the word *communism*, of the distinction between the external and the internal enemy. Together with this collapse, another distinction becomes impossible, one that separates the law from the violence external to the law. Civil war becomes inevitable, and a new legality must be founded from the ashes of the old legality's defeat—a defeat that from the Francoist point of view was nothing but the logical outcome of liberal legality's potential for self-destruction.

The anecdote contains *in nuce* the motifs that Jesús Fueyo expands on in other works in which he analyzes the topic of the historical crisis of liberal legality and the creation of a new legality based on legitimacy. Let us restate those motifs. From a position outside of official Republican legality in both a professional and geographical sense (as a renegade general about to be stationed in Morocco) Franco announces his decision to intervene and rebuild the state by putting into practice his pledge to defend Spain from communism at whatever cost. Instead of correcting an existing situation, he inaugurates a new and different principle of political rule: authority. Franco reacts to Alcalá Zamora's reassurance that he will successfully control communism with a counterpromise to eliminate it. I believe that this counterpromise is what Fueyo, in his definition of legitimacy, calls the "vocation of legacy": "'*Legitimacy*' is the sign and the cipher of this vocation of legacy, which unfolds [*se resuelve*] institutionally and politically as the tradition of authority."[40]

In positing Franco as an embodiment of the principle of authority and as the founder of a legacy, Fueyo situates Francoism within the larger context of Western political history, which in his view is characterized by the long demise of a principle of authority that must be revived. Despite the fact that the term *authority* later became associated with individuals who possess an exceptional real or symbolic power due to charisma or superior social position, in the Roman tradition *auctoritas* was a strictly legal concept disconnected from a person's external attributes, including profession or political position. In private law, auctoritas referred to the property of the paterfamilias, who granted legal status to actions of those who possessed the necessary faculties or capacities but were not legally authorized to act on their own behalf.[41] In the realm of public law auctoritas pertained to the Senate, in contrast to *potestas*, or the power to rule and make decisions for the community, which pertained to the magistrates as representatives of the Roman people.

In *State of Exception* Giorgio Agamben analyzes the interplay between auctoritas and potestas as a crucial factor in the development of the Western idea of law in relation to politics and life. Agamben quotes a passage from Fueyo's 1956 essay "La idea de 'auctoritas': Génesis y desarrollo," which was originally published in a volume honoring Carl Schmitt on his eightieth birthday. The starting point of Fueyo's as well as Agamben's analysis is the function that auctoritas held in the private and public life of ancient Rome. In that context auctoritas was differentiated from potestas, which was attributed to the legally elected representatives of the Roman people. Only if the power of legal representatives were suspended in an abnormal situation, such as a war or a power vacuum (*interregnum*), did those who held auctoritas assume certain functions, to which they were entitled exclusively due to the lack of potestas, and never in order to simply assume power.

Agamben's analysis of the pair auctoritas and potestas focuses on different historical instances, ranging from Augustus's Rome to fascism to the

Guantánamo detention center, as examples of the tendency of the Western conception of law to inextricably link auctoritas and potestas, so that the former refers to the dignity that the community attributes to those things that symbolize its political existence and the latter refers to the power to create and enforce the law. The link between auctoritas and potestas manifests itself particularly in those situations in which the realms of law and life, both individual and collective, intersect to the point of becoming indistinguishable. One example of this would be when, during a state of exception, the sovereign suspends the law in the name of protecting life. The opposite case—the fusion of the sovereign's life and the law—would be Ernst Kantorowicz's paradigm of the king's two bodies (the physical one and the symbolic, immortal one), in which the physical body of the sovereign is elevated and venerated as the representation and embodiment of law.[42] For Agamben these examples, as well as the cases in which the power of fascist leaders was attributed to their immediate and almost mystical relationship with the community, are manifestations of a long-lasting tendency in Western juridical thought that sees law as "identical with—or immediately articulated to—life."[43] The purpose of Agamben's analysis of the state of exception is to break the fiction that ties auctoritas and potestas to the idea of law as identical to life. For him, it is a task of a new type of politics, different from biopolitics, to work against the synthesis between law and life that makes it impossible to distinguish between auctoritas and potestas, between the public and the private, between the law's creation and its application, between the legal norm and the state of exception.

The route Fueyo takes is very different. Like Agamben he is interested in how the separation between the principles of auctoritas and potestas in Roman law eventually led to their fusion. However, whereas for Agamben the possibility of the fusion between auctoritas and potestas is a crucial and politically dangerous component of the Western conception of law, for Fueyo the lack of distinction between the two terms and their overlap in the concept of sovereignty means that the entirety of Western political history is to be interpreted as a long process of corruption of the notion of auctoritas. Despite Fueyo's elaborate historical analysis of that corruption, the conclusion his essay reaches is remarkably simple. Once auctoritas became identified with potestas—and the two notions became fused in the concept of sovereignty—the only path to recovering the meaning of auctoritas was through reviving the experience of authority. This amounts to declaring that, just as in the case of love, freedom, or happiness, the only way to know authority is to feel it (the only other way would be to feel the lack of it). Of course, this is not quite how Fueyo phrases his claim. In his words, "La 'autoridad' es la respuesta de principio a esa situación, porque es el principio de las respuestas" ("Authority" is the principled/principal answer to the situation [of the historical insecurity of an era] because it is the beginning/principle of answers).[44] The only correct way to pose the question of the meaning of authority in an insecure era—*La época insegura* is the title of the book from which the quote comes—is to posit authority as an answer.

How does Fueyo arrive at the conclusion that authority is the principled answer, the "principle of answers," to the crisis of his era? And what does that answer mean, or perhaps reveal? His analysis of the idea of auctoritas begins with the Romans, for whom participation in politics was inseparable from the condition of being a Roman citizen, a member of the community. It was not a question of political rights but of civic identity, aside from which there was nothing more important or more fundamental (such as religion or individual convictions). This experience of politics as the true meaning of life in a community was based on the Roman distinction between auctoritas and potestas. This was not a social distinction based on difference in class, profession, or status, Fueyo observes. Rather, the distinction itself was the trademark of the Roman conception of politics, which in turn captured the Roman way of life as it developed through history. In the context of a form of life based on the distinction between auctoritas and potestas one could not, properly speaking, impose auctoritas. It could only be invoked or claimed. Taking as his example the reign of Augustus, Fueyo emphasizes that the one who held the position of auctoritas was precisely *not* a dictator. Augustus himself emphasized this when he established that his position, while endowed with an "august" authority, in no way entailed a destruction of the existing legality or the invalidation of the constitution from the republican period of Roman history. The legitimacy of his auctoritas, Fueyo emphasizes, came entirely from its association with the principle of continuity of the polity and the sense of respect for its foundations.

More than being simply one, or even the leading, principle of Roman politics, Fueyo continues, auctoritas signified a respect for that community's founding principle. In that sense, auctoritas was the principle of principle, a meta-principle. Using poetical language that anticipates Agamben's observations about the fusion of law and life, Fueyo defines Roman auctoritas as "the principle that expresses the originary sense of the community . . . [that] invokes life in common [*convivencia*] in its pristine significance . . . and consecrates the power that achieves public recognition as a bearer of this significance, in which . . . the life-giving [*genesíaco*] *factum* of political existence announces its presence as an ideal of life."[45] It would hardly be possible for a legal scholar to use loftier language in order to capture the meaning of an institution.

Fueyo attributes the decay in the notion of auctoritas to Christianity. By introducing the difference between the transcendental and the mundane realms, Christianity interrupted the fusion between politics and life that was contained in the Roman interpretation of the pairing of auctoritas-potestas. Through the figure of Christ as a symbol of redeemed existence, Christianity both elevated the value of individual life and devalued politics to a mundane concern.[46] The shift in the relationship between auctoritas and potestas that took place under the auspices of Christianity eventually produced a specifically modern notion of sovereignty. In Fueyo's view, the gradual confusion between auctoritas and potestas, and their merging in the notion of sovereignty, represents a founding moment of modern politics that must be comprehended if one is to assess correctly the politics of the time, including the Cold War or Francoism.

In the Christian paradigm, the relationship between auctoritas and potestas is still the founding principle of the political, Fueyo further observes, but it is now based on a new kind of duality. Auctoritas belongs entirely to the religious realm, while the worldly power of rulers (potestas) lacks a legitimacy (auctoritas) of its own. The relationship between auctoritas and potestas ceases to constitute, as it did in Rome, a dynamic principle of communal life that unfolded as an interplay between legitimacy and legality. It becomes marked by a split between the worldly order of rulers, which lacks an intrinsic legitimacy of its own, and the absolute authority of the religious principle, which resists a complete translation into the categories of worldly power. For Fueyo, the symmetry established in Christianity between a divine auctoritas divorced from potestas and a potestas lacking full auctoritas produced a mutual attrition of the two categories, which would lead to an undermining of the principle of authority.

This attrition was a result of two parallel processes, he argues. At the conceptual level, instead of representing two sides of the coin of legality as they did in Rome, auctoritas and potestas began to refer to two connected yet necessarily different spheres of power: on the one hand, the Pope, and on the other, the emperors and kings. This separation and doubling of powers led to an undermining of the initially distinct roles of the two spheres, which marked the Church as the bearer of auctoritas and political leaders as holders of potestas. In a move analogous to Franco's declaration that Republican legality was a *mere* legality that needed to be defended (or dismantled) by adding to it a new principle of legitimation (anticommunism), Fueyo argues that the pair of auctoritas-potestas began to crumble as soon as the modifier "mere" could be added to either of the terms. Once auctoritas could be seen as mere auctoritas—as authority without power—the limit separating the terms could no longer be sustained, and auctoritas had to include some potestas and vice versa. The same goes for potestas. Gradually, the justification of royal power began to be formulated in terms analogous to those used to describe the properties of the Church dignitaries, and, from there, the elements of spiritual auctoritas became associated with royal potestas.

At the historical level, Fueyo observes, this tension between ecclesiastical and secular leadership and their competing claims over the title of auctoritas and the exercise of potestas was resolved with the creation of the notion of sovereignty, in which the two terms blended indistinguishably. Sovereignty does away with the distinction between auctoritas and potestas, replacing the highly symbolic frontier between them with a concrete geopolitical notion of a border that demarcates a given political unit, which is theoretically and practically uncontestable within its borders. It is impossible to contemplate another concept that would limit or oppose sovereignty because the only border of sovereignty is another sovereignty.

For Fueyo the loss of distinction between auctoritas and potestas was the origin of post-1945 Europe's historical crisis. The nature of that crisis becomes clearer, he notes, through examples of contestation of European domination that represent a threat or an exception to its political ideals. In this group Fueyo includes struggles for independence in European colonies, the alternative to the European order represented by communist Russia, and the specificity of the Spanish regime. The latter example, however, Fueyo deems radically different from the other two. As we shall see, Franco's regime was an exception to the exception, a case that began as an exception but ended up fully within the space of the rule.

Fueyo argues here and elsewhere that the incapacity of the modern era to perceive the distinction between auctoritas and potestas manifests itself as a crisis of authority, which further deepens the gap between legality and legitimacy. In his essay "La agonía de la legitimidad" he criticizes the French revolutionary aspiration to transform the idea of freedom into the basis of a universal human order. He writes: "In order to establish a principle of order in the name of freedom, or any other name, one needs to start with a historical concentration of authority, and in order to proclaim a universal order it is necessary to possess hegemony peacefully."[47] Unlike revolutionary principles, which supposedly possess a validity of their own and aspire to assert that validity by imposing it as a universal principle, the principle of authority manifests itself as a concrete historical instance. One either has authority or does not; one either does or does not embody the concentration of properties that will establish a new principle. In other words, the measure of authority is its capacity to establish the institutions able to maintain order in authority.

Unlike legality, which represents a formal and abstract set of rules and norms, legitimacy is a vital and historical principle. To elaborate this point, in his 1956 article "La razón vital de la legitimidad" Fueyo refers to none other than José Ortega y Gasset, who at the time of his death in 1955 was being celebrated by intellectually and politically restless students of Madrid University as Spain's liberal philosopher par excellence. Despite Ortega's reputation as a "maestro liberal," his 1941 essay "Del imperio romano," which is the focus of Fueyo's article, shows Ortega's liberalism to be debatable at best. His critique of liberalism, and Fueyo's interest in that critique, represents a return to origins. On the one hand, it is a return to the origins of the Western notion of freedom, which, Ortega argues, Romans interpreted in the most creative and historically meaningful way, embedded in the notion of *libertas*. On the other hand, it is a return to the origins of modern liberalism, a theme that appears in somewhat ghostly fashion through Ortega's critique of the loss of the original sense of libertas and the ensuing misinterpretation of the authentic meaning of freedom, which he attributes to liberalism. Fueyo's return to Ortega one year after the latter's death reflects his desire to refresh the stale atmosphere of the present by reawakening the *pedagogía regeneradora* (regenerating pedagogy) of a writer who has already attained the status of a classic.[48] The historical lesson Fueyo finds in Ortega has to do with the relationship of the present political moment to the past and the future.

Ortega's formulation, which brings together philosophy, history, and politics, oscillates around the difference between two conceptions of freedom: Roman libertas and the liberal conception of freedom, the latter of which, he argues, constitutes a narrowing down of a singular notion of freedom to freedoms in the plural. Similar to Fueyo's interpretation of auctoritas, Ortega's reading of libertas departs from a radical difference between Roman and modern conceptions of politics. To capture the meaning that politics had for the Romans, he draws on the distinction between two key notions of his philosophy: ideas and beliefs (*ideas y creencias*). Whereas ideas are purely rational conceptions about a certain aspect of reality, beliefs are notions about the world defined by the fact that they are held in common. Beliefs in Ortega's sense are not something that belongs solely to an individual or even to a group so as to differentiate it from another group. Rather, they belong to the very nature of the social. Beliefs preexist ideas and determine a deeper meaning of the political, which for both Ortega and Fueyo is contained in the notions of *concordia* and *discordia*. The former refers to the social cohesion that results from the existence of commonly held fundamental beliefs, while the latter names the breakdown of social cohesion that occurs in the absence of such beliefs. In talking about Roman politics, Ortega uses the term *creencia* in two senses: as that which stands at the origin of certain social institutions, on the one hand, and belief in the political institutions themselves, on the other.[49]

The most fundamental belief, as Ortega points out and as Fueyo agrees, is articulated as an answer to the question of "who should rule" in a given society at a given moment. It is that question, and not the related one of "how much should rulers rule" that represents "the ultimate and radical question in the life of the state."[50] Without mentioning explicitly the terms *legality* and *legitimacy*—which is what Fueyo will proceed to do, inspired by Schmitt—Ortega points out that the question of belief informed the nature of Roman institutions and Roman conceptions of law and political freedom to such an extent that, without taking belief into account, the true meaning of libertas becomes virtually incomprehensible for the modern, rational mind trained to associate political freedom with the idea liberalism has of it. Liberalism, obsessed by the question of how much the ruler should rule and convinced (erroneously) that freedom consists in limiting the power of the state over the individual, remains blind to the question of who should rule.

Fueyo takes up this point from Ortega's essay and expands on it. He describes the difference between the question of "who should rule" and "how much one should rule" as "a systematic cut between the principle of legitimacy of the political order and the constitutional scheme of its legal functioning."[51] Immediately, he makes it clear that this is neither a technical nor, much less, futile question for Francoism. The systematic cut between the two terms marks the difference between "those who think it is unimportant who should rule provided that they rule within 'such and such' a system and those who believe that the system does not matter if a particular person is in charge." Fueyo continues: "The former is called liberalism, no matter how much it calls itself monarchic; the latter is called autocracy, no matter how charismatic it declares itself."[52] The latter sentence contains a barely veiled criticism of the groups within Francoism that advocated a legal transformation of the regime into a monarchy while simultaneously denying that Francoism was, or should be, an autocracy that rests on the charisma of the leader. Both of these attitudes are shortsighted, in Fueyo's view.

Ortega's analysis allows Fueyo to add another twist to the problem of the relationship between liberalism and authoritarianism, or between legality and legitimacy, beyond their simple opposition. Ortega offers a critique of liberalism on two levels. First, he argues that liberalism should not be seen as having a monopoly on defining freedom. Second, he suggests that if we accept the liberal definition of freedom as the only or the best possible one, we may actually be forfeiting the meaning of what he calls "la vida como libertad," which is the unique experience of freedom itself.[53] Ortega's observations develop out of his insight into the uneasy relationship, or tension, between these two incommensurable notions of freedom. In order to capture that tension, it is important to recapitulate the path that takes Ortega from Rome to liberalism and back to Rome or, at least, away from liberalism.

The meaning of libertas captures the sense of loyalty of the Roman people toward their political institutions, a loyalty that manifests itself as a respect for law. Romans associate the law with the continuity of the polity, given that the law represents the foundation of institutions such as the Senate and the *auspicia*. (In ancient Rome, the *auspicium* was a form of divination derived from the observation of the flight of birds, thought to provide the clues indicating whether a certain course of action, private or public, had the approval of the gods. Roman magistrates interpreted the auspicia that concerned public matters.) In Rome, the validity of the law does not stem from its formal legal properties. In other words, it does not command respect simply by the fact of its existence. Instead, something is considered law, and circumscribes the field of legality, *because* it is respected and valid for all. The constitution—argues Ortega in a sentence that could pass for a definition of the material constitution—"is valid when there is an underlying agreement [*acuerdo subyacente*]."[54] Liberalism, which erases the unified and totalizing sense of libertas by shattering freedom into specific individual freedoms, buries the experience of freedom under a series of legally established criteria that determine the conditions under which each freedom is to exist. This accounts for the different relationship between law and (individual) freedom in liberalism, where an individual is free solely with respect to the law, which is to say that each freedom exists as long as it is not legally suspended. Ortega does not miss the opportunity to remind liberals of the fact that what defines their notion of freedom is not only its primacy but also its relative value, evident in the fact that each constitution establishes the possibility of the suspension of freedoms under certain conditions. With its tendency to legally consecrate certain freedoms, which includes the possibility of suspending them, the liberal constitution does not so much rest on an underlying agreement but instead on the limiting of underlying disagreement.

A particularly valuable aspect of Ortega's essay, for Fueyo, is the third conception of freedom it puts forward, one different from both the Roman and liberal views. In Rome the law is an objective representation of what it means to be Roman. The mixture of that internal sense of belonging and the objective character of law—or, to use Ortega's terms, the fusion of belief and politics—determines both the nature of freedom and its scope. Roman freedom is both completely identified with political institutions and completely limited by them: "For the Roman, . . . state power [*poder público*] has no limits; the Roman is 'totalitarian.'"[55] Ortega's decision to put quotation marks around the word "totalitarian" is a mischievous reminder to those reading his book in 1941 that in Roman society a total belief in the law and the state converged with a complete sense of freedom.

For his part Fueyo appreciates Ortega's ideological ambiguity, which he interprets as a lack of bias on the philosopher's part and proof that Ortega is an eminently political and practical thinker in tune with the times, which demand a repudiation of facile distinctions between liberalism and totalitarianism.[56]

Compared with the complete and yet totally limited Roman sense of freedom, the liberal idea of freedom is, for Ortega, an ideological construct that is inevitably partial. Liberalism confuses individual freedoms with freedom in both a theoretical and practical sense. First, it limits the meaning of freedom to the practice of certain freedoms that, according to its own logic, the state can suspend without therefore negating freedom. This, in Ortega's view, is proof that freedom is never limited to any one form and that one can feel free, even when some of one's freedoms are temporarily suspended in the name of freedom. Second, by ignoring the fact that practicing certain freedoms under certain conditions does not amount to exhausting the possibilities of different forms that freedom might take, liberalism ignores the most important, constitutive, aspect of freedom: it has many forms, and the form in which it is practiced determines *what* it is and *if* it is. Out of the similarity and difference between Roman and liberal notions of freedom—a belief in freedom that de facto limits freedoms versus concrete freedoms that stand for (or pass for) freedom—a third conception of freedom emerges that Ortega calls "life as freedom" and describes as one where "people [*hombres*] live within the institutions they prefer [*instituciones preferidas*], whichever those might be."[57] It is not strange that this position would appeal to a Francoist legal theorist like Fueyo. Ortega's quote can be read as an indirect legitimation of the Francoist regime that, while not conforming to a liberal conception of freedom, established institutions that the Spanish people preferred at that particular historical juncture, at least according to less-than-reliable official referendums.

The idea of "life as freedom" announces a crisis of the liberal notion of freedom and aims to disrupt the identification between freedom and political freedoms. Instead of guaranteeing individual freedoms by circumscribing freedom to the question of "how much one should rule," freedom in Ortega's sense, subsequently taken up by Fueyo, is the result of an implicit agreement within society about a more fundamental question of "who should rule." By focusing obsessively on the former question, liberalism ends up placing artificial limits on the exercise of power. As a result, it actually curtails the meaning of freedom in the sense in which Ortega and Fueyo conceive it: a freedom that arises as a product of societal consensus on "who should rule" and that materializes itself through the shape of the institutions preferred by that society. The confusion of liberal freedoms with freedom itself leads to the suppression of a more authentic and *vital* conception of freedom, which Ortega relates to the Roman tradition of libertas and which, as Fueyo insists, is never far from the tradition of auctoritas.

Ortega's critique of the notion that liberalism should have a monopoly on defining political freedom is embraced fifteen years later by Fueyo as a way of resisting liberalism without thereby rejecting freedom. Fueyo writes: "But if legitimacy is the tradition of one concrete form of life in common, then no legitimacy can be taken as a universal principle of order. Rather, the important thing is that no people vote on the freedom of the world, so that every single people could fashion their own freedom, with or without voting."[58] The allusion to Francoism as a legitimate way of creating the institutions and the kind of freedom most appropriate for Spain is all but spelled out here. So is Fueyo's critique of the attempt to posit liberalism as a universal regime of political freedoms. One consequence of conflating political freedoms with freedom as such, he argues, is the ideological expansion of liberalism; the other, somewhat paradoxically, is the narrowing down of the authentic notion of freedom by reducing it to a formal, legal question. The expansion of liberal freedoms in the West, as well as the domination of the party in the countries of the Soviet Bloc, represents, for Fueyo, one of the main features of life in an "insecure era," to wit, the substitution of ideas and ideals with ideologies.[59]

What ties together this critique of the dominant ideologies of the era with Fueyo's more strictly theoretical concern for questions of freedom and authority is the idea that the ideological expansion of power is itself a symptom of the crisis of the function of authority in the modern world. Unlike the expansion of power that takes place through the imposition of a single, ideologically shaped notion of freedom—what Fueyo describes as an attempt on the part of a single country to vote on the freedom of the world—the function of authority, or authority *as* a function, serves the purpose of containing and limiting power. By its very definition—by the fact that the consolidation of authority presupposes the establishment of a peaceful hegemony or homeostasis among different groups—authority does not, strictly speaking, represent an imposition of power but instead its limitation and containment. In that sense, the expansion of power through the instrument of ideology stands in contrast with the consolidation of power via authority. Fueyo illustrates this function of authority in relation to Franco in an essay entitled, significantly, "Hispaniae moderator."[60] Here Fueyo argues that Franco as a figure of authority neither creates nor single-handedly secures power but instead allows it to come into being by limiting (moderating) the interplay of different forces. It is in the space between the free interplay of forces and the simple continuity of power, between the instability of power and its quasi-biological permanence, where one should locate Fueyo's attempt to overcome the finality of Francoism by defining the function of authority in opposition to the liberal idea of freedom. And what better way to illustrate the interplay between authority and freedom in the context of Francoism than to envision the encounter and the abysmal reflection between Ortega and Fueyo—the Francoist legal scholar who advocated a change within the regime by appropriating the critique of liberalism from the philosopher whom the more recalcitrant Francoists denounced as a liberal par excellence?

Francoism was obsessed with liberalism and legality not because the regime was keen on expanding political freedoms but because it had to distinguish itself from totalitarianism without embracing the status of an interregnum that would lead to the reestablishment of liberalism. For the authors analyzed here the question of the regime's legal structure was indeed vital because, without it, the survival of the regime depended solely on the length of Franco's life. Copious and convoluted theoretical writings as well as the often more telling autobiographical and journalistic accounts analyzed in this chapter make patent the difficulty, not to say impossibility, of the enterprise of legally securing not just Franco's succession but the regime's continuity. Far from subscribing to the idea that the Spanish dictatorship was an anomaly in post-1945 Europe, Francoist legal scholars believed that by looking for a novel articulation of the relationship between the notion of the rule of law and the regime's politics they had positioned themselves fully within the Western intellectual and political tradition, the future of which hinged on the battle between liberalism and totalitarianism. In different ways they sought to adapt Francoism to new historical realities and accommodate the unchanging aspects of the regime to the necessities of change. Increasingly they focused on problems that the Spanish regime shared with other European societies and that required finding an appropriate legal formula to balance economic development with spiritual principles, ideological sectarianism with political cohesion, and the maintenance of power with the preservation of the society's core beliefs.

The paradox shared by the writers analyzed here is that, each in a different way, they collaborated in the consolidation of Francoism while also anticipating its inevitable end. By further reducing the power of the Falange and failing to strengthen the influence of the Movimiento Nacional, Arrese contributed to the triumph of a less ideological and more administrative approach to government. Fraga's interpretation of the regime's material constitution all but spelled out his conviction that Francoism would have to change substantially in order to survive and that the key to its future lay in anticipating the conditions of its orderly transformation. Finally, Jesús Fueyo critiqued the liberal conception of freedom as synonymous with (individual) freedoms and recuperated Ortega's idea of freedom that is rooted in a particular set of beliefs instead of an abstract system of legal rules. While combating the sense of immobility that emanated from the uncertainty about the future of the regime, these authors illustrate different ways in which the thought of the regime's end was necessary to stimulate and propel its movement forward.

CHAPTER 2

The Movement of Divergence

Dionisio Ridruejo from Totalitarianism to Liberalism

Dionisio Ridruejo's poem "Romance de la empresa vendida" (Romance on a sold-out undertaking) contains in a nutshell the formulation of the issue that runs through this entire chapter: Ridruejo's critique of Francoism as an aberrant political system that transformed the Spanish political landscape into a desert. The metaphor of the desert captures Ridruejo's vision of Francoism as a political hiatus founded on the absence of a legitimate political contract between the regime and the population. The absence of such a contract meant that, following the initial period of consolidation, the regime's existence was plagued by uncertainty over its future. The price of that uncertainty was much higher for the Spanish people because, by excluding the possibility of reasoned political discussion about life after Franco, the regime sacrificed care for the collective future to a strategy of postponing the inevitable: the moment of its political end. Francoism was unable to secure the future, and the uncertainty that this generated was permanently at odds with its claims to normalcy. The political desert of Francoism produced a mirage of political stability intended to hide the lack of a true political contract between the rulers and the ruled, without which the regime could never survive Franco's demise.

Ridruejo's "Romance," addressed directly to the members of the Falange, was written during the author's 1957 imprisonment on charges of instigating and collaborating in the 1956 student demonstrations at Madrid University. In the poem he reflects on the Falange's role in the formation of Francoism, declaring that the time has come for the party to cut its support for the regime. Through a somewhat veiled poetic overview of the party's history the poem invokes the memory of the past in order to justify the author's invitation to those members of the Falange still loyal to its original spirit to abandon their political enterprise. The claim that the Falange should embrace the defeat of its cause despite being on the victorious side in the Civil War reappears throughout Ridruejo's writings.

In this particular instance Ridruejo calls attention to the fact that the growth of the Falange, from its early foundation as a minority party of intellectual elites to becoming the nucleus of the only legally permitted political organization under Francoism, did not represent an advancement or fulfillment of its ideals. On the contrary, as Ridruejo claims, that growth entailed a betrayal of the Falange's own promise. The poem argues that the Falange's weakness had come about as a result of its disproportionate and artificial growth during the Civil War: "eras muy tierno de huesos / para carne tan espesa" (too tender were your bones / for such a thick flesh).[1] The torrent of new members that swelled its ranks almost overnight—giving birth to what Ridruejo calls "la Falange de aluvión"— and the untimely death of the party's leader in Alicante prison in 1936, radically transformed the role and profile of the Falange. From a small but influential grouping whose symbols (the yoke and arrows) invoked tight unity and uncompromising loyalty toward the movement's dreams and ideals, it evolved into a herd without a leader. The yoke, an agricultural metaphor of the Falange's unity, lost its metaphorical significance when the party was reduced to an instrument of its new leader, General Franco, and the traditional social elites who reestablished themselves in power after the Nationalist victory in 1939. The Falange's vaguely formulated political ideas and antiquated symbols turned into something else once they were put to new use:

> Eran viejas cosas, nobles
> si sirven para leerlas

pero que, usadas, bien pueden
volverse contra su empresa

They were old, noble things
if one aspires to read them
but, once used
they may turn against their purpose. (304)

When a metaphoric yoke (*yugo* in Spanish) is used as an actual yoke, it responds to the necessities of the one pulling it and not to the desires and ideals of those who are pulled by it. Having lost the control of its "yugo," the Falange became subjugated.

The poem underscores the difference between the nobility of the Falange's original cause and its later status as an instrument serving goals it could not identify with. Not only was the Falange instrumentalized but it was made to serve a purpose foreign to its own. Ridruejo's plea to abandon the enterprise is rooted in his own grief as a former Falangist leader who, soon after the end of the Civil War, became disillusioned and increasingly critical of Franco's regime. He is warning his comrades that as long as Francoism continues to use the party and its symbols as instruments for its own purpose, the continuous betrayal of the Falange's cause will be disguised as loyalty to its original project. As the poem's title suggests, Francoism legitimizes its own victory by using symbols borrowed from the Falange. In that sense, any Falangist who professes loyalty to those symbols is, or has become, a soldier in an army that was defeated the moment its flag was raised in celebration of another's victory. Therefore, for Ridruejo, accepting defeat is the only way to acknowledge and overcome the loss that resulted from an ill-begotten victory.

The fact that the Falange was transformed into an instrument in the hands of the new regime revealed Francoism's internally conflictive nature. While the Falange, subsumed into the "Movimiento Nacional," represented a power that was not its own and that it could not use, the regime continued to count on the Falangists' unquestionable loyalty to Franco.

In order to ascend the summit of power, the Falange had to lose sight of its main goals, but, having reached that summit, the mountain on which it was standing only revealed the deserted landscape surrounding it. In Ridruejo's poem, the word *desert* refers both to the Falange's utopian dream that it abandoned in the process of pursuing it—while engaging in bloodshed and carnage on the road to victory—and to the absence of hope, the collapse of utopia, that resulted from the acknowledgment of the Falange's betrayal by those who falsely appropriated its ideas.

> Cuando llegaste a la cumbre
> y volviste la cabeza
> viste a los amos probando
> el látigo y las espuelas
>
> When you reached the summit
> and looked back
> you saw the masters trying out
> the whip and the spurs. (307)

For Ridruejo, who at the time of writing the poem was publically distancing himself from the Falange, arriving at the mountain summit means reaching a point that combines hindsight and foresight, allowing him to assess the Falange's original intentions based on the results they produced as well as to grasp the nature of Francoist power by assessing its fruit. The conclusions he delivers in his poetic address to the Falange are the consummate expression of personal and political disenchantment. It is clear to him that Francoist power is a fruit of the Civil War victory, but, as such, that power grows and sustains itself only on the weakness and defeat of those who did not partake in the victory. Francoist power is a fruit that grows on a barren land and from the seed of the defeated. The purpose of Ridruejo's poem, therefore, is to invite the Falange to reap the fruit of its own defeat by giving up a power that is someone else's harvest of the group's early, and perhaps mistakenly planted, seed.

When Ridruejo asks the Falange to reap the fruit of its own defeat—
"Todavía queda tiempo, / .... / para volverte guadaña / contra tu estéril
cosecha" (There still is time, / .... / for you to become a scythe / against
your sterile harvest)—he is suggesting that the organization should either
disband, which means disappearing into the ground and *becoming* ground
that might nourish new seed—"Vuélvete sangre de pueblo, / vuélvete
trozo de tierra" (Turn into blood of the people, / turn into a chunk of
land) (313)—or that it should relinquish power by cutting itself off from
the fruits of victory it still enjoyed (official positions, material benefits,
public displays of its symbols, and so on). In this second sense Ridruejo
is inviting the Falange to rid itself of excess members, to prune its own
tree in order to grow smaller—and perhaps stronger?—again. Without
cutting itself off from power, the Falange will continue reaping its sterile
harvest of fruits that grow on the barren land of another's victory or that
grow by virtue of annulling their own seed.

Dionisio Ridruejo's Anabasis

In the essay "Fascinating Fascism," which analyzes the process of historical rehabilitation of one of the pivotal figures of Nazi art, film director
Leni Riefenstahl, Susan Sontag calls attention to two different ways that
controversial historical figures are dealt with, one that is characteristic
of totalitarian regimes and another of liberal ones.

> The rehabilitation of proscribed figures in liberal societies does not hap-
> pen with the sweeping bureaucratic finality of the *Soviet Encyclopedia,*
> each new edition of which brings forward some hitherto unmentionable
> figures and lowers an equal or greater number through the trap door
> of nonexistence. Our rehabilitations are smoother, more insinuative. It
> is not that Riefenstahl's Nazi past has suddenly become acceptable. It
> is simply that, with the turn of the cultural wheel it no longer matters.
> Instead of dispensing a freeze-dried version of history from above, a
> liberal society settles such questions by waiting for cycles of taste to
> distill out the controversy.[2]

Sontag eloquently describes the diverging mechanisms by which two emblematic twentieth-century political regimes settle their accounts with the past. While a Soviet-style, totalitarian version of history relies on the guillotine-like efficiency of the official truth, which annuls controversy by making differences of opinion into a matter of life and death, liberalism lets history itself resolve the question of acceptance of what previously seemed unacceptable, leaving the faculty of taste in the position of a judge able to discern the difference between the tolerable and the intolerable, the appealing and the unappealing. The liberal treatment of the past is based on a false sense of continuity, which consists in preserving only the palatable aspects of the past while ignoring those deemed unpalatable. By contrast, totalitarianism creates a sense of discontinuity by imposing a radical break between the present and the past, erasing some aspects of the past as if they had never existed while resuscitating others that were thought dead.

In the context of the historical struggle between totalitarianism and liberalism in twentieth-century Spain, the political trajectory of writer and intellectual Dionisio Ridruejo (1912–75) stands out as both unique and exemplary. Unique, because Ridruejo is the most famous case of an intellectual who defended both causes, with equal power and engagement, at different points in his life. Exemplary, for the very reason that, having been a prominent figure in the fascist Falange before becoming a champion of the liberal opposition to Francoism, Ridruejo's trajectory embodies not only the contrast and conflict between the two ideologies but also a satisfactory resolution of that conflict through a transition to liberalism, which, moreover, was not predicated on an ideological conversion or disavowal of his previously held beliefs. It would appear that, in Ridruejo's case, the conflict between two rival ideologies did not play itself out following either the Soviet-style model of violent erasure of the past or the liberal strategy of its neutralization.

Current interpreters of Ridruejo's work still struggle with the seeming paradox that his shift from fascism to liberal democracy did not hinge on a sudden conversion or an outright rebellion against his previously held ideas. In his introduction to the 1961 book-length essay *Escrito en España* Ridruejo refers to his embrace of democratic convictions as "el descubrimiento del Mediterráneo" (the discovery of the Mediterranean), that is, as not quite a discovery but an encounter with something that was already there.[3] In the same text he describes his ideological transformation not as a simple change of mind or heart but as a coming into its own of an already-existing set of ideas, once they were thought differently, without being subordinated to the demands of action: "My ideas started out as the usual ones, but when they were thought through in another way, and without any plan whatsoever with regard to action, they in effect ended up being different [terminaron por ser otras]."[4]

Ridruejo's assessment of his ideological trajectory stands at odds with Santos Juliá's belief that, since liberalism and totalitarianism are warring and mutually exclusive ideologies, any intimation that a former fascist could embrace liberalism without thereby relinquishing all sense of coherence and continuity must be problematic at best and disingenuous at worst.[5] Ridruejo's statement also complicates Jordi Gracia's description of the process by which the staunch Falangist gradually yet inevitably grew out of his youthful fascination with fascism, aided by his sharp intelligence and sense of personal integrity, his "morbosa integridad" (pathological integrity).[6] What Ridruejo describes is a curious trajectory that consists of continuing always in the same direction but arriving at an ideological destination different from both the original point of departure (violent rejection of liberalism) *and* the originally desired destination (fulfillment of the totalitarian project). Instead of tracing a straight line that connects two distant points—his totalitarian past and his liberal future—or one that would proceed in a zigzag fashion, crossing the impermeable border that divides two hostile realms, Ridruejo's statement maps out the trajectory that he had to traverse in its entirety in order for his ideas to become different and yet not be completely at odds with what they were, or turned out to be, all along. At the same time, his statement neither affirms an ideological purity and loyalty to an origin nor proclaims the inevitability of his ideological point of arrival. Instead, it emphasizes the trajectory itself: a not necessarily planned movement between two ideological points whose relative proximity (his ideas started out being the same as the ones he previously held) underscores their, also relative, distance (eventually, his ideas ended up being different).

The trajectory Ridruejo describes evokes the notion of *anabasis*, which Alain Badiou employs in his book *The Century* as a way of thinking through the historical experience of the twentieth century. Referring to Xenophon's *Anabasis*, which offers an account of the wandering and eventual return home of Greek mercenaries left adrift after the death of their Persian employer, Badiou describes the term as "the free invention of a wandering that *will have been* a return, a return that did not exist as a return-route prior to the wandering."[7] Similar to what happens in Ridruejo's description of his trajectory, anabasis describes a wandering that, originating in a sense of being lost, creates a previously nonexistent path of return to a point of departure, which, even if it is a new one—as was the case with Ridruejo—can be recognized as such only retrospectively. Ridruejo's account of his ideological transformation, and Badiou's assessment of the anabasis of the twentieth century, allow us to not lose sight of the complex and uncertain nature of the trajectories they describe by focusing either on the certainty of destination (Ridruejo's embrace of liberalism) or the primacy of origin (his totalitarian "deviation").

I analyze here the role that notions of movement and absence of movement play in Dionisio Ridruejo's poetry, essays, and poetic prose written between the end of the Spanish Civil War and 1956, the year when he officially became a member of the opposition to Francoism and a proponent of social democracy. In contrast to scholars who tend to view Ridruejo's ideological shift in biographical terms—as a belated and unsatisfactory conversion, or as a gradual evolution—this chapter asserts the importance of literature for grasping the nonlinear nature of his passage from totalitarianism to liberalism. My reading examines the complex nature of Ridruejo's trajectory in light of a broader issue of the differences and similarities between totalitarian and liberal conceptions of politics in terms of the role each assigns to movement and its opposite (immobility, rest, or stability). In *The Origins of Totalitarianism* (1951), Hannah Arendt claimed that movement was a lynchpin tying the ideology of totalitarian regimes to their practice. "In the interpretation of totalitarianism," says Arendt, "all laws have become laws of movement. When the Nazis talked about the law of nature or when the Bolsheviks talk about the law of history, neither nature nor history is any longer the stabilizing source of authority for the actions of mortal men; they are movements in themselves."[8] Totalitarianism requires a whole-scale social mobilization in order to transform the proclaimed laws of nature and history—racial domination in the case of Nazism, dictatorship of the proletariat in Stalinism—into the ruling principles of social existence. The totalitarian enterprise of designing a machine-like society that operates according to implacable natural and historical laws uses up all human energies and demolishes any sense of social stability or continuity.

I aim to show that preoccupation with movement is a constant throughout the different stages of Ridruejo's political commitment and through the different genres in which he wrote. This preoccupation emerges in the early 1940s, a period of his disillusionment with the Francoist regime for its failure to implement a totalitarian conception of politics based on a guiding role of the party-movement (Falange or Movimiento Nacional) in the establishment of a totalitarian state. Following his 1942 resignation from the positions he held in the regime, Ridruejo's dwindling hopes for the fulfillment of the Falange's role as an ideological avant-garde engender a sense of existential and political uncertainty, which is a subject of the cycle of elegies composed during the first year of his exile in Andalusia. In "Elegía ante la mar," the poetic subject experiences a mixture of calm and unrest associated with the stasis of the sea, a repetitive and unstoppable movement that combines rest and motion, thereby dissolving a sense of purpose and suspending any kind of simple, linear relationship between means and ends, path and goal. The broader point of the chapter is that Ridruejo's distancing from totalitarian ideals depended on the abandonment of the instrumental conception of movement in general, and political movement in particular.[9] In the sections of this chapter devoted to the book of poetic prose *Diario de una tregua*, I focus on Ridruejo's depiction of the landscape of rural Catalonia that emanates rootedness, stability, and a sense of limits. His characterization of the Catalan period (1943–48) as a space of truce (*tregua*) and respite from the pursuit of political goals anticipates his later characterization of liberal democracy as a kind of politics that does not reduce action to the pursuit of preset goals. Of particular relevance here is the parable of the swimming lesson, which appears in an episode from the *Diario* and is taken up again in the 1956 letter to the Falange, where Ridruejo confirms his commitment to a democratic future and refers to himself as a swimming instructor for new generations of Spaniards. Becoming a swimming instructor and teaching the young how to move in an unpredictable and threatening environment (the murky waters of Francoist politics) entails a change in the conception of the nature of political action. The role of swimming instructor is not that of directing movement but instead of transmitting skills to help one stay afloat. As a metaphor for a noninstrumental conception of movement, learning to swim does not lead to an end that is different or separable from the process itself; the meaning of the action is inherent in the movement necessary to carry it out.

The goal of my reading is not to revisit Ridruejo's political trajectory in order to ascertain the authenticity or timeliness of his ideological shift. Not only have such analyses already been carried out, notably by Santos Juliá and Francisco Morente, but their underlying approach calls into question the meaning and relevance of the very notion of ideological conversion, both with respect to Ridruejo's work and more generally. As we can see through the example of Juliá and Morente's works, the very demand for a conclusive and timely ideological conversion of those who once boasted of their antiliberal convictions already presupposes that doubts have been cast on the veracity and/or timeliness of that conversion or retraction. One has to wonder how the demand for the conversion of former fascists differs *structurally* from the position of the liberal intellectuals from the period of the Second Republic who chose to live in Franco's Spain. As Gracia has shown, the acceptance of such figures as José Ortega y Gasset and Gregorio

Marañón by the victorious regime was contingent upon the unsatisfiable demand that they offer a mea culpa, even when they had already willingly sacrificed their liberal credentials on the altar of anticommunism and the defense of an historical continuity they thought the dictatorship would provide.[10] A broader question here is how one can assess the sincerity and validity of an ideological shift when that shift is preemptively denied at the very moment it is expected, or even demanded, by the victorious regime or paradigm. Slavoj Žižek poses an analogous question in the context of the fall of communism in Eastern Europe. In particular, Žižek points to the paradoxical situation of the Eastern European communist parties in the period leading up to the democratic transition. Even as they were expected to uphold their promise to organize democratic elections, the representatives of the communist regime were supposed to continue playing the only role available to them, that of the enemies of democracy: "Communists were expected to assume the impossible position of pure metalanguage, saying, 'We confess, we are totalitarian, we deserve to lose the election!'—just like the victims of Stalinist trials."[11]

The ways in which Gracia, Juliá, and Morente approach Ridruejo's trajectory in the context of Francoism certainly differ—and are often in disagreement.[12] Yet, despite these differences, all three writers examine Spain's not-too-distant past from the standpoint of our present, the time of victorious liberalism. From that privileged vantage point, any detours on the path toward liberal democracy appear either as deviations that must be duly denounced and corrected or as temporary interruptions in the flow of the liberal tradition that, in the long run, create conditions for that tradition's restoration. That is to say, for these writers, the victory of liberal democracy is retrospectively inscribed in our reading of the past, either as a censure of those who belatedly embraced it or as a recuperation of those who, sometimes despite themselves, kept the flame of the liberal spirit alive.

Ridruejo's path from totalitarianism to liberalism does not proceed in a linear fashion, as these notions of conversion and continuity suggest, but instead depends on two connected movements, reminiscent of the figure of anabasis. One is a movement that, originating in a violent reaction against liberalism, proceeds in a direction of fulfillment of a totalitarian social project. Another opposing yet related movement originates in the failure of his totalitarian aspirations and, through a gradual divergence from his previous, increasingly impossible, goals, leads toward an alternative conception of politics, which he will recognize as liberal democratic. Rather than as a simple succession of stages or an incongruent linkage between mutually exclusive positions, Ridruejo's trajectory can be more productively assessed by rethinking his politics and literature in relation to these two movements. The movement that pursues the fulfillment of totalitarian goals ends in failure once he deems those goals unreachable. The failure of totalitarianism pushes him off course and generates a different kind of movement, the errancy of anabasis, which entails a different conception of both beginnings and endings. The path from totalitarianism to liberalism is neither inevitable nor direct. On the contrary, it is predicated on a sense of loss, not only of his totalitarian ideals (or illusions) but also of an idea of politics that is predetermined by an absolute and unquestionable goal. Ridruejo's remaking of his trajectory, following the loss of his totalitarian ideals, will entail a search for a noninstrumental conception of politics in which beginnings and ends are not given but are constantly recreated and reassessed in relation to the paths taken and not taken, paths that open up with and through movement or lead to dead ends. While the full trajectory of Ridruejo's movement is something he discovered only upon arriving at the destination—which is how he saw his 1957 incarceration in Carabanchel prison, where he officially became an enemy of the regime—it is in the poetry written in early 1940s where his search for an alternative kind of movement effectively begins.

Movimiento without Movement

Before turning to Ridrejo's poetry, and subsequently to some of his other poetic writings, I would like to trace the changes in his political ideas during the period leading up to and following his resignation from the Francoist state apparatus, made official in his 1942 letter to the dictator. Ridruejo's ideas about politics do not represent merely a source of background information for interpreting certain motifs in his poetry. Rather, a grasp of the nature of his political discontent is integral to identifying a central theme in the cycle of elegies Ridruejo wrote during the year he spent in Andalusia, in exile from Madrid and from active politics. I argue that the failure of the Falange's project of creating a new society finds its poetic elaboration in a double movement of Ridruejo's elegies that combines a lamentation for the loss of his world (the world of fascist utopia) and an intimation of a wandering return—his own and that of the world around him—to a new beginning.

Ridruejo's disillusionment with the failure of the Falange's project of building a "new world" and his search for an alternative path back to the world should be read in relation to, although not as a simple translation or allegory of, the conflict between totalitarianism and liberalism and their respective conceptions of the political. In *Totalitarianism and the Modern Conception of Politics*, Michael Halberstam argues powerfully against viewing liberalism and totalitarianism solely through their own ideological prisms, as mutually opposed. Instead, for Halberstam, liberalism and totalitarianism represent two rival visions of the political or, more specifically, rival attempts at realizing a modern project of human emancipation in the realm of politics. Their irreconcilable differences should therefore not obviate the fact that, like other modern ideologies (for example, socialism or communism), liberalism and totalitarianism seek to transform politics into a vehicle of human liberation from the shackles of entrenched traditions, received ideas, and inherited meanings. In that sense, their mutually exclusive ideas about the concrete forms of politics, or the nature of emancipated humanity, should not obscure a shortcoming common to both: their inability to respond to the danger that Halberstam deems inherent to the modern project of emancipation and that he describes, following Hannah Arendt, as the loss of the world and, concomitant with it, the loss of the meaning of politics.

Totalitarianism, in Halberstam's words, "haunts the modern ideal of political emancipation."[13] It does so by providing the modern ideal of emancipation with its most sinister fulfillment, contained in the idea that society, which the modern era views not as something given but as a product of human action, can indeed be (re)constructed deliberately and at will. As Arendt put it, totalitarianism proclaims that "everything is possible, if only one knows how to organize the masses for it."[14] Liberalism approaches politics in a radically different way. While totalitarianism aspires to build from scratch, as it were, a new society that is totally and fully emancipated from inherited ideas and relations, liberalism is rooted in the idea of an autonomous society that exists not inside of, nor independently from, but on the edges of the political. For liberalism, the function of politics is none other than to preserve, secure, and protect those edges that allow society to exist and thrive by harboring a liminality that is safeguarded from undue encroachment on the part of political power. In liberalism, the realms of the political and the social continuously limit and push against each other, so that more power on one side automatically means less on the other. That differential between political interference and social autonomy is, for liberalism, the measure of freedom.

Halberstam's main point, that "neither liberalism nor totalitarianism can be understood without the other," implies that totalitarianism is not only a radical and destructive reaction against liberal politics but also a critique of, and a response to, certain tendencies existing in liberalism.[15] The foremost of those tendencies concerns the way in which liberalism seeks to fulfill the Enlightenment ideal of human emancipation in the realm of politics. The project of human emancipation is based on the idea that our relationship with the world depends on concepts and laws that are creations of the human intellect rather than existing in the world independently of us.[16] The basic principle of any emancipatory project is the notion of "society as artifact," that is, society as not an objective order whose meaning is given, but a product of the relationship between the human subject and "the space of intelligibility that we call 'world.'"[17]

From the standpoint of liberalism, the relationship between individuals and the social is a function of human demands for self-realization. That means that the goal of politics is not to determine who we are or should be but rather to remove impediments standing in the way of our legitimate aspirations to become who we want to be. At the same time, the liberal approach to society is based not on immanent but on external factors, which means that society has no intrinsic criteria for setting its own goals, and its only measure of success is the extent to which it allows individuals to meet their goals.

In opposition to liberal politics, which focuses on the notion of procedure or process based on the interplay of individual interests, totalitarianism sees itself as a politics of meaning. And the differences between the two do not end there. While the liberal approach to reality is pragmatic, the totalitarian approach is ideological. While liberalism seeks an external criterion of legitimation (individual interests), totalitarianism excludes references to any external sources of legitimacy, such as religion or tradition. While liberalism avoids assigning purpose or meaning to the social universe, totalitarianism aspires to construct a society "pregnant with meaning, a society that bears the plenitude of its own reality within itself."[18] The liberal vision of the world is that of a "technical product" formed by our rational action and made to fit our needs.[19] Totalitarianism, on the other hand, constructs the world as if it were an aesthetic object, which obeys its own logic and produces a hermetic fit between the image social actors have of the world and the place they occupy in it. By attempting a radical reconstruction of the social in accordance with a preexisting ideological model, totalitarianism exacerbated, but also managed to foreground, the problem of the "loss of the world" shared by many emancipatory projects. At the same time, the totalitarian attempt to create a new society serves as a reminder that, by subordinating the world of politics to the management of individual interests, liberalism became blind to the fact that, as Arendt put it, "in politics not life but world is at stake."[20]

Halberstam's account of the complex relationship between liberalism and totalitarianism affords a possibility of moving away from the issue that dominates existing discussions of Ridruejo's politics: the question of *when* he finally abandoned his fascist beliefs and, related to this, whether we should trust his own account of the process and grant a former fascist the privilege of being remembered as a predecessor of Spain's transition to democracy. It is important to insist here that the nature of the struggle between liberalism and totalitarianism in Spain cannot be comprehended in terms of ideological binaries and a linear succession of events in which the victory of Francoism is seen as the necessary consequence of the defeat of liberal democracy.[21] Rather, as Ridruejo seemed to understand better than any of his contemporaries, there was no simple connection between the defeat of liberalism and the fulfillment of the totalitarian project; the latter would not follow as an automatic result of the former. A whole new conception of politics and a whole new approach to social reality needed to be built. But as Ridruejo discovered soon after the end of the Civil War, instead of establishing a new model of politics and society, the Franco regime reestablished an old form of dictatorship propped up and made inviolable by military victory. Ridruejo's disillusionment with a regime that he saw as having betrayed the Falange and appropriated it for its own ends subsequently evolved into a more general critique of the instrumentalization of politics. In the process, the sense of having lost his way allowed him to rethink the nature of his goals and to move from a totalizing to a noninstrumental conception of politics.

Ridruejo's distancing from the regime, which started immediately after the war and became definitive with his 1956 incarceration, was motivated by that sense of betrayal. However, a deeper issue fueling Ridruejo's discontent had to do with the differences and similarities between the "new" regime and the despised and finally dismantled "old," liberal Spain. During and immediately after the Civil War, Ridruejo reaffirmed his (and the Falange's) commitment to the imperative of creating a new Spain, a task whose prelude was the process of disintegration and re-foundation that the war represented. The war was both a final step in the disintegration of the old Spain and the first step in forging a new Spain and a new world. "We want to be the parents of generations that dream of dominion over the earth," proclaimed Ridruejo in 1940.[22] No matter how persuasive such dreams of ruling the world were for a young Spanish fascist at that particular moment, he was also convinced that the Civil War was just one step—a decisive one, but insufficient and incomplete. As he reiterated in several essays from the 1940s and early 1950s, the only thing that could ensure that the nationalist victory would be a lasting one in the creation of a new Spain was *movimiento* (movement). This word should be understood both in reference to Ridruejo's perception of the role of the Movimiento Nacional in the new regime as well as in the context of his continuous emphasis on politics as movement, as *andar* (walking). As he wrote in 1953: "But the act of force [el hecho de fuerza] is always limited to making possible a new direction. It does not exempt us from tracing a new path, nor, above all, of walking down it [de andarlo]. . . . Historically speaking, health consists primarily in walking [en andar]."[23] Ridruejo, the most brilliant of the Falange's orators and its one-time chief of propaganda (he was occasionally referred to as Spain's Goebbels) could certainly talk the talk, but could he walk the walk?

The notion of politics as andar brings together two related ideas: that of finding a new destination and that of constructing a common path leading to it. In Ridruejo's vision of Spanish politics and the Falange's role in it, the two were intrinsically connected: There could be no new path without establishing a common goal, and the existence of a common goal presupposed that political actors were walking together in unison. Ridruejo believed that the Franco regime had failed to do either of these things. Moreover, the political context in which he sought to implement his vision was so fraught with difficulties that the very conception of politics as andar or movimiento only brought into sharper view the obstacles and impasses on his and the Falange's path, which were transforming their efforts into aimless drifting. Not only did Franco and many Falange's intellectuals have radically different ideas about the nature and function of the Movimiento Nacional but those differences made it evident that the regime and the party presumed to be its ideological backbone were in fact moving in different directions.

The clearest formulation of Ridruejo's discontent with the direction of the regime was his 1942 letter to Franco requesting that he be relieved of all official functions. As he argued at the time, the growing distance between his ideas and the regime's political reality had transformed those functions into a burden that he needed to shed by returning to "el lugar de origen: la vida privada" (the place of origin: private life).[24] The reasons for Ridruejo's distancing from the regime were in part ideological. Francoism had turned out to be something different from what he as a Falangist had hoped and fought for: a totalitarian regime whose policies would faithfully realize the party's ideological tenets in all spheres of life—politics, economy, culture, law, and so on.[25] Aside from the question of ideology, there was the issue of method. Rather than dwelling on the fact that his and the Falange's aspirations remained unfulfilled, his letter stressed the way in which those aspirations were being systematically undermined. Adopting the privileged vantage point of an insider on his way out, Ridruejo laid out a scathing critique of Francoism and the role it assigned to the Falange.

Francoism, he declared, found itself in a double bind. It functioned in a way that was at odds with fulfilling the purpose for which it was constituted, that of carrying out a national revolution—which, in Ridruejo's view, had to be fascist, because all other ideological options reeked of a return to the old (be it in the form of liberalism, monarchy, or some kind of coalition of oligarchic forces). Three years after the end of the Civil War, that revolutionary program—or, as he called it, "realización histórica refundidora" (the refounding historical realization)—had not been implemented, and, given the regime's modus operandi, it was becoming clear that it never would be: "esto lleva camino de que no resulte ya nunca" (this is on track to never happening).[26] This failure of implementation had resulted from a skewed relationship between the three elements representing the pillars of the regime: el caudillo himself, the Movimiento Nacional, and Spanish society. First, Franco could not be called a dictator in a true sense of the term: "the dictator cannot be the arbitrator [*árbitro*] among contradictory forces, but the leader [*jefe*] of the force that incarnates the revolution."[27] Second, the Falange, the presumed political force in charge of the revolution, was actually not holding the reins of power, whether within the Movimiento Nacional or in the government. Finally, there was not even the most minimal sign of a new collective project capable of mobilizing society—"an enterprise capable of creating better forms of life and a collective ideal for this nation."[28] In effect, Francoism was almost the exact opposite of the kind of regime Ridruejo and the Falange aspired to. However—and here lay the paradox of the situation—while the Falange's efforts to realize its political project within the regime were being systematically undermined, the group nonetheless continued to be essential for the regime's functioning. The thrust of Ridruejo's 1942 critique of Francoism was a condemnation of the regime's superficial use of the Falange's symbols while keeping in check the Falange's revolutionary ambitions, thereby maintaining the power solidly in the hands of the dictator and his traditional support base: the army, the Catholic Church, and various right-wing groups. Not only was Francoism using the Falange as a public face while remaining largely hostile to the organization's political goals, but in order for the Falange to keep its share of symbolic power, it had to pay the highest possible price. With the future of Francoism and the outcome of World War II still largely uncertain, the Falange was left with the option of either forfeiting its totalitarian ambitions, thereby languishing within the regime, or serving as the target of an anti-totalitarian reaction, thereby perishing along with the regime.

> Everything seems to indicate that the Regime is sinking as an enterprise, although it sustains itself as a contraption [*como "tinglado"*]. In effect, it has no strong and authorized base of its own, and the crisis of discontent is growing. One day the collapse [*derribo*] could happen quite easily. And then we Falangists would fall as accomplices into the debris of a politics that was not ours. . . . It is not a matter of avoiding death. But—for God's sake!—let us not die confused with what we detested.[29]

World in Movement

As we have seen, Ridruejo's post–Civil War engagement with politics had as its guiding principle the notion of *movement*. This notion referred simultaneously to the idea of politics *as* movement and to the

Movimiento Nacional as a would-be embodiment of that idea. The purpose of political action was precisely to tie together the two elements: politics *as* movement and the politics of the Movimiento. In practice, that meant organizing the Movimiento in a way that would enable it to realize its vision of politics as movement (primarily by virtue of its unification around the Falange and el caudillo) and endow it with the power and dynamism necessary for the fulfillment of the Falange's revolutionary goals. For Ridruejo the politician, the goal and the path—the common purpose and the power (*dynamos*) needed to materialize this vision—constituted two sides of the same coin. In that sense, his abandonment of active politics was in no way a repudiation of fascism but a reaction against the immobility of the Movimiento, which substituted a sense of dynamism grounded in common goals for an entirely formal conception of unity based on perseverance and a will to survive against all odds.

My reflection about the connection between politics and movement in Ridruejo's literature starts with the analysis of the motif of movement in the poem "Elegía ante la mar," written in exile in Andalusia. As I have argued, Ridruejo's passage from fascism to liberalism cannot be understood as a natural evolution nor as a simple change of direction or political orientation. Rather, both his ideological shift and the nature of his trajectory rested on a search for a conception of movement that would differ from an instrumental model of political action in which the path is predetermined by the goal. In his post-1939 poetry, Ridruejo comes to terms with the failure of his political aspirations and with his ensuing existential crisis by attempting to articulate an idea of movement that originated in a sense of being lost, of lacking a goal and direction.

The type and conception of movement we encounter in Ridruejo's elegies, which were completed in 1945, diverge markedly from his idea of movement in totalitarian politics. In the elegies—particularly in "Elegía ante la mar"—the emphasis is on the interplay between movement and rest, which, throughout this book, I interpret in reference to different meanings of the Greek term *stasis*. In *Geo-filosofía de Europa* Massimo

Cacciari refers to the deep connection between stasis and sea in Greek thought. For Cacciari, stasis, in the sense of upheaval within the polis, is essential for understanding the deep link that Greek thought established between democracy and the conquest of the sea. He brings up Plato's claim that the aspiration to conquer its neighbors through control of the sea (*thalassocracy*) stands at the root of Athenian democracy: "La talasocracia es la que impone la forma democrática. El dominio del mar exige que el pueblo que mueve las naves tenga el mando" (Thalassocracy is what imposes the democratic form. Domination of the sea demands that the people moving the ships have control).[30] Athens's special relationship with the sea and its loyalty to the principles of dynamism, inventiveness, and technical prowess that the control of the sea requires went hand in hand with a discovery of freedom associated with readiness to be uprooted and to venture into the unknown. This had two important effects. While, on the one hand, it created a sense of restlessness and instability associated with the idea that power belongs not to those who are entitled to it (aristocracy) or to the wisest (philosophers) but to those able to identify their private interests with the interests of the polis, it also established a long-lasting analogy between the passion for venturing out to sea and intellectual pursuit.

In my reading of Ridruejo's elegy, stasis refers not only to lack of movement but also to the kind of movement, associated with the sea, that speaks to the unpredictable nature of ends, or even defies the very notion of an end. By juxtaposing the frantic movement of the world and the constant becoming of the sea, Ridruejo's elegy accomplishes a dual task of reflecting on the deep failure of his vision for a new world, all the while pointing to the exemplarity or even grandiosity of a failure that seems inevitable in retrospect, that is, in the light of how the movement of the sea reflects and unravels the movement of the world. Both reinforcing and opposing each other, the two types of movement—that of the world and that of the sea—relate to a larger topic of this chapter: the relationship between totalitarianism and liberalism and the nature of Ridruejo's passage from the former to the latter.

From its very first lines "Elegía ante la mar" presents contrasting images of stillness and movement, juxtaposing them with images of war and peace. The poem opens with the following hendecasyllabic verses:

Estoy sentado ante los hondos llanos
de las aguas del mar. Detrás la tierra
fatigada de muertos y derrotas
aleja mansamente sus escombros.

I am seated before the deep plains
of the sea's waters. Behind me, the land,
weary of deaths and defeats,
quietly dispels its debris.[31]

The poet's own lack of movement contrasts both with the fluidity of the sea he is facing and the recently extinguished bellicose fury of the land, to which he is turning his back. His stillness ("estoy sentado") singles him out, isolating him from both the human and natural worlds, which exist in and through movement. While the movement of the human world is a result of agonistic activity whose passing leaves death and ruin in its wake, the natural world exists simply *as* movement in multiple forms: the spring sky recedes before his eyes ("primavera / hace huir a sus cielos / hacía sí mismos"), murmuring trees palpitate ("el rumor de los árboles palpita"), the breeze carries sounds along ("y discurre una brisa con pájaros en celo") (462). Not only is the lyrical "I" the only element characterized by the absence of movement, but his very presence within the natural idyll connects the outward sense of stillness with references to strife and turmoil.

Different meanings of stasis are implicitly addressed in two successive questions that immediately follow the poem's opening. First, the poet asks himself: "¿Qué abandono, o que aguardo / tan sorda y levemente, tan sin prisa?" (What do I relinquish, or what do I await / so mutely and softly, so without hurry?), only to continue in a more probing tone: "¿Por qué he llamado 'un mundo' / al creador empeño de los hombres / que no quieren pasar como las ondas?" (Why have I called "a world" / the creative exertion of men / who do not wish to pass like the waves?) (462). The first question is an expression of the poet's uncertainty regarding his present state, depicted as a placid, and almost indifferent, wave-like motion back and forth in time ("¿Qué abandono, o qué aguardo?"). The second question deploys the motif of the sea in constant motion in order to express personal and collective anguish regarding a frustrated human project ("creador empeño de los hombres / que no quieren pasar como las ondas"). In the first instance, a temporary suspension of movement reflects a lack of direction related to the poet's uncertainty about his point of departure or destination. In the second, the incessant movement of the sea stands in contrast with human desire for permanence, which encounters its limit in the inherent instability of the human-created world. In other words, the absence of movement, which produces a sense of placid indifference, contrasts with the agonistic movement of the world that turns against itself.

The poet's regret for having named "a world" what is a mere product of human desire to avoid passing like the waves announces a special, albeit conflictive, relationship between the human—that is, the social—world and the sea. Through the encounter with the sea, Ridruejo's poem turns into a meditation on different meanings of stasis as they manifest themselves in a conflictive relationship between the world, *his* world, and the sea. In particular, he focuses on the way in which a world in stasis, in constant agitation and struggle with itself, encounters its limit in the implacable presence of the sea, which shatters the poet's sense of tranquility even while inviting it. This conflict is exemplified by the passage of the poem that expands on Ridruejo's second question:

> ¿Por qué he llamado "un mundo"
> al creador empeño de los hombres
> que no quieren pasar como las ondas?
> La creación de Dios vuelve a los ojos.
> Un mundo no se rompe puramente

como un fanal de vidrio. Pero hay sueños de mundos que se pudren
poco a poco y que claman y resisten,
y que engendran y matan.
Hay mundos que agonizan con fuego y con raíces,
se adentran por las almas y las van ensanchando
o las van destruyendo
con resplandor sublime de ilusiones
junto a hogueras de angustia.
Y, al fin, cuando aquel otro,
el impasible mundo, se ha desencadenado,
quedan rotos, desiertos y en cenizas
ante el sueño del mar.

Why have I called "a world"
the creative exertion of men
who do not wish to pass like the waves?
God's creation returns to the eyes.
A world does not break cleanly
like a glass lantern. But there are dreams of worlds that rot away
bit by bit and that cry out and resist,
and that engender and kill.
There are worlds that expire with fire and with roots,
penetrate souls and expand them
or destroy them
with sublime radiance of illusions
next to bonfires of anguish.
And, in the end, when that other,
the impassible, world, has come unchained,
they are left broken, deserted, and in ashes
before the dream of the sea.

The beginning of the passage establishes a distinction between the
human, historical world and divine creation: not only is the historical world
not created pure and whole, as if by divine fiat, but it also does not "break

cleanly" ("no se rompe puramente") like a glass lantern that shatters into pieces. Rather, the historical world is born and vanishes "impurely," driven by its own feverish movement that breeds dreams of other worlds, fueled by restlessness and discontent with the existing world. In the historical world defined by violence and stasis (again, in the Greek sense), dreams of other worlds are born through a process of fragmentation and multiplication—suggested by the plural "hay mundos" following the phrase "por qué he llamado 'un mundo.'" This movement of the world that both breaks and multiplies itself by creating dreams of other worlds cannot attain completion or fulfill the aspirations of those engaged in the creative effort of dreaming or attempting to build a world that would not "pasar como las ondas." Rather, the fluctuation of the world perpetuates itself in the movement of the lines from this section of the poem, which is a reflection of the stirrings of the poet's soul in tension between rebellion and repentance, between desire for a new world and sorrow for the destiny of the world that generates dreams of other worlds and perishes together with them ("Hay mundos . . . / que se adentran por las almas y las van ensanchando / o las van destruyendo"). That is why the last part of the section, beginning with "Y, al fin" (And, in the end), announces not so much an ending to the struggle as a decisive point in the battle of the world with itself and that of Ridruejo with his soul: a point when stasis or the violent movement of the world ends up shattering the dreams of other worlds only to find itself shattered in the encounter with "aquel otro, el impasible mundo," which, like the sea, continues to move, indifferent to the drama of history.

In Ridruejo's poem, the movement of the sea inverts and complements the movement of the world. In contrast with the vertiginous movement of the world that, unable to achieve peace and stability through stasis, finds itself broken and in pieces, the continuous back-and-forth movement of the sea distances the poet from the feverish activity of the world while returning him and the world to the prospect of beginning anew. As the poet Luis Rosales, Ridruejo's friend and a member of the Generation of 1936, observed in his reading of the elegy discussed below, the sea cleans the poet of the detritus of the past.[32]

Combined, the contrasting movements of world and sea form the double trajectory of anabasis. In Badiou's description, anabasis names a trajectory that combines two diverging principles: a "principle of lostness" and that of an "unprecedented return," or the invented path of return that arises out of the experience of wandering.[33] Anabasis in Ridruejo's poem likewise consists of a double movement, one arising from the impasse associated with the poet's sense of having lost his world (after all, the poem is an elegy), and another that announces the possibility of a new beginning that originates precisely in coming face to face with the failure to reach the desired end.

In Ridruejo's poem, the sea functions as a reminder of his failure to create a new world. Rather than achieving the desired end (fulfillment of the fascist utopia of a world that would be both new and "would not pass like the waves"), he contemplates the destiny of his world in the incessant, repetitive movement of the sea, which annihilates any illusion of permanence and dissolves the dreams of other, future worlds. Ridruejo wonders: "¿Cada hombre, Señor, ha de llorar su mundo? / ¿Cada hombre ha de crear al mundo, de sus ruinas? / ¿Cada hombre ha de olvidar y soñar nuevamente?" (Lord, must every man weep for his world? / Must every man create the world, out of its ruins? / Must every man forget and dream anew?) (464). While serving as a reminder of the failure of his aspirations, which, far from attaining the desired end, had led to the opposite outcome (the crumbling of his world together with his dreams of the new world), the presence of the sea also announces the imperative to start again. In fact, the poem alternates the lines where the sea appears as a formless living abyss that devours any memory of human presence— "una terrible vida sin figura" (a terrible, figureless life) (463)— with lines in which it announces an alluring promise, a siren's song of the future that brings an ever-renewed possibility of beginning again. Speaking in its own voice, the sea calls itself "yo, madre del mañana, / que es también el ayer y late en el instante / del hoy que eternamente os acaricia y sufre" (I, mother of tomorrow, / that is also yesterday and pulses in the instant / of the now that eternally caresses you and suffers) (466).

In its continuous movement, the sea represents a noncoincidence of beginning and end, which can manifest itself negatively or positively: negatively, as the impossibility of envisioning a future, since both future and past dissolve in accordance with the irrevocable rhythm of the waves, and positively, as a possibility of freeing the poet from illusions of permanence in order to allow him to begin anew, unencumbered by the past. In keeping with the double meaning of the Greek word *arché* or the Spanish *principio*, we can say that the sea is both a promise of a new beginning (principio) and a testimony to the historical principle (principio) that signifies the absence of fixed paths between the points of departure and arrival, thereby making it possible to begin again even in the aftermath of a catastrophic failure.

This broader value of Ridruejo's elegy, as not merely reflective of the poet's confusion and yearning for a new beginning but emblematic of the historical vision of those Spanish poets who at one point sided with Franco's regime, was not lost on Luis Rosales. In his reading of Ridruejo's elegy Rosales transforms the poem into a manifesto of a poetic generation that regarded the sea in general and the Mediterranean in particular as a symbol of both an individual and a collective—as well as a notably European—cultural imaginary.

Rosales's essay "A Dionisio Ridruejo" opens with a description of an indeterminate "someone" (*alguien*) who is gazing at the sea and concludes with a direct address to Ridruejo himself, whom the author calls by his first name, "Dionisio"—particularly significant in this context not only because of the mythical Dionysus's link with the sea but also because the concluding part of Rosales's essay reveals that, in the same way that "alguien" is "Dionisio," the sea before him is not just any sea but must be the Mediterranean. Like Ridruejo's poem, Rosales's essay depicts someone gazing at the sea, leaving behind a ravaged land that pains and oppresses him. This contemplation of the sea and the distant horizon is a specular voyage of sorts as well as a voyage of anabasis. It snatches the gazing subject away from a given place and moment in time—"no todas las tardes nacen para morir" (not all afternoons are born to die)—only to bring him back to the auroral moment when the sea and the eye meet as if for the first time: "En una tarde de éstas, alguien puede nacer en su Mirada" (One of these afternoons, someone could be birthed in his Gaze).[34] Rosales's celebration of someone who, purified from the debris of an historical shipwreck, listens to the pulsating blood streaming through his veins—"el árbol de la sangre y el árbol de las olas; los dos mares" (the tree of blood and the tree of waves; the two seas)—becomes more restrained when he addresses Ridruejo: "Pienso yo que ese mar que mirabas, Dionisio, había que ser el mar Mediterráneo" (I think this sea you looked at, Dionisio, must have been the Mediterranean).[35] Rosales knew well that Ridruejo, after his rupture with Francoism, lived in proximity to the Mediterranean, so the "I think" and "must have been" should be read as deliberate emphases. This careful naming of the Mediterranean as an historical and geographical referent of the sea from Ridruejo's poem conveys the idea that, more than just a physical location and a source of poetic inspiration, the Mediterranean is a privileged site for rethinking and remaking the course of both European history and the history of a poetic generation.

Rosales describes the Mediterranean as "un mar hecho por el hombre, es decir, recreado, inventado, vivido y modelado por el hombre, como una estatua" (a sea made by man; that is, recreated, invented, lived, and modeled by man, like a statue). Rather than a simple invocation of common European cultural origins, the composite image of the sea-as-statue depicts history being (re)made not only in human likeness but also in the likeness of the sea, a constantly changing pattern of the paths taken and not taken, moving matter that precariously links origins and destinations. The Mediterranean, concludes Rosales, might be the only complete word ("palabra entera") Europe has ever uttered, except for another word, which names a new continent: "América, cuyo destino es acabar de decirse a sí misma."[36] Historical and poetic meanings of the sea have to be expressed with two words (two shores, two worlds), one that names the fluid nature of what is deemed complete (the Mediterranean as an image of European history) and another (America, or the new world) that projects itself onto the future.

Rosales's essay is the message of a poet and friend reaching out to Ridruejo, who, at the end of "Elegía ante la mar," finds himself "solo y par, con el vago sabor del Paraíso / ante el dolor del parto, la fatiga del surco / y el hambre dolorosa de Dios en la memoria" (alone and paired, with the vague flavor of Paradise / facing the pain of childbirth, the fatigue of the furrow / and painful hunger for God in the memory) (466). Aside from its religious tone, the relevance of this passage lies in its evocation of the motif of "the two-in-one" ("solo y par"), which, according to Arendt, describes the condition of the thinking subject since Socrates, who expressed the duality in disavowing it, claiming that "it would be better for me . . . that multitudes of men should disagree with me rather than that I, *being one, should disagree with myself.*"[37]

The product of a soul-searching meditation facing the sea, Ridruejo's poem embodies the complex nature of stasis, understood as both the absence of movement and an unstoppable, self-perpetuating movement with no foreseeable end in sight. Yearning to overcome the inner schism between who he once was and the one he is not—not anymore or not yet—Ridruejo reflects on the collapse of his world. All the while he seeks to ward off the twofold danger of paralysis or resignation, which would make the creative movement, of the self and of the world, impossible. As he comes to terms with the collapse of his dreams of the new world, he moves away from a certain conception of politics that culminated in the organized frenzy of totalitarianism, which, as Arendt showed, aspires to control subjects and the world by subordinating them to the laws and necessities of political movement. For Ridruejo at the time of writing this elegy, the only *poetic* alternative to the perils of *political* movement is the discovery of the hazardous yet promising movement of the sea that dissolves the opposition between movement and its absence, between the undying desire for a new world and the always lurking possibility of failure or dead end. In "Elegía ante la mar," he discovered his poetic Mediterranean, a discovery he would complete in the mid-1950s with a rediscovery of its political equivalent: liberalism, which does not predetermine the course of political action with the certainty of an end.

Peace of Many Pieces: Catalonia and After

In order to elucidate the nature of what *will have been* Ridruejo's (re) turn to liberalism, it is crucial to examine the way in which the tropes of movement and stability or repose function in the poetic prose work *Diario de una tregua.* This work, written during the author's exile in Catalonia, captures the newly found experience of stability, which stands in apparent contrast with the movement of the sea in his poetry. And yet, as we shall see, while providing a sense of order and stability, the Catalan landscape also exemplifies a dynamic interplay between the part and the whole. The exile in Catalonia functions as an interlude in Ridruejo's life, a period of *tregua* (truce) before his return to active politics. But it is precisely in the diary he wrote during that interval of peace where we can find the first articulation of the trope of the swimming lesson that encapsulates the liberal and anti-Francoist political position Ridruejo adopts in the mid-1950s. I discuss this trope in relation to his definitive abandonment of the instrumentalist vision of politics combined with the development of a skill that permits one not to be swallowed by perilous currents.

Ridruejo lived in exile in Catalonia for four years, from 1943 to 1947. The initiative to settle in this region after the first location of his exile, the Andalusian village of Ronda, came from his Catalan friends, who persuaded him of the practical advantages the move would entail, including better prospects for improving his financial situation, which had become difficult after he resigned his posts in the regime, and the possibility of enjoying more freedom of movement under the benevolent eye of the leadership of the Catalan Falange. Recently married to painter Gloria Ros, sister of writer Samuel Ros, his friend from the war days, Ridruejo accepted the arguments of his friends and moved with Gloria to the Mediterranean coast, from which he would make occasional escapades to Barcelona. *Diario de una tregua,* a book of poetic prose dedicated to "Gloria, catalana," is a literary fruit of his Catalan exile, a kind of homage to Catalonia and a testimony to the crucial role that the region to which Ridruejo was linked by the bonds of marriage, friendship, and exile played in the author's political and intellectual biography.

Diario's prologue reveals Ridruejo's deep fondness for the rural landscape of coastal Catalonia, a region set between the rugged mountains and the sea and parceled out, in compliance with these natural limits, into a constellation of small, diligently cultivated peasant holdings. He barely mentions the industrial, urban, and entrepreneurial Catalonia, which exists only at a distance, as a looming presence he wishes to keep at bay. In transforming the landscape into one of the main protagonists of his diary Ridruejo tapped into a venerable tradition of writers for whom the landscape of another Iberian region, that of Castile, served as inspiration for meditations on the reasons for the downward spiral of Spanish history from the 1600s onward. At the same time that Ridruejo was writing his diary, Pedro Laín Entralgo, his comrade from the war years—a distinguished intellectual and rector of Madrid University from 1951 to 1956—published *La Generación del 98* (1945), part of a larger project that aimed to summarize, systematize, and reclaim the heritage of different generations of thinkers who grappled with the issue of Spain's decadence and the country's marginality with respect to modern Europe. The final version of that larger project was published in 1955, causing much splash among intellectuals loyal to the regime, primarily because of its title: *España como problema* (Spain as a problem). The 1945 volume, which opened with an "Epístola a Dionisio Ridruejo," contains a lengthy meditation on the role of the Castilian landscape in the works of the members of the Generation of 98 that can be productively contrasted with Ridruejo's vision of Catalonia.

The purpose of Laín's project was to reverse the trend of national decadence by creating a synthesis of attitudes from two opposing camps: those who attributed Spain's decadence to a stifling tradition represented by the Catholic Church, and others who blamed it on the lack of patriotism of liberal intellectuals and their fascination with foreign ideas. In striving for this synthesis, Laín, who describes himself as a "Catholic historian,"[38] approaches both Spanish history and his own political biography through the operation of *religare,* a word understood in its etymological sense of "linking again." Creating or restoring the unity of a Spanish tradition irremediably split between liberal and traditionalist camps demanded that Laín align himself with everything "pure and excellent" in that tradition, regardless of the camp in which it originated (673). This attitude of a certain tolerance toward the ideas of the defeated was the reason why Laín's enemies accused him of being a crypto-liberal Falangist. José Luis Villacañas recalls Laín's characterization of his participation in the Civil War in terms of the impetus to "overcome or somehow try to overcome, in my conscience and my conduct, that bloody division of my people."[39] After the war and following the dismantling of the Falange's original ideological project, Laín's aspiration to synthesis shifted entirely to the realm of pedagogy, where he dedicated himself to tasks of "teaching, integrating and learning" (673).

Much was at stake for Laín in the endeavor of writing a history of the four generations of Spanish intellectuals—from Menéndez Pelayo's to his own—in order to prevent future outbreaks of stasis by overcoming the confrontation between opposing camps: traditionalist and liberal, nationalist and Europeanist, triumphant and defeated. Without that synthesis, neither Spain's future nor the two facets of his biography—his militancy in the Falange before and during the Civil War and his academic mission after 1939—could come together into a coherent project. In other words, advocating the value of synthesis in his overview of Spanish intellectual history was a precondition for bringing together two facets of his biography: Laín the Falangist and Laín the professor. The integrity of Laín's commitment depended on framing his two endeavors (political and intellectual) as examples of a search for synthesis in two different spheres of action (war and pedagogy). The first problem with this gesture was that the very aspiration to synthesis grew on the soil of fratricidal violence, past and present. The second was that neither of Laín's spheres of action could be justified solely on its own terms, but had to complement, and be complemented by, the other. The professor's defense of an intellectual synthesis was built on the ground of the bloody division of the Civil War, and the self-assertion of the Falange as a political synthesis between the Left and Right echoed the professor's conviction that only the assimilation of some of the ideas of the defeated—those deemed "pure and excellent"—could bring closure to the conflict that had led to the war. Laín's account of Spanish history and his intellectual biography is based on what could be called mimetic appropriation, on applying the same idea of synthesis to different spheres that end up mirroring each other.

This gesture of mimetic appropriation of the past is also present in Laín's account of the vision of the Castilian landscape among the writers of the Generation of 98, which I briefly address before engaging with Ridruejo's significantly different approach to the landscape of rural Catalonia. In *España como problema* Laín argues that the Generation of 98's image of Castile had left an indelible mark on subsequent generations' perception of Spain's historical reality. Their treatment of the Castilian landscape, full of harsh and desolate tones but rich in poetic details and emotional nuances, left the younger writers with a sense of debt that Laín describes as simultaneously patriotic, aesthetic, and linguistic. By acknowledging this debt, he is inserting the youth of the Falange into an uninterrupted intellectual lineage in which they occupy the place of the "grandsons" of the Generation of 98. The older generation's image of Castilian landscape as a metonymy of Spain's historical decline in the modern era was one of the elements that contributed to the Falange's sense of patriotic mission. Laín quotes none other than José Antonio Primo de Rivera's affirmation of the proximity between the Falange's vision of Spain and that of their predecessors: "Our [Falange's] patriotism also came about by way of critique" (338). The same notion of patriotism born of critique compelled the Falange to love Spain precisely because they did not like it (what Santos Juliá called "amar porque no gusta").[40]

The writers of the Generation of 98 did not find the landscape of Castile appealing for its natural beauty or admirable as a testimony to human labor; it was neither paradise nor home. Instead, they saw it, in Antonio Machado's words, as "a chunk of the planet," a fragment severed from the whole.[41] As the setting of their physical and existential voyages, the Castile that appears in their texts is not a self-contained and autonomous reality but an intellectual projection. Their vision of Castile is a product of multiple mediations and filters interposed between the eye and the reality it observes. Instead of describing the Castilian landscape, the writers of the Generation of 98 seek to comprehend it in relation to something else: the landscapes of their native regions, their personal memories, or the historical and cultural reminiscences they inscribe onto the austere and impoverished land. It is as if, lacking the appeal of other landscapes, the somber Castilian countryside were an inert backdrop onto which a melancholy patriotic gaze superimposed layers of images and meanings.

Laín's account of the Generation of 98's approach to the Castilian landscape contrasts with Ridruejo's vision of Catalonia. The Generation of 98's inward-looking search for the causes of Spain's decadence and the Falange's dissatisfaction with the course of Spanish history lead Laín to approach the stark and desolate Castilian landscape as a representation of that Spain he and his comrades loved and did not like. It was the insoluble bond of stasis as internal conflict that tied him and the Falange to their intellectual grandfathers, most of whom were liberals, and that turned their unhappy love of Spain into a search for synthesis. In contrast to these multiple mediations, in Ridruejo's *Diario de una tregua* rural Catalonia is a land whose different properties—physical, economic, cultural, and aesthetic—depend on an underlying quality that connects them all. That quality has to do with the importance of natural and human-made limits in creating the landscape of the Catalonia that Ridruejo learned to love, a land parceled out into a conglomerate of small rural properties that form a common *oikos*, "home and hearth." It is through the dynamic interplay between a part and the whole that the love of limits becomes a key to Ridruejo's vision of Catalonia. In the same way in which the Catalan landscape speaks to the importance of each part for the composition of the whole, the work's structure of a diary that condenses the period of four years into one natural year (four seasons) emphasizes the impor-tance of each day or scene for the text as a whole. In other words, both thematically and in terms of structure, *Diario* instantiates the sense of stability and rootedness in space and time as the most salient "lesson" the author learns while observing his surroundings and engaging in prosaic, everyday activities. The fact that dynamism and liveliness do not stand in contradiction with stability and peaceful conformity—or with "complacency with the existence of limits"—that he sees all around, points to a relationship between movement and rest that is very different from the one found in *Elegía ante la mar*.[42] Whereas in *Elegía* the repetitive and unstoppable movement of the sea resembles immobility, the *Diario* focuses on dynamism that is found in stability. Whereas the stretches of Laín's Castile vanish into the horizon, replicating the movement of thought in search of an ever-escaping synthesis, in Catalonia Ridruejo learns that the very possibility of movement depends on encountering the internal and external limits that allow one to stop and to pause, to look and orient oneself.

As stated before, Laín describes the human aspect of the Castilian landscape in terms of its ability to awaken reverberations of patriotic feeling in different generations of Spaniards. This patriotic feeling is a traveling emotion. It goes from one generation to another and moves inward from the land to the observer's eye and the heart, where it rebounds and returns transformed into a vision of common historical destiny. Ridruejo, by contrast, finds the Catalan landscape important not as an origin or a destination but as a fruit, a product of human activity and a witness to the form-giving, world-creating capacity of human efforts. Instead of generating the utopian impulse of creating a new world, which Ridruejo examined in the elegies, that world-creating capacity manifests itself in carving out the limits of one's world, making one's home in the world that is constituted by, and comfortably situated within, its limits.

Ridruejo's decision to elevate rural Catalonia into a part that stands for the whole, complete with the descriptions that speak of "the happy federation of rustic properties," "pleasant inclines covered with soft, easy-to-cultivate soil," and "civilized and curious farmers" (14), raises the question as to whether the *Diario* is the work of an author eager to replace fascist utopia with bucolic fantasy. The response, although decidedly negative, merits further elaboration, because it is closely related to the issue of the interplay between the part and the whole as a trope that marks this particular stage in Ridruejo's movement from a totalitarian to a liberal conception of politics. The landscape of rural Catalonia is important not as a natural idyll but as an emblem of the virtue that this book attributes to Catalan culture as a whole: love for the limits. This is so because what is true for Catalonia, namely, the fact that it inhabits a limited space between the mountains and the sea, is particularly true for its rural hinterland. Due to its internal structure and to the nature of its relationship with its surroundings, agricultural Catalonia can be seen as a part that embodies the importance that the limits have for the existence of the whole. "Mystery has almost completely vanished, beauty is a fruit, the emotion is enjoyment and sweetness. But is all of it, all of this land, like that? One might say that *everything in this land that is not its whole* [todo lo que no es su todo] is like that. But then this land allows itself to be seen in detail better than in its totality" (14, emphasis added). This passage plays on different usages of the word *todo*, which simultaneously designates all of something (toda esta tierra), everything that is, or belongs, to something (todo lo que es), or an abstract totality (su todo). The play on different meanings of *todo* indicates that the Catalonia that is the subject of Ridruejo's diary is not just a concrete geographical given; that is only one of the meanings of *todo*, not the only one or the whole one. On the other hand, neither is Catalonia some imagined, abstract totality divorced from the concrete reality that one is able to experience directly and clearly ("Mystery has almost completely vanished"). Ridruejo's conclusion is that *everything* in Catalonia, its whole *and* its parts, is better seen in detail. The totality of which this passage speaks is not a given or just a sum of its parts; instead, it is a result of the harmonious coexistence and mirroring of the parts in the whole and the whole in its parts.[43]

Ridruejo's book is a chronicle of his encounter with a concrete geographical and human reality: Catalonia, whose guiding principle is inscribed in the very nature of its landscape and identified with the way of life for which that landscape provides a setting. Instead of referring to an abstract principle or an ideal goal, love for the limits is what makes possible the harmonious coexistence of two dimensions of the Catalan landscape—natural and human-made—while rooting them in the same principle. The notion of rootedness is crucial for Ridruejo's experience of Catalonia: "'Not a place, but landscape,' that is what I could say about my native land, the upper Duero river, which stretches out mirrored in eternity, in the passing of life. On the other hand, I would have to say about this one, the land I inhabit now, that it is, above all, a residence and place of abode" (14). Whereas his youthful memories of Castile awaken images of errancy against a background of vast and fleeting vistas, his Catalan landscape is associated with symbolic and concrete attachment, a sense of place rooted in the cultivation of soil and rewarded by its fruits. Not only are the two landscapes different in terms of their physical features, but this very difference reveals contrasting principles that Ridruejo associates with Castile and Catalonia, respectively: errancy as opposed to stability, uniformity as opposed to variety, restlessness and striving for the infinite versus conformity and aversion to the infinite, daily struggle with the hostile environment versus quiet enjoyment in daily existence. "Starting from this—small world that dominates, grounds and provides—one can also arrive at certain spiritual associations: love of the limit and of work, passion for definition and for wealth, love of form and of planning. Aversion to the infinite. Excellence, perseverance, taste for ownership—to own and be owned—, tendency to order and stability, sense of humor. Finally, and above all, passion for life and the enjoyment" (15). After four years in Catalonia, this "man from the other landscape" (15) became so accustomed to that "human land" [tierra de los hombres] (16) that, when he finally left, he had become another man, altogether different from the one who had been abandoned by, or expelled from, the first landscape.

The transformative, even therapeutic, effect that the four years spent in Catalonia had on Ridruejo's life and his political ideas is closely related to the way in which his poetic experience of the natural setting can be read as a correlate for his commentary about his relationship with his Falangist past and with the *nature* or *topography* of Francoist power, that is, the regime's inability to unify its components into an ideologically coherent whole. Rather than a simple integration of the parts within the whole,

Ridruejo's diary examines the dynamic interplay between the two, so as to alter the habitual perspective of the relationship between things small and big, things that move and those that remain static. The diary's entries note the slightest indications of a change in the environment by which a new season announces itself while the preceding one is still in full swing, thereby rendering visible an otherwise invisible pattern of seasonal change. This method of locating change within continuity, the big (seasons) in the small (moment in a day), goes hand in hand with Ridruejo's talent for altering the perspective in such a way that everything grandiose and terrifying in nature—all those things that belong to the Kantian sublime, such as the beauty of the stars or the power of the storm—become adequately captured and comprehended by attending to the smallest detail of everyday life: a walk through the hills surrounding the house, the eye of a cat that reflects the outline of a room on a stormy night. In Ridruejo's book, the small contains the big, so that, often, what is smallest turns out to be bigger than the biggest: a kitten stepping through tall grass is more dignified than a lion traversing a jungle.

This notion that the big is contained in the small is one of the lessons Ridruejo learned from the beautifully cultivated Catalan landscape. His praise for the humanized nature of that landscape goes hand in hand with offering his book as an illustration of those lessons. In Ridruejo's book, adopting a human scale means examining each thing or moment against the background of a diverse, constantly moving and changing world, in which everything, animal and human, close and distant, old and new, big and small, achieves its place and measure. The entry dated August 17 describes a stroll through woody hills recently refreshed by a brief and much-needed summer rain. The narrator captures the vivid intensity of the colors after the rain. He admires the detail and the precision with which different dimensions and components of the landscape come together to form a coherent picture: "Everything is big, because everything is small. The diminutive and rich topographic diversity recreates the unity of an entire world. That peak over there seems too high, inaccessible; fifteen minutes of an easy hike and we are already at its top. Down there, that house and that man walking seem very far, but they still preserve their size. How everything human grows in a world of such meticulous brevity!" (112).

The episode plays with the notion of measure and perspective, not merely to depict the beauty of the Catalan landscape for readers but, more importantly, to show how the human and the natural both complement and enhance each other. The passage describes how, looking down from the hill he was climbing, the narrator is able to see the entire valley, visually putting together the diverse pieces that compose it. The variety and arrangement of the elements lead him to see in this minute portion of the Catalan landscape an image of a complete and unified world. However, what truly establishes the proportions of that miniature world—or world in miniature—is the figure of a man walking in the distance, a distance that, Ridruejo observes, is suddenly reduced by the large size of the figure compared to the smallness of the background. The presence of the human figure generates a multiplicity of perspectives that truly make the scene what it is. Not only does the man seem bigger against the background of the suddenly diminishing landscape, but the small valley, which the human presence made even smaller, also ends up reflecting an entire world, becoming a beautifully shaped universe adjusted to human measure. In a sense, this interplay between human presence and landscape makes everything in the scene grow, including those things that get comparatively smaller. To put it differently, the scene is an example of how the man and his surroundings enhance each other, of how human activity transforms the natural setting into an image of the world that grows in beauty and complexity by virtue of being created and experienced as limited.[44]

Several tropes that encapsulate Ridruejo's vision of the Catalan landscape—aversion to the infinite, beauty as a fruit, a world of meticulous brevity, a part that contains the whole—underscore the author's conception of Catalonia as a world whose dynamism is a function of what he calls "love of the limits." In terms of Ridruejo's political biography, following the collapse of the totalitarian utopia of creating a new world, Catalonia offers an image of a concrete, tangible world. The love of limits that the *Diario* evokes reflects the author's discovery of his love for the world that is constructed and experienced as finite and stable. The very structure of the text introduces a sense of temporal and spatial limits within which it is possible to register the continuum of change and stability that emerges from movement. The interplay of change and stability in the *Diario* does not comply with the notion of movement subordinated to a determinate goal or end, as was the case with Ridruejo's conception of the role of the Falange within the Movimiento Nacional. It also differs from the self-propelled movement of the sea, which has its *telos* within itself and seeks never to end. Rather, as I argue next, in the *Diario* we encounter an example of the conception of political movement that Ridruejo would spell out in the mid-1950s as he assumed the role of companion and mentor to a new generation of Spaniards who were achieving their political maturity under the Francoist yoke. According to that new conception, encapsulated in the metaphor of swimming teacher, movement is not to be instrumentalized at the service of an end. Rather, capacity for movement is commensurate with the potential—and the skill—to resist and overcome the forces that seek to impede movement or subjugate it to a pursuit of an externally imposed end. This noninstrumental conception of movement and political action leads to the embrace of liberal democracy, which Ridruejo would accept as an unforeseen, and yet logical, point of arrival to a career that started off with the commitment to fascism.

Ridruejo's Two Bodies: Swimming Instructor

The years 1942, when Ridruejo abandoned the posts he held with the Franco regime, and 1956, when he was imprisoned for participation in student protests, marked the starting and ending points of his transition from serving as a prominent member of the coalition that claimed victory in 1939 to becoming an officially recognized dissident and enemy of the regime. In many of his writings between 1942 and 1956 Ridruejo expresses his disagreement with the Franco regime while stopping short of disavowing his fascist past. If this was a contradictory attitude, then the reasons for that contradiction should be sought not so much in his personal resentment toward the Francoist establishment or in his loyalty to the cause of the Falange, but in the paradoxical nature of the Falange's position within Francoism. The latter's appropriation of the Falange's symbols, coupled with an abandonment of its ideological principles, meant that the Falange would exist as long as, and to the extent to which, reference to it was necessary for Francoism's own survival. For Ridruejo, any kind of relationship with the "original" cause, be it rupture or loyalty, was complicated by the existence of the Francoist Falange, which he referred to in a 1942 letter to Franco as "this thing whose only purpose is to trouble our consciousness."[45] Although calling the Falange "this thing" implied that it was no longer Ridriejo's thing, what mattered was the fact that it still existed. As it happens with other ideologies when their agendas are appropriated by rival ideologies, the problem with the Falange was not that its cause continued being alive but that the empty shell—the ghost—of that cause was not yet dead.

The originality and, dare one say, the consistency of Ridruejo's relationship with Francoism, on the one hand, and his own fascist past, on the other, resided in his realization that, had the Francoist appropriation of the Falange been solely a problem for the Falange and those loyal to its ideology, then it would not have been a problem at all. Had that been the case, the Falangist cause would have died, whether peacefully or violently, in a futile effort to revive its project and reclaim the place that presumably belonged to it. Something much more serious was at stake, and it had to do not only with the Falange's past but with Spain's future. Ridruejo's move from fascism to liberalism was predicated on his conviction that Francoism, instead of building a new society around a new totalitarian ideology, now risked unleashing, under radically different circumstances, a crisis analogous to the one that had led from the Second Republic to fascism and civil war. Francoism was replaying the same scenario and structure of crisis that had motivated Ridriejo's initial embrace of fascism.

While the liberal regime of the Second Republic had proved unable to control the forces of revolution that were fueled by its own internal contradictions, the Franco regime, itself brimming with contradictions, used conflict, both internal and external, as an opportunity to perfect its strategies of survival and adaptation. Rather than building a new society, the main item on the Francoist agenda was its self-preservation. Unfortunately for the regime its formula for survival rested on two pillars, both of them unsustainable in the long run. On the one hand, Francoism relied on the passivity of the population, which Ridruejo saw as a product of long-standing ills in Spanish society: excessive individualism, lack of solidarity, incompetence, and political disorientation on the part of the socioeconomic elites, combined with their tendency to usurp power.[46] On the other hand, the regime's intransigence not only precluded any possibility of reasoned public discussion about the political future but also fostered collective passivity as the only acceptable response to the uncertainty surrounding the evolution of Spain's political system. Anxiety about the future was the regime's dirty little secret, barely hidden behind the façade of its unity and will to permanence. Ridruejo feared that a society like Spain, in which regular channels of political change were blocked and a clearly defined common political project was nonexistent, would compel those who were the most concerned about the future—the young—to opt once again for revolutionary violence as the only available model of change. A new generation of Spaniards, those born in the aftermath of the Civil War and who were coming of age in the late 1950s, faced a dire and, for Ridruejo, all too familiar political dilemma: either revolution—this time communist, and not fascist—or something he viewed as equally unacceptable, namely, conformism and passivity: going with the flow.

An interpretation of another motif—a swimming lesson—deployed at two different junctures in Ridruejo's writings can illuminate Ridruejo's evolving conception of political change, a conception that is closely related to his ongoing reflection about his own personal and political trajectory. The motif in question first appears in an entry of the *Diario de una tregua* as a memory of a boy—presumably young Ridruejo himself—who is being taught how to swim. It reappears in his 1956 report to the Falange concerning the student protests in February of that year, in which Ridruejo claims for himself the role of a swimming instructor for new generations of Spaniards. In both cases the motif of the swimming lesson has more general political significance insofar as it exemplifies a direct relationship between the "what" (the art of swimming) and the "how" (learning to conduct oneself in the water), between the process and the outcome, the method and the goal. In the *Diario*, the boy glimpses the experience of swimming through a learning process that does not lead to mastering the skill; hence, the importance of the swimming lesson lies in its failure. In the 1956 report, the hope of negotiating the murky waters of Francoist politics exists precisely because the young *can* be taught how to swim. The motif of the swimming lesson offers the hope of crossing the river—be it the river of Ridruejo's life, the river of history, or the turbulent river of politics—and getting to the other side, particularly when there is no bridge, no preestablished or necessary link, between the two shores (here and there, then and now).

In the April 16 entry of Ridruejo's *Diario*, the memory of a swimming lesson offers a narrative framework for an allegorical and deceptively simple account of Ridruejo's political biography. The element that sets the stage for the lesson consists of the narrator's observations about what he calls "children's civilization" (36). The latter is not that different from the adult version of civilization except for the fact that, among children, certain features of the adult world, such as the drive for possessions or the will of the stronger to assert dominance over the weaker, appear in an unrestrained and extreme form. Children's tendencies toward possessiveness and control are comparable only to their dread of being or looking different, of standing out from the rest. However, these tendencies fall apart during experiences such as recreational outings to rivers, Ridruejo observes, reminiscing about his own past. There, "artificial differences . . . disappear and . . . other, real ones, . . . prevail. Those who are poor can be as beautiful as little gods. And the rich [can be] as pitiful as worms. . . . Air and water wash away the residues of culture and put to test the quality of the clay" (36). Unlike the static hierarchy that characterizes children's civilization when they are clothed, both literally and metaphorically, the unclothed children who go to the river to swim form a dynamic society based on free competition and individual prowess. Here, Ridruejo's allegory of two different types of society—one based on prestige and the other on competitiveness, one rigidly stratified and the other dynamic and entrepreneurial—and his sympathy for the latter are fairly straightforward. But it is here where the motif of swimming lesson is introduced, posing a different kind of relationship, that between a boy and his swimming instructor, which is irreducible to either social model. Unlike relationships based on the primary and direct domination of one child over another through power and performance, the relationship of an adult swimming instructor to his young trainee represents a form of what one might call secondary or indirect domination. Here, the difference between the boy and the adult is not established through mere exercise of power but is presupposed from the very beginning. That difference, although given, is not fixed or unmovable; instead, it reflects both parties' unequal, yet changeable, standing with respect to a third element, in this case the ability to swim and to find one's bearings in a new environment (water).

At the point where the episode moves from general observations about children's behavior to the memory of a specific swimming lesson, Ridruejo's writing shifts registers, replacing the allegory of two different kinds of society with a presumably autobiographical account of an event whose allegoric content is not readily decipherable. The memory recalls a group of children who are attempting to swim in the swift waters of the river, close to a dam. The challenges they face in staying afloat become an opportunity for an adult to instruct them on how to swim with a proper style—like men and not like dogs, as the narrator puts it (37). In the midst of the commotion among the boys who are trying to perfect their masculine swimming technique and abandon their former, canine, style, the narrator focuses on a boy, presumably himself, "whose body changed, who came across a body that would never again be able to sustain itself in the water, as if someone had tied a block of lead to his foot" (37).

The boy, whom the teacher had used as a guinea pig for a staged rescue lesson, discovers his new body during the very brief interval between the moment he starts to sink and the instant the teacher pulls him out of the water. "The adult," writes Ridruejo, "left him by the sticky edge, where he submerged himself into a big bubble similar to another world. He was neither a dressed nor undressed child any more. A few instants in the haze of death had made him into an individual, revealing to him the innermost kernel, untamable, and impossible to share [*incomunicable*]" (37).

The crux of this account of swimming-practice-turned-rescue-lesson is to be found in the quick succession of events that progress, not without some drama, from an innocuous beginning to an unexpected outcome. A more general relevance of the episode is connected to the fact that, at the end, the protagonist finds himself in a position diametrically opposed to the initial one: he goes from being just one of many boys learning to swim—his being used as a guinea pig underscores his status as a stand-in for an entire species—to becoming someone defined by a sense of irreducible individuality, which originates in the experience of near drowning. The succession of events that constitutes the narrative core of the episode is full of reversals, such that the outcome of each action represents not only a consequence of the previous one but also its flip side. It is as if we were watching a scene in which each action is reversed by the reaction, each cause stood on its head by the effect it produces. The boy who is made to feel that he is almost drowning gets saved by the instructor for whom drowning is just a method for teaching how to stay afloat. Subsequently, the relief of recovering the ground under his feet, which the protagonist would have experienced in the aftermath of his rescue, gets reversed by the sense of abandonment and isolation that he associates with being left on the shore. The shore is not a safe haven but a sticky edge, a limit to which he is bound by his fear of drowning and by the discovery of loneliness that delineates the contours of his new body. Secluded within the limits of that body, which will "never again be able to sustain itself in the water," he hovers within a bubble that forms a boundary between two environments, air and water. The experience of almost drowning is what produces his new self, born out of the marriage of attempt and failure, as a point of connection between two opposing forces that become inextricably linked through him: the water that has the potential of taking him away and the land to which he is bound by the fear of drowning.

The relevance of this episode for our understanding of Ridruejo's political trajectory—an issue that, in turn, is related to a broader question regarding the role of literature in providing a deeper, more nuanced, and more truthful vision of his politics—is to be found in his autobiographical account of an individuality that emerges not only *out of* the experience of drowning but also *in response* to it. That is, the protagonist's acquisition of one of the most cherished values of the liberal mind-set, the sense of the limits of individuality that is experienced as irreducible and untamable, occurs not only as a product of the experience of drowning but also as an antidote to it. What defines the value of individuality for the protagonist is that he owes the knowledge of its existence to the experience of almost losing it. The boy's new identity is not a simple or static product of the near-drowning experience. Rather, it is a complex self whose present combines memory and anticipation, memory related to the passing of something that is lost forever (his old body) and anticipation that names the existence of something able to counter the loss (his sense of individuality). In an essay about Hermann Broch, significantly entitled "No Longer and Not Yet," Hannah Arendt observes that, for Broch, living requires "that we forever 'stand on the bridge that is spanned between invisibility and invisibility and nevertheless . . . are caught in the stream.'"[47] Paraphrasing Arendt, we could say that in his account of the swimming lesson, Ridruejo portrays a boy, himself, who came out on the other shore of his new self while feeling the weight of his old body still pulling him down. In order to surmount the rivers of history and get to the other side of the experience of almost drowning, the adult Ridruejo needed to help others not get caught in the stream.

The moral of the youthful swimming lesson is inscribed in the acceptance of the two-fold failure, that of the lesson and of the protagonist himself. The memory of that failure, the sensation of being caught in the stream, becomes a bridge between the old body that almost drowned and the new one, which is not and will never be, a body of a swimmer. This brings us to the second swimming lesson, in which Ridruejo assumes the role of a swimming instructor for younger generations of Spaniards, who in 1956 were starting to publicly express their disaffection with the regime. Incarcerated in Carabanchel prison on the charge of being an instigator of the student demonstrations of that year, Ridruejo wrote a letter to the leadership of the Falange in which he explained the nature of his commitment to the students' cause and addressed the issue of his apparent betrayal of the cause he had supported in his youth. Concerning his motivations, he writes: "My main concern, that which has forced me . . . to be active and speak my mind, is principally the following: that no one in Spain end up again under the spell of ideologies or formulas of political magic, because the Spanish problem is the problem of conduct, of the sense of responsibility, of the laboriousness and intelligence of the Spaniards."[48] From this declaration he reaches the following conclusion: "Those who expect anything from any kind of formula and are not determined to demand the most of themselves, they, in truth, don't hope for anything, except perhaps to fish in turbulent waters [*pescar a río revuelto*]. And, in turbulent waters one doesn't need to know how to fish but how to swim. That is what I have tried to be, especially with the young, a swimming teacher."[49]

A deeply personal and political message, one that resonates strongly through Ridruejo's life and his writing, hinges on the relationship between the two swimming lessons, one that deals with the aftermath of the individual experience of drowning and another in which the art of teaching the young to swim requires instructors first to learn the lesson themselves in order to put themselves into the students' shoes, or their skin. These two moments encapsulate the process of change in Ridruejo's conception of politics, defined on one side by the failure of the totalitarian option and completed on the other side by his embrace of the cause of liberal democracy. In Ridruejo's biography the failure of the totalitarian option, symbolized by the Falange's contradictory role under Francoism, becomes the motif for his rejection of the ideology and cause of totalitarianism. In other words, the rejection of totalitarianism occurs only in retrospect, after the Falange emerged victorious from the Civil War but failed to achieve its political goals. Addressing the critiques that view this sequence of events as a sufficient reason to question the integrity of his transformation, Ridruejo argued that the nature of political action requires comprehending the importance of the relationship between ends and means for politics. Politicians judge the validity of their motives, or the integrity of their methods, primarily in light of the goals they aspire to. In other words, rather than just a feature of his biography, the phenomenon of one's inability to judge the motives and methods of one's actions except in relationship to preset ends, and the tendency to question those ends only after failing to achieve them, is a characteristic of political behavior as such. A "politician"—writes Ridruejo—

> tends to judge based on the ends. Only when I perceived the latter in all of their crude reality, everything else became patent and terror regained its true face of an intolerable evil. . . . . I do not think that this process of judgment coming out of disillusionment, or differed judgment, psychologically, constitutes anything exceptional. The majority of people who have forged their moral humanism after certain undue hopes of theirs were shattered, or who lived firsthand the experience of terror, got to rebel against terror and justify their reaction as a rebellion against terror, only because they had previously experienced the failure of their hopes.[50]

Ridruejo's questioning of the Falange's goals, which occurs as a consequence of its failure to achieve them, replicates the temporality of the first swimming lesson. There, the boy's failure to keep himself afloat is retrospectively elaborated in the protagonist-narrator's account of the lesson as an event that produced his new body by way of the experience of sinking. Transposing this example onto Ridruejo's political commitment, we could say that his distancing from fascism came on the heels of his conviction that the Falange's history exemplified an ill-fitting combination of ideology and practice, which resulted in not achieving desired goals, or rather in achieving goals different from those intended. The Falange's failure was inscribed in the fact that, in order to reach its goals (victory in the war, foundation of a new state), it resorted to the means (creation of a broad coalition of traditional right-wing forces) that were incongruent with the final ends (total state). Ridruejo's 1956 letter called the attention of the Falange's members to the unsustainable paradox of their position:

> Falange which came to July 18 [1936, the outbreak of the Civil War] as a project of totality . . . emerged from the war transformed into a part. . . . Not only was it a part with respect to the defeated half of Spain, but also within the alliance of forces comprising the victorious half. Its assimilation of the values of the left was dissolved in a forced loyalty to the values of the right. . . . It lent its form—which, in retrospective, is its most questionable element—and could not impose its reformist substance except in quantities so diminished that they do not even remotely resemble the origin.[51]

In other words, in the aftermath of the Civil War, the Falange not only got something different from what it aspired to, but the very thing it got—a portion of power granted to it by Francoism—had the effect of annulling, retrospectively, the validity of its original aspirations, which aimed for a complete overturn of the old liberal state and the establishment of a revolutionary fascist state.

A perverse mixture of liberal and totalitarian features is how Ridruejo describes the Francoist regime in his most ambitious political-historical work, *Escrito en España* (1962). On the surface, the civic passivity of Spanish society under Francoism more resembled the conformist contentment of the "free world" than the asceticism of obedience characteristic of totalitarian societies. "Like the obedience in absolutist regimes, our inhibition is something imposed. Like the conformism of free citizens, it is something that is accepted . . . without too much opposition."[52] This combination of conformism and oppression served to uphold the political system based on the similarly problematic mixture of an apparent pluralism and the equally apparent unity of the regime. While apportioning power through limited competition among insiders, Francoism continued to divide Spanish society into two separated and amorphous camps: the victors and the defeated.

Learning to swim functions as an alternative to two futile political options afforded by Francoism: fishing in the murky waters of Francoist politics or belonging to an unmovable and ill-defined whole comprising the quasi parts that owed their existence to the regime. Once Ridruejo accepted the inevitability of the Falange's debacle and concluded that an evolution of Francoism through internal reform was impossible, he publically affirmed his political and ethical commitment to averting the possibility that Spanish society, and particularly its youth, be forced into another political dead end. While imprisoned at Carabanchel, Ridruejo wrote "Romance de los estudiantes presos" (Romance of the imprisoned students), a joking parody of Jorge Manrique's famous "Coplas por la muerte de su padre," in which he portrayed himself as one of many Spaniards, particularly the young, whose lives were like rivers flowing to their final destination, which is in jail ("Nuestras vidas son los ríos / que van a dar al penal").[53] Many lives flowed into Carabanchel. For some of them (Ridruejo), the events of 1956 were a point of no return, while for others, the young opposition to the regime, it was a point of departure. Despite the time-space that stood between the ex-Falangist and the future leaders of anti-Francoist opposition, there was a certain symmetry between the long road Ridruejo took to get where he was and the distance of their destination that presaged a long journey ahead. Coming from different ideological shores and with the horizon of fulfillment of their common goals still remote, the only place where Ridruejo and the students could meet was in the river.

Ridruejo's role as swimming instructor consisted not so much in teaching the young the technique of swimming—which, if judged by that early lesson, he himself never mastered—but primarily in encouraging them to venture into the political waters without fear and with the knowledge of a few basic skills that would allow them to keep from drowning. "'Let's see if you really know how to breathe freely.' 'Let's see if you really know how to proceed with justice.' 'Let's see if you really are capable of rescuing lovingly the one who is drowning, even if he is an enemy, instead of smacking him in the head and letting him sink, which is the way we do things around here.'"[54] Rather than pointing to a goal that the young should reach, Ridruejo's task was to help them avoid the failure that results from conceiving political action in accordance with totalizing goals and without concern for the relationship between the goals and the methods employed to achieve them.

Ridruejo's ideological transformation was grounded in the conclusion, put forward in his 1956 letter, that the Falange resembled its enemy, communism, in its common tendency to posit lofty ends and try to accommodate reality to the ideal by resorting to reprehensible means. Here, he came full circle with respect to his past convictions, by portraying fascism and communism as two sides of the same totalitarian coin, much the same way Arendt did in her book on totalitarianism, written around the same time. From there to embracing the idea of liberal democracy as the only acceptable political alternative, there was only one small step, one that, in 1956, Ridruejo was willing to make publicly. He makes it clear that his positive view of democracy is not that of a starry-eyed neophyte but of someone who has come to terms with the idea that democracy is the only civilizational achievement for which he is ready to fight. Rather than an ideal goal or absolute end, for Ridruejo liberal democracy is the only solution to the dead end of his own development. Totalitarianism, according to Ridruejo, is a tyranny of ends, which in practice degenerates into a straightforward tyranny of means; such as, for example, when total submission to the party becomes the criterion of loyalty to the revolution. On the other hand, the most valuable aspect of liberal democracy is the compatibility between ends and means, between the democratic idea and the concrete practices and procedures without which the idea remains just an idea.

One might argue that Ridruejo's reasoned—not starry-eyed—embrace of liberal democracy articulates a position not significantly different from one that many members of the Francoist regime would adopt later, when they became active participants in the process of democratic transition.

Following Franco's death, democracy simply made more sense and, moreover, did not require reckoning with the dictatorial past. Instead of arguing in favor of or against Ridruejo's political choices, this analysis of his tortuous political path aspired to show that any approach to politics—Francoist or democratic—that is built on the suppression of stasis obliterates the very core of democratic politics, which is its agonistic openness.

CHAPTER 3

Paradoxes of Francoist Stasis

Miguel Espinosa and the Art of Protest

In 1956 a reliable insider within the Francoist regime, likely Manuel Fraga himself, discouraged publication of what would have been Miguel Espinosa's first novel, a baroque allegory of a despotic power, entitled *Historia del eremita*. The assessment that the novel, despite its merits, was unpublishable had significant, albeit unforeseen, consequences not only for *Historia del eremita* but also for Espinosa's literature as a whole. Instead of putting the project aside, over the course of the next eighteen years he would write two more complete versions of the novel.[1] By the time the third and final version, *Escuela de mandarines*, was published in 1974, just a year before Franco's death, Espinosa had spent two decades (1954–74) writing, expanding, and reworking the text with the devotion of an artisan whose commitment to producing an object—a book about Francoism—demanded time, sharpened skill, and vision.

Rather than thwarting its future, the period during which the book was kept out of the public eye became a necessary ingredient in its production. Those two decades of Espinosa's life and the life of Francoism proved formative in more than one sense and, as such, remain inscribed in the differences of form and substance between the first and the last version. In both cases, the narrative centers on the protagonist, named Eremita (Hermit), who travels to the capital of an oppressive regime in which power is wielded jointly, although not always harmoniously, by the sovereign—a prince or dictator—and a cast of mandarins, who are the keepers and sole interpreters of the state's founding text, known simply as "the Book." In the first version of the novel, *Historia del eremita,* circularity is the dominant feature in the narrative of the protagonist's life as well as the regime's history. Eremita's departure from the city and his return, at the end of the novel, to the utopian natural setting that is his place of origin mark his rejection of the cyclical movement of history from one unrest to another—from the establishment of princely power in fratricidal wars to the unraveling of the alliance between political and spiritual authority (the prince and the mandarins), which paves the way for another cycle of violent power struggles followed by the establishment of an even more sinister kind of order.

Eighteen years later, in *Escuela de mandarines,* the protagonist's life and the regime's history unfold in a different order of temporality, one not circumscribed by the turbulent cycle of power, which Eremita had condemned in the first version of the novel by returning to the world outside history. Rather than describing an inescapable historical circle, the 1974 version places side by side two competing and yet intimately linked forms of life, the regime's and Eremita's, both defined by their capacity to endure. The duration of the regime, now called "Happy Governance," is measured in billions of years. It stretches from the mists of the past, populated by events and figures whose meaning is all but forgotten, to the nebulous present, in which the Book has lost its status as the depository of foundational truths and is treated as an allegory, a mere pre-text for the regime's continuous self-interpretation and refashioning. The regime has done away with any notion of time or history and, with it, the idea of change; it sees itself as timeless and eternal. The term *year* has lost its meaning pertaining to the calendar and is reduced to representing a mere number.

Although blissful oblivion and a lack of concern with its own history are the main features of the regime in the final version of the novel, the passage of time left a decisive imprint on the process of the book's transformation. Against a background of the Francoist regime's endurance, the decades that separated the first and the last versions (1954–74) constitute a sort of interregnum—an interstitial period of conflicts and tensions with no clear end in sight. Rather than being ousted or imploding under the weight of its internal ideological divisions, after the government reshuffle of 1958, Francoism entered a new phase centered on economic progress and the normalization of its international status. As I argued in chapter 1, despite being immune to true change or transformation, Francoism was nevertheless constantly preoccupied with its future. With his first novel blocked from publication in 1956, Espinosa created the two subsequent versions during a period in which his project grew in parallel with the regime it allegorized. The historical referent and its allegory were being created simultaneously—in real time, as it were.

My reading of *Escuela de mandarines* starts from the premise that the form and the very existence of Espinosa's novel are examples of critical reflection about the essence of Francoism and its capacity for endurance. I examine in depth the connection between the duration of Francoism and the nature of Espinosa's novel, a connection the author himself established in a letter to Jean Tena:

> El libro podría calificarse, a mi juicio, de utopía negativa del fascismo español . . . ; por utopía negativa entiendo la exposición de lo que no debe ser. También podría definirse como un intento de descripción ontológica, o sea, en su real ultimidad, del fascismo, tal y como ha florecido en España durante cuarenta años; la obra quiere pintar, pormenor a pormenor, una sociedad fascista, en su totalidad y en cada consecuencia. Como solo en España, si hacemos excepción de Portugal, ha perdurado el fascismo casi medio siglo, creo que solo desde aquí podría pergeñarse la obra que describiera su ser inmoral.

> The book could be qualified, in my judgment, as a negative utopia of Spanish fascism . . . ; by negative utopia, I mean the exposition of what should not exist. The book could also be defined as an attempt toward an ontological description of fascism—that is, in its real finality—as it has flourished in Spain for forty years; the work seeks to portray, detail by detail, a fascist society in its totality and in every consequence. Since

only in Spain—excepting Portugal—has fascism endured for half a century, I believe that only from this place could a work be produced that would describe its immoral being.[2]

Not only the form and substance of Espinosa's novel but also his writing method, based on sustained observation of the regime's quotidian reality—"pormenor a pormenor"—were a way of giving an account of two processes that unfolded simultaneously and thereby both reflected and limited one another: the author's persistence in expanding and perfecting a book deemed impossible to publish and the longevity of the regime that condemned it to obscurity until a year before the dictator's death. For Espinosa, writing was a response to a double impossibility: the impossibility of ending the book without anticipating the complications entailed in the other ending, that of Francoism, whose endurance acted both as a stimulus for continuing the book and an obstacle for finishing it. In that sense, there is a deep *structural* connection between Espinosa's novel and the history of the regime he hated so passionately, a hatred that itself became an enduring bond tying him to Francoism. The very magnitude of the novel's final version—600 pages, 488 character names, a lengthy apparatus of footnotes—is both a testimony to the lasting ignominy of Francoism/Happy Governance and an attempt to preserve its memory for posterity. In fact, one must wonder whether the scant critical attention given to *Escuela*—even compared to Espinosa's other novels— might reflect not just the novel's difficulty but also the desire to forget the complexity and enduring impact of Francoism: its repressive nature and its success at ensuring stability and social conformity that allowed it to last and to end peacefully.

The strong bond of animosity that tied Espinosa's writing to the existence of the regime whose end he passionately desired evokes the complex set of ideas embedded in the Greek notion of stasis, a conflict between fellow citizens that introduces, in Nicole Loraux's words, a "bond of division" among them.[3] A similarly paradoxical bond links Espinosa's book to the destiny of the seemingly interminable regime of Francoism and its fictional incarnation, Happy Governance. Espinosa's will to continue with the writing process became a peculiar form of protest: While he resisted concluding the book before the regime ended, finishing the book after Franco's death potentially risked diminishing its impact. The 2012 publication of the first version, *Historia del eremita*, and its differences with the final version show that the author's fascination with and detestation of Francoism grew stronger as the regime personified by el caudillo neared its end. In this chapter I argue that the measure of Espinosa's incommensurable, abiding struggle with Francoism is found in the 1974 novel's portrayal of Happy Governance as an unending regime that, together with enforcing immobility, introduces restlessness within the regime and generates protest among the dissident characters, who are absent from the first version.

The possibility of comparing the first novel and the last, considerably longer and more complex version, offers an invaluable heuristic tool for analyzing Espinosa's novelistic project as a form of protest. My argument about the ontological, ethical, and aesthetic tenets of protest focuses on what I deem to be the most significant contributions of the 1974 version, namely, the proliferation of figures of dissidents and the addition of philosophical disquisitions about the role of literature in the context of political oppression. Building on Dimitris Vardoulakis's account of the democratic potential of stasis, I argue that different forms of protest in Espinosa's novel reflect his conception of "being in common" or, in Vardoulakis's terms, "being with."[4] A fundamental element of this conception of being is the proliferation of (chance) encounters, which informs the sprawling structure of the novel. For Espinosa the writer and his protagonist, protest is not just an activity but a form of life that serves as a venue for the exploration of the ontological, ethical, aesthetic, and political dimensions of being.

Approximately half-way through *Escuela de mandarines*, Espinosa inserts a commentary about the hypothetical event of its publication: "El hijo de Maravillas Gironés escribió en la Tercera Provincia Oriental, lejos de la Ciudad, y su obra pudo ver la luz porque los hijos de Casilda y

Lala Fulvia, los famosos Formulario y Sonsibio, censores locales, tanto la despreciaron que la dejaron editar" (The son of Maravillas Gironés [the name of Espinosa's mother] wrote in the Third Eastern Province, far from the City, and his work could see the light because the sons of Casilda and Lala Fulvia, the famous local censors Formulario and Sonsibio, despised it so much that they allowed it to be published).[5] In this mixture of real and fictional names, which is deployed throughout the book, Espinosa's derogatory invocation of famous local censors contrasts with the gesture of honoring his mother's name, which he, the anonymous author, reveals and invokes for posterity as a reference to his origin. While connecting the history of his book to the memory of a woman who would otherwise remain anonymous—using the name of Maravillas Gironés as a protective shield guarding the absence/presence of his own name—Espinosa also pays tribute to the lasting glory of the censors. That very questionable glory echoes in the sounds of their and their mother's names and manifests itself through the exercise of authority over the book, which enters the public realm carrying the indelible stain of their scorn. So convinced are they of the book's—and the writer's—irrelevance that their scorn becomes a sufficient criterion for allowing its publication. Scorn that signifies approval, merit that denotes irrelevance, lasting glory that is a confirmation of another's lasting marginality: such are the ruling paradoxes in the history of Happy Governance. These paradoxes, I argue, are related to the nature of Espinosa's book, which grew by defying its own ending and that of the regime. In that sense, the temporality of the book and the regime it describes exemplify a complex, nonbinary relationship between immobility and movement constitutive of the Greek notion of stasis.

Muddy Foundations

José Luis Bellón observed a surprising tendency among critics to ignore the connection between *Escuela de mandarines* and the history of Francoism.[6] In light of that oversight, it should come as no surprise that no critical account of Espinosa's novel—including Bellón's—has noticed the somewhat obscure but crucial mention of the recurrence of civil wars in the history of Happy Governance. In contrast to the first version of the novel, which contains an entire section entitled "Guerra civil," the 1974 novel omits the term *civil war* altogether. The event of civil war does not disappear, but the term does. I would argue that this disappearance constitutes the site of Espinosa's reflection on the status of civil war in the history of Happy Governance and Francoism. More specifically, Espinosa's account of the fictional polity's history speaks to a gradual replacement of politics by economy as a source of legitimation of a regime founded on fratricidal violence.

The section on civil wars in *Historia del eremita* narrates a struggle between three proconsuls—each one at the helm of an army of mercenaries—who turn against each other after overthrowing the existing princely regime. In *Escuela de mandarines*, the story of the three proconsuls, now referred to as "Los degolladores" (the slaughterers, or the butchers), becomes less prominent. The struggle for power between the cruel, power-hungry, and ignorant "butchers" is more significant for the references it elicits to two other civil wars, mentioned seemingly in passing, often in footnotes, as if to illustrate their status as remote events that some members of the regime evoke with a sense of embarrassment and others with nostalgia and pride. One of these wars is marked by popular uprisings in various provinces, which the proconsuls suppress before overthrowing the prince and turning against each other. Another takes place 560,770 years later, when the proconsul Silvestre organizes an expedition that annihilates the last remaining descendants of the "municipalists," the provincial rebels defeated by the proconsuls.

It is this second war, which confirmed and consummated the almost six-hundred-thousand-year-old defeat, to which Espinosa gives the proper name "Batida," or "Rastrojo." The following quote, found in a footnote, is how he describes the event of Batida:

Como sabemos, los Procónsules Cirilo, Salvador y Calvo reprimieron el levantamiento de los municipalizantes hacia 1030030, causando más de novecientos mil muertos. Ciertos supervivientes se refugiaron en unos bosques pantanosos, donde devinieron, con el tiempo, raza nudista y sin lenguaje, ajena a toda civilización. Así transcurrieron 560,770 años, hasta que en 1590790, el Procónsul Silvestre decidió exterminar la especie, iniciando la llamada Batida o Rastrojo, guerra contra el más indefenso pueblo del mundo, que "por no saber trabar vocablos, no podía sustentar doctrina alguna, ortodoxa ni heterodoxa."

As we know, the Proconsuls Cirilo, Salvador, and Calvo repressed the uprising of the municipalizers around 1030030, causing more than nine hundred thousand deaths. Certain survivors took refuge in some swampy forests, where over time they became a naked race without language, alien to all civilization. Thus transpired 560,770 years, until in 1590790 the Proconsul Silvestre decided to exterminate the species, thereby initiating the so-called Batida or Rastrojo, a war against the most defenseless people in the world, who "because they did not know how to stutter out words, were unable to sustain any doctrine whatsoever, whether orthodox or heterodox." (220)

Espinosa's description of the outrageous nature of the genocidal event draws attention to the words he uses to name it. There is an unsettling, even unbearable, proximity between the event and its name. The term *batida* names a military operation to which neither the name of war, nor that of civil war, can be legitimately applied. How can one call "war" the extermination of an entire species that is characterized by its utter harmlessness and defenselessness? How to give the name "civil war"—a confrontation between members of the same political "family"—to an expedition against people whose lack of language and civilization deprives them of the ability to name their family and communal bonds and thereby to establish their common genealogy? Can one properly assign the status of enemy to a group whose long defeat remains inscribed on the bodies of its members, their nakedness standing not just for the absence of clothes but of shelter more generally?

All these questions swarm beneath the surface of Espinosa's matter-of-fact, encyclopedia-style entry on the event of the Batida. He forgoes offering a definition of the word itself, even though its choice might strike the reader as strange and archaic, although not more so than the Francoist designation of the Spanish Civil War as a *cruzada*, a term whose echoes are heard in *batida*. Sebastián de Covarrubias's 1611 dictionary of Spanish language does not contain an entry for *batida* but offers a useful explanation of the verb *batir*. "Batir," he says, comes from the Latin "batuo," meaning to strike or to hit, which forms the root of the noun "batalla." The meaning of "beating someone into the ground" comes from the Hebrew "bat," translated into Latin as *desolare* (to desolate, devastate).[7] In a more contemporary usage, the noun *batida* belongs to the terminology of hunting, or the manhunt, as in the phrase "batir el monte," to overrun the terrain that offers shelter for animals or criminals.[8] *Rastrojo*, the other name Espinosa gives for *batida*, is an agricultural term that describes harvested land containing traces (*rastro*) of crops, which are usually burned in order to fertilize the land (896).

The two terms name multiple forms and layers of violence: beating into the ground, overrunning a terrain, eliminating natural shelter, denuding and burning land to increase its yield. All of these violent acts are gathered under the name of the event during which imperial armies left bare the swampy terrain inhabited by a naked race comprising descendants of the survivors—traces of traces—of another war. That first war, as Espinosa points out (once again in a footnote) was waged against the provinces that challenged imperial rule by claiming their right to the collective ownership of land.[9] The period of almost six hundred thousand years that separates the two wars undermines any idea of a chronological or causal connection between them. Rather than following chronology or causality, that connection is to be found elsewhere. The elements common to both events—violence and land—underscore their difference. While the first civil war was waged in the provinces that rose up against the imperial power demanding collective property rights, the second constitutes the gratuitous destruction of people who do not and cannot rise up because they lack the land and the ground upon which to stand. Deprived of a stable terrain to cultivate or build on—Espinosa refers to the "receding mud" of the swamps—the history of the naked race testifies to a loss of ground or foundation. Over time, the defeat and the muddy terrain of marshes swallow up—they make recede—the foundations of their civil and political existence: language, kinship, property, technology. Deprived of the faculty of "combining words" (*trabar vocablos*), they cannot "uphold any doctrine."

Speaking of words, references to stasis—the word *and* the event—seep everywhere into Espinosa's account of the extermination of the naked race, at least as I read it. The story of the naked race, which Espinosa reduces to its bare bones—how it came into being and ceased to be—compresses in time and space the succession of different civil wars. It encapsulates the *longue durée* of the regime's history, a history so long that the regime has lost its durée and cannot help but repeat itself, redefeat the defeated, beat the beaten down. Both the event of the Batida and its name exist as a way of insuring the foundational role of civil war—and its forgetting—in the history of Happy Governance. The duration of forgetting is embodied in the race whose existence outside language and civilization both preserves and perpetuates the erasure of the event that brought it into being. The members of this race are the last, most feeble traces of the harvest of a remote civil war, ready to be leveled down. While avoiding the term civil war, the words Espinosa uses to name the extermination of the naked race evoke another kind of foundational violence: encircling and beating into the ground someone barely able to stand, or returning to the soil of war that which was once harvested from it.

Rather than perpetuating forgetting, Espinosa's deliberate omission and replacement of the term *civil war* by *batida* and *rastrojo* draw attention to the nature of this multilayered violence, aimed at nothing less than the *extermination of the descendants of the survivors of the rebels* from another civil war. If there was ever a civil war whose name one could not bear to utter, this would be it. Instead of simply naming another civil war in a long series of civil wars, the terms *batida* and *rastrojo* metaphorically expose and lay bare the dubious, unstable foundations of the regime built on the destruction of the last traces of resistance, the last vestiges of an internal rebellion.

As I discussed in the introduction, the Greek term for internal rebellion, *stasis*, derives from the verb *histemi*, to stand, to assume an erect bodily position, which in politics translates into claiming and defending one's stance in confrontation with others. Batida and Rastrojo name actions diametrically opposed to those grouped under the rubric of stasis as civil unrest. Their purpose is to ensure that no one remains standing on a muddy terrain that shelters those who exist outside language and hence outside the civic, political realm. But, there is another facet to the "heroic" undertaking of Batida/Rastrojo. By annihilating the inhabitants of the swamps, the regime also builds its own foundations on a muddy, receding terrain. It marches on, building its own history on nothing. This is so because the naked race was the only presence still standing—however precariously—and holding on to the ground that, in the absence of that race, reverts back to its natural state of instability; it becomes nothing but permeable, moving, and sinking soil. While the action of standing that is the origin of stasis implies the existence of a ground on which to stand or rise, the existence and eventual annihilation of the naked race underscores the muddiness and instability of the ground on which Happy Governance is erected.[10]

Interlude: Stasis as Threshold

In *Stasis: Civil War as Political Paradigm*, Giorgio Agamben analyzes the role of stasis, or civil strife, at two paradigmatic moments in Western political thought: ancient Greece and the 1651 publication of Hobbes's *Leviathan*. In both cases, stasis is a contradictory phenomenon: it poses a threat to the existing order, while also being necessary for its reestablishment. But whereas in ancient Greece the latent memory of civil strife remains intrinsic to the way in which the polis thinks its unity, the Hobbesian conception of sovereignty expels stasis outside of politics, into the state of nature.

Greek thought locates stasis at the point that Agamben calls the "threshold of politicization," where the alliances commanded by the realms of family and city, *oikos* and *polis*, clash and contaminate each other.[11] Stasis (fratricidal war) casts both family and polis into disarray. It turns the members of the same polis (the same political family) into enemies and ruptures existing family bonds for the purpose of the creation of new political alliances. Stasis politicizes family bonds: members of the same family turn into enemies, and strangers become brothers. Politicization runs contrary to depoliticization, the latter being defined as the primacy of the family and oikos over participation in the affairs of the polis. Politicization requires the citizens to put other alliances aside and act for the common good, as equals. In the Greek polis, as Agamben reads it, there is a tension and a precarious balance between politicization and depoliticization, which are not merely opposed but instead sustain and limit each other. Family is not merely subsumed into the polis, and neither is politics reduced to oikonomy, the management of the common household.

While seeing fratricidal war as a peril and misfortune, Greek culture offers examples of an attitude that, instead of simply rejecting stasis, attempts to negotiate the extremes of politicization and depoliticization. At one end of the spectrum stands Solon's law (from the early sixth century BC), which punishes with ostracism those who, during an outbreak of stasis, remain on the sidelines and refuse to take sides.[12] On the other end of the spectrum is the law of amnesty, instituted in 403 BC, which mandated that past divisions within the polis be forgotten following the cessation of hostilities. Whereas Solon's law condemned the refusal to take sides during civil strife—depoliticization—the law of amnesty sought to put an end to excessive politicization, the refusal to put internal divisions behind. By locating Greek stasis at the threshold of politicization and depoliticization, Agamben reads it as *pharmakon*, both poison and remedy, a trace of discord and division, which makes the thought of unity inseparable from the possibility of conflict.

In Hobbes's *Leviathan*, civil war also occupies an ambiguous position, signaling the collapse of sovereignty, which is nevertheless necessary for its reestablishment. The emblem that appears as the frontispiece of *Leviathan* illustrates the Hobbesian conception of sovereignty, which is aimed at creating unity out of multiplicity, single people out of a multitude of bodies. Through the mechanism of political representation, the sovereign, whom Hobbes calls a "mortal god," gathers within the same "body politic" a multitude that would otherwise remain scattered and, for that very reason, unrepresentable. There is a certain circularity in the Hobbesian idea of sovereignty, which is closely related to the role that civil war plays in his theory. The vicious circle, or what Dimitris Vardoulakis calls "the ruse of sovereignty,"[13] postulates that only unified people can be represented and only the sovereign can unify people through the mechanism of representation. The "people" does not exist outside the pact with the sovereign. More specifically, without that pact, the people stop existing as *demos* and constitute merely *laos* or *plethos*, a crowd or multitude, which, for Hobbes, is a nonpolitical entity.

This is where, in Agamben's view, civil war enters the picture. For Hobbes, it is impossible for the people (*demos*) to legitimately rebel against the sovereign, because once the covenant with the sovereign is broken, the people (understood as demos) cease to exist, and dissolve into multitude, *multitudo dissoluta*. For a dissolved multitude to reconstitute itself as demos, it must first pass through the stage of civil war, a natural state of disorder (*status naturalis*), which concludes with the victory of one group. Here also, civil war occupies a threshold: this time between the dissolution of sovereignty and its reestablishment. In Agamben's terms, civil war represents the threshold of the disappearance of the people (*ademia*).[14] That means that demos exists only in that interstitial space where the disunity of the civil war subsides to give space—or, like Batida, to clear the ground—for the reestablishment of unity and the rise of a new sovereignty. Once this sovereignty is reestablished, the people, subsumed in the figure of the sovereign, are again absent as demos and present only as a population, subject to sovereign rule and protection.

Castes and Sects: From Imperial Conquest to Opus Dei

How does Agamben's analysis of stasis contribute to Espinosa's account of the relationship between civil war, politics, and economy in his fictional polity? The basic feature of Happy Governance is the absence of stasis, not just in the sense of the fading memory of the history of civil wars but also in the sense of an apparent lack of internal dissent. The regime of Happy Governance rules over an immobile, pacified, and depoliticized society. In his Parmenides lectures, Heidegger reflects on the etymology of the Latin *pax* (peace) as a derivation of *pango* (to fix). For Heidegger, this connection between peace and the action of fixing, that is, encircling and keeping someone in place, reflects the process of imperial domination, where "the fallen are not destroyed" but are kept within "the limits fixed by the dominating ones."[15] In proximity to Heidegger's account, a pacified society of Happy Governance is also vertically fixed, divided in six castes: two are considered originary (people and mandarins), three are auxiliary (civil servants, mayors, and gendarmes), and one is transitory (apprentices to mandarins).

A scene in the novel captures the relationship between the castes. All the inhabitants of a village—members of different castes ("little people," mayor, gendarmes)—are summoned as audience for a government official sent to teach them how to recognize an enemy. Not only is everyone in the village obliged to attend, but, according to state law, at every official gathering, each caste must be represented. If there are no actual representatives of a caste in attendance, then a member of another caste assumes the task of representing them, filling in the space of the absent caste. This ritual of representation indicates that the castes are seen as separate universes—impersonating a caste other than one's own shows the unlikelihood of aspiring to actually occupy its place—and yet each caste makes sense only in relation to the whole.

Instead of an optical illusion that forms unity out of multiplicity, as was the case in *Leviathan*, in Happy Governance political representation is a mere convention, a spatial arrangement of bodies meant to imitate— even parody—the ordering of the social. Each caste has a fixed position in the social hierarchy, inferior or superior to others, and yet all castes are self-enclosed entities, conjoined by separation. Espinosa emphasizes the paradox of that nonrelationship by noting that in Happy Governance each caste has its own gods, its own heaven and afterlife. Given the exclusivity of the relationship between castes and their divinities, gods belonging to one caste both confirm and invalidate the existence of other gods. Put slightly differently, all gods are true and false at the same time. A passage from the Book of Mandarins that Espinosa quotes in one of the footnotes spells this out: "Las castas son libres de pugnar entre sí e injuriar incluso a sus respectivos dioses, pues cada una usufructúa su dios y su cielo verdaderos, que hacen falsos a los demás. De tal forma, todos los dioses y cielos son falsos y verdaderos a un tiempo" (The castes are free to fight among themselves and even to insult their respective gods, for they each make use of their own true god and heaven, which causes the others to be false. In this way, all gods and heavens are true and false at the same time) (241).

Not only has Happy Governance colonized the afterlife and turned gods into appendages of different castes, but it has managed to create a peculiar kind of theocracy without one true god. What we have here is an atheological politics based on the idea that no god is true without also being false—gods that belong to one caste are automatically false for the others—or an apolitical theology, where every caste believes in its own gods precisely *because* they are false for others and are therefore true for the caste that upholds them. In this farcical distortion of theocracy, the existence of different gods mimics the existence of castes as the foundation of the worldly *and* otherworldly existence. The ordering of society in castes, held together not by what unifies them but by what divides and stands between them, repeats in reverse the hierarchy between heaven and earth, up and down. In Happy Governance, earth does not ascend to heaven through the promise of salvation for all. Instead, heaven is brought down to earth as a representation of the perpetuity of the castes, which are separated from each other for eternity. The purpose of the gods is to serve as a guarantee for each caste's conquest and preservation of its own fixed place.

Another purported quote from the Book of Mandarins asserts that "la mediocridad de los dioses oficiales [es] un principio de seguridad" (the mediocrity of the official gods is a principle of security) (241). How are these gods mediocre and how does their mediocrity ensure security?

Although the book does not give an explicit answer to this question, one can surmise that the gods are mediocre because, being both true and false, they are not defined by their divine essence but by the status given to them (true for some and false for others). Happy Governance, which Espinosa at one point defines as "the union of gods and property owners," does not believe in a sovereign divinity that orders the world according to its will or mandate (185). Instead, the regime itself ensures the distribution of gods and their roles. In order to be believed, gods have to be partial to the interests of individual castes. Through the mediocrity of its gods, the regime of Happy Governance ensures an almost universal complicity. Beginning with the mandarins, who, as "prestamistas de los dioses" (moneylenders of the gods) give or lend the gods their roles, everyone—every caste and every god—is a participant in the system to which they owe a guarantee of their existence (241). All the members of Happy Governance, gods and humans alike, are indebted to the system that secures their place and ensures their complicity.

But what is the basis, the grounds, of that complicity? Here I briefly turn to Espinosa's account of a particularly influential sect formed in the course of the Batida. The sect, known first as the "Sociedad de los Vinculados" (Society of those Linked Together) and later as the "Unión Imperial de los Santos" (Imperial Union of the Saints), expanded so "fiercely" that "en menos de treinta años ocupó los institutos públicos, se adueñó de la economía, señoreó los Centros de Estudios Universales, y acabó por nombrar y deponer Dictadores" (in fewer than thirty years it occupied the public institutes, took ownership of the economy, seized control of the Centers of Universal Studies, and ended up naming and deposing Dictators) (331n6). "Los vinculados" is likely a veiled reference to Opus Dei, the lay Catholic organization founded in Spain in 1928, whose influence in education, economy, and politics became notable in the second phase of Francoism. Although the foundation of Opus predates the 1936–39 armed conflict, *El Camino*, the principal work of its founder Josemaría Escrivá Balaguer, was not published until immediately after the Civil War.

More important than Espinosa's jab at Opus Dei is his account of the sect's uncontainable expansion in the aftermath of the Batida. The key to that success lay in promising its followers the kingdom of this world and the other, finding in the possession of material goods (wealth, success, prestige) the path to spiritual benefits. This "eminent nonsense," as Espinosa calls it, spread like wildfire among those whose passions, mobilized during the period of the Batida, were further stirred up by the sect's contradictory pronouncements. "Los vinculados"—the bound ones—of the novel bind together paradoxical principles: heroism and conformism, "caudillismo" and meekness, glory and comfort. Their imperial conquest of heaven started from the domination of the ground wiped clear during the Batida. In other words, they harnessed the fury of war and turned it into a different kind of enterprise: that of conquering eternity by fostering material interests and egoistical passions.

Springing from the unstable ground of the Batida, a seemingly futile enterprise of conquering a swampy terrain and annihilating a race submerged in self-oblivion, the furious expansion of "Los vinculados" testifies to the zeal with which it bound passions unleashed in the war in pursuit of a determinate goal: transforming individual prosperity into a path—*el camino*—to eternal life. The "eminent nonsense" of that idea resides, for Espinosa, in its basic logical inconsistency. The hypothesis of the existence of two realms—this world and the other—rests on their antinomy, without which the very concept of an "other" world, envisioned in either religious or political terms, makes no sense. The trick of offering in the same package the benefits of this world and the other, while nonsense on one level, strikes one of the characters of Espinosa's novel, a dissident by the name of Mitsukuri, as objectively evil, because a simple nonsense becomes evil when it turns to action in order to fulfill its objectives. In the case of "Los vinculados," the apparent inconsistency of its principles holds the key to the sect's purpose: that of stirring up the desires of gullible spirits, exalting their selfishness and stimulating their appetites.

A novelistic embodiment of the all-consuming greed hidden behind the facade of spirituality is the character of Molicio, a member of "Los vinculados" and the owner of a vast honey production empire—hence his name, derivative of *miel* and *molicie* (softness, comfort)—whom Eremita describes as "el individuo más contento que nunca vi de sí mismo" (the individual most contented with himself I ever saw) (325). Molicio, who equally rejoices in his wealth and his orthodox beliefs, derides the uselessness of Mitsukuri and Eremita's criticism of the sect in the face of a soon-to-be universal planetary expansion of the mentality of "Los vinculados." "Ahora dominamos la Feliz Gobernación . . . mas pronto lanzaremos nuestros pioneros . . . a cuantas naciones pueblan la esfera" (At present we dominate Happy Governance . . . but soon we will send off our pioneers . . . to however many nations populate the globe) (329). The sect's expansion is a result of a disturbingly simple logic. By glorifying greed and selfishness, that is, by bringing into its fold an increasing number of individuals ruled by the belief that they can accrue material and spiritual benefits while acting solely in their own interest, "Los vinculados" will in fact end up ruling the world. While continuing to offer their services to the state, God's earthly representative, the sect's members, duly organized and bound together, will not rule only Happy Governance but will proceed to conquer the globe.

From the standpoint of this utilitarian logic by which everything is the means to an end, the highest end can only be a total domination: conquest of the world by binding together an ever-growing number of members, one by one, and infiltrating states beyond Happy Governance, one by one. A promise or prediction of that potentially infinite expansion can also be heard in Escrivá Balaguer's message to Opus Dei's members: "The harvest is bountiful and the laborers are few."[16] The meaning of the Obra (Opus) is to enlist more workers (*operarios*) to do its work until finally the entire earth is mobilized and ready to stand at its service. Referring to the bees as his sisters (*hermanas abejas*) as well as his workers—agents in the process of production whose benefits are reserved solely for him— Molicio embodies the ideology of the sect that seeks to encircle the planet within the parameters of its enterprise, at once economic and spiritual. What generates Molicio's self-contentment is not just his wealth but the spectacle of nature, in this case the bees, working for him and producing the honey his ships take to remote countries and ports.

In "The Question Concerning Technology," Heidegger finds the essence of modern technology in the transformation of nature into "standing-reserve [*Bestand*]."[17] By framing nature as a source of energy, technology challenges the earth to work and become an agent that contributes to the enterprise of the human domination of the world. Like Molicio's bees, nature is put to work in order to facilitate human planetary conquest. By achieving the status of "standing reserve," earth's human and nonhuman potential becomes framed as a productive source ready to be conquered and used or, employing Escrivá Balaguer's terminology, harvested. By making productivity into an essential component of Opus Dei—God's work—the sect turns not just bees but also God into an instrument or a tool.

While Molicio's predictions about the universal appeal of "Los vinculados" speak of the latter's ambitions to encircle the planet within the capitalist productive frame, Espinosa's account of the alliance between economic, spiritual, and political interests under Francoism adopts a deliberately small-scale, provincial point of view. A well-known aspect of Espinosa's biography is that he is a writer from the provinces who, except for a brief three-year period (1961–64), spent his entire life in Murcia, the capital city of a region that at the time was one of the poorest in Spain, having previously been one of the last bastions of the Republican regime before falling to the Nationalists in 1939. In *Escuela de mandarines*, but also in *La fea burguesía* and *Tríbada: Theologiae Tractatus*, Espinosa's most famous novels, the social milieu of the provincial capital acquires the status of a microcosmos, an ecosystem whose small scale allows the writer to observe characters and events before him as if they were placed under a magnifying glass.

As Espinosa himself confirmed in an interview, the stifling environment of the University of Murcia, at the time the newest among Spanish universities, where he studied law, provided the inspiration and material for his vitriolic portraits of mandarins.[18] Much more than a personal vendetta, Espinosa's depiction of the presumptuous "catedráticos" and their assistants was a critique of the institution that was the breeding ground for Francoist elites. In her study of the University of Salamanca during the rectorate of Antonio Tovar (1951–56), historian Isabel Ramos Ruíz describes the creation of the Francoist university culture, including the establishment of the Colegios Mayores, institutions whose name and function were inspired by the imperial model of Spanish Golden Age student residences.[19] References to the imperial past could not hide a more prosaic reality of the Francoist era in which a speedy construction of new student residences anticipated one of the enduring features of Spanish capitalism—its reliance on the construction and real estate market—and in which different factions of the regime waged a fierce battle for control of the university. Simultaneously with the decline of the influence of the Falange grew the power of the religious actors Opus Dei and Acción Católica, both of which were promoting a veritable "asalto a las cátedras universitarias" among their members.[20]

Given this context of struggle for spiritual and economic power being fought out at the Francoist university, it is not surprising that Espinosa's novel would make a student residence into a site of a bloody battle for the future of Happy Governance. The "Rebelión de los becarios," or "the rebellion of the mandarins' apprentices," is the only outbreak of stasis as an act of civilian (nonmilitary) sedition in the entire novel. Together with questioning the future of Happy Governance, this rebellion shows that the power of Happy Governance resides not in the "higher" realm of ideas and eternal principles but in the "lowly" sphere of bodily cavities, the mouth and the stomach, which process the consumption of food. Returning to Agamben's analysis of stasis as a threshold between politics and economy, we can say that behind the facade of a regime that emerged from the "crusade" of the Civil War with the mission of restoring traditional Spanish Catholic values, Francoism implanted a form of domination whose principal instrument was the economy, understood in a broad sense of the management of the needs of the population through the governance of the common national household. As Barberillo Autodidacto, one of the dissident writers quoted in Espinosa's novel, puts it: "Sobre el hambre y su apaño se levantó la Gobernación Mandarinesca" (Over hunger and its remedy arose the Mandarinesque Governance) (199).

The "Visceral Register" of Rebellion

Of the six castes composing the regime of Happy Governance, it is the temporary one—the *becarios,* or apprentices to the mandarins—that best illustrates the intimate relationship between hunger and power.[21] While the other five castes are defined by their fixed place in the social hierarchy, the becarios, as the only nonpermanent caste, are unique in that their existence is measured in temporal terms. As future mandarins, the apprentices are defined not so much by what they are but what they will become. The time span of the caste of apprentices is limited to the period of three thousand years that it takes to complete the course of their studies. During that time they consume a strictly prescribed amount of food: twenty thousand *quintales* (a hundredweight) of soup in the first millennium, four thousand cows in the second, and fifty thousand ostriches in the third. Other aspects of their life are also regulated, from the number of pillows on which they sleep (three) and the clothes they wear (*calzones clausurados,* pants sewed up to prevent masturbation) to the bodily posture they adopt to manifest their contrition and gratitude for the privileges awarded to them. In the universe of Happy Governance apprentices play the role of *sustancias sumisas* (submissive substances), not yet fully formed exemplars of the species of mandarins who are kept behind the walls of their residences like larvae in their cocoons.

Given the submissiveness of the becarios, any intent on their part to question their status as a temporary caste would pose an existential threat for the regime, whose future depends on a regulated reproduction of the ruling castes. Such an existential threat materializes during the rebellion of the apprentices, which takes place during the rule of Silvestre, a proconsul who exterminated the naked race. The rebellion starts when an apprentice by the name of Fustos begins advocating the elimination of time constraints on the status of apprentices. If all the other castes are eternal, then why shouldn't apprentices represent the future eternally? If they are the keepers of the regime's future, why should their futurity be limited? Couldn't futurity be their essential and not just temporary feature? Undoubtedly, these questions are a commentary on the paradoxes contained in Francoism's efforts to secure its own future. In order to make the connection between the rebellion of the apprentices and Francoism more evident, Espinosa quotes Fustos's claim that apprentices "sólo responden ante dioses y ante la Historia" (respond only to gods and to history) (193). Apart from putting *dioses* in the plural, this phrase replicates exactly the definition of the exceptional historical status of el caudillo. The apprentices' demands bring up the question of how a regime that claims to defend eternal and unchanging principles can depend on el caudillo's life. The outrageous nature of those demands encapsulates Espinosa's condemnation of the regime's desire for perpetuity, which rests on something as perishable as the flesh of cows and ostriches that the apprentices consume, and as insatiable as their desire for infinite enjoyment of privileges.

The rebellion of the apprentices shakes the very foundations of Happy Governance, not because they want to overthrow it but because they are the true believers who take the power at its word. They interiorize the regime's claims to perpetuity and wish to remain a temporary caste forever. This attempt at stretching orthodoxy to its limits provokes fury among the regime's establishment, and for a very logical reason. If apprentices are by definition docile and submissive, it is because they owe their existence to the regime. They are indebted to the regime not only for who they are (apprentices whose studies are financed by the state) and what they aspire to be (mandarins) but also for who they were and are not any more (children from poor families). As one mandarin puts it, of all people, apprentices are the least innocent of beings in the world.

The only solution to the impasse introduced by the rebellion is the physical annihilation of the caste, which is carried out systematically by Abilio, a soldier-priest at the head of an army that destroys and pillages the apprentices' residences and slaughters eight hundred thousand of the caste's members. In the course of the operation, many secrets come to light, among them the wide-scale forgery of official records, thanks to which apprentices extended their studies well beyond the allotted time. In other words, they were de facto enjoying the unlimited privileges that the rebellion aspired to consecrate publicly and make into law (*de iure*).[22]

The most scandalous example of the forgery is the case of Falca, who cheated the state long enough to consume six hundred thousand cows instead of the four thousand that were officially assigned to each apprentice. The excessiveness of Falca's transgression and his willingness to collaborate with the authorities by divulging other secrets of the caste transform him into a collective hero, symbol of multiple abuses hidden under the appearance of "submissive substances." Falca's excesses turn him into a living legend. Not only is he spared from the slaughter, but he becomes the inspiration for a cycle of six hundred thousand poems dedicated to him, one for each cow. As the stories and songs celebrating Falca spread from mouth to mouth, hundreds of commemorative plaques and monuments in his honor appear almost overnight. In the first version of the novel, Espinosa even refers to the creation of the legend of Falca's ghost, who, after his death, started appearing in the countryside, provoking nocturnal orgies and scenes of demonic possession, particularly among women who succumbed to the seductive power of his boundless, perhaps not explicitly erotic but certainly carnal, appetite.

The rebellion and ensuing slaughter of the apprentices, followed by the appearance of Falca's legend, serve as a background for a poem incorporated into the novelistic account of the rebellion, entitled "Cow Five Hundred Thousand and One." To judge by its title, the poem is an homage to the hero who, having already devoured five hundred thousand cows, tackles the first ruminant of the new era. The number "one" in the poem's title both adds this cow to the preceding five hundred thousand and sets it apart, given that it opens up the count to cows not yet consumed. The question implicitly addressed in the poem's title is not "How many?" but "How many more after this one?" Paraphrasing Derrida's take on *à venir* as "the future to come," we can say that the title of the anonymous

poem is open to the future of "cows to come." But this is not a poem
about one particular cow that represents all cows consumed—or yet
to be consumed—by the apprentices. It is, however, a poem about one
particular apprentice who is elevated to the status of an example, not just
of his caste but of what the poet refers to as "our race." Here is the poem
in its entirety:

VACA QUINIENTOS MIL UNO
En la cueva de la boca,
allí donde efecto y causa se confunden,
celado del Sol y de toda Historia,
guardas tu secreto, casto Falca,
símbolo y prueba de nuestra raza.
Tú, que convertiste el placer en resignación,
y que juraste olvidar el colorido
de los frutos, porque vivir es triste,
como enseña la Escritura,
conoces de la lengua lo que la lengua no dice.
Grande es tu ejemplo, divino becario,
pues transformaste el goce en trascendencia,
sabiendo encontrar dioses en el estómago,
y ganar, como manda el Libro,
las dos vidas que nos ofrece la Ortodoxia.

COW FIVE HUNDRED THOUSAND AND ONE
In the cave of the mouth,
there where effect and cause are confused,
concealed from the Sun and from all of History,
you guard your secret, chaste Falca,
symbol and proof of our race.
You, who converted pleasure into resignation,
and who swore to forget the color
of fruits, for living is sad,
as the Scripture teaches,

you know about the tongue what the tongue does not say.
Great is your example, divine becario,
for you transformed joy into transcendence,
knowing how to find gods in the stomach
and to gain, as the Book mandates,
the two lives that Orthodoxy offers us. (199)

The first five lines state that Falca is a keeper of certain knowledge about his race that his example reveals, for which he offers proof. However, that knowledge is kept secret. More specifically, it is knowledge of the secret that Falca possesses by keeping it hidden (concealed) in his mouth. There is an ambiguity about Falca, which is associated with the cave of his mouth as a site that both holds knowledge and hides it from the sun and history, not allowing it to come to light. Through references to cause and effect, Espinosa connects the cave of Falca's mouth to the Platonic cave, although with a twist. In the myth from Plato in *Republic*, the knowledge of the appearances—the shadows on the wall seen by those imprisoned in the cave—is just a reflection, an effect of the light whose source (cause) remains unseen. In Espinosa's poem, however, the knowledge found in the cave of Falca's mouth is precisely that the cause and effect—the apprentice's desire to continue eating and his complicity with the regime that feeds him—are indistinguishable.

The secret knowledge kept in the cave of Falca's mouth is therefore different from the philosophical metaphor found in Plato's myth, which separates shadow and light, (mere) appearances and (true) reality. Like the apprentices' sewed up pants (*calzones clausurados*), designed to pose a barrier to the satisfaction of the male sexual appetite, the chaste Falca's mouth remains closed, although as the poem's readers or listeners know, it is neither idle nor empty. In fact, while closed, it is also extraordinarily full and active, and that precisely is its secret, or the most tangible of its secrets: the amount of flesh Falca consumed prior to being discovered.

The poem barely conceals the phallic connotations of Falca's insatiable appetite, which can be heard in the proximity between his name and the word *falo* (phallus). Phallic references are present in the connection the poem establishes between eating and power, between the process of ingestion and the experience of communion with the power whose secret is stored and restored in the apprentice's mouth and belly. It is by continuing to eat more than he is allowed that Falca gets closest to internalizing the double secret of his bond with that power. He, more than anyone else, has identified the process of assimilation of the regime's teachings with the unlimited consumption of the benefits that are generated by belonging to the power.

As the second sentence of the poem indicates, the poet associates the knowledge hidden in Falca's mouth with the apprentice's ability to assimilate or, quite literally, swallow the teachings contained in the Scripture. "You who converted pleasure into resignation / and who swore to forget the colors / of fruits . . . / know about the tongue [language] what the tongue [language] does not say." Falca is a keeper of the truth whose essence consists in not leaving the mouth, not being voiced in language but savored by the tongue. Falca, who became a popular hero for the countless subjects of Happy Governance preoccupied with the procurement of food, transformed his mouth, tongue, and stomach into political organs par excellence. Protecting his secret and showing his eternal conformity with the power that feeds him, Falca's closed, silent mouth speaks about the nature of power, about how the unequal distribution of food is a primary token of exchange between the ruler and the ruled, a way of instilling obedience.[23]

Like the enigmatic and often ambiguous text of the Scripture, Falca's hermetic silence binds together different registers of the regime's power: overt (exoteric) and hidden (esoteric), public and secret, literal and figurative. The poem suggests that Falca's apparent defiance of orthodoxy, his violation of the rules that govern the life of an apprentice, is in fact a way of interiorizing a deeper meaning of the book's principles. It is by eating his way through and beyond the apportioned amount of time and allotted number of cows that Falca erases the border dividing the activity of eating flesh from the process of internalizing the gifts of power that enter his mouth and disappear in it. A site of consumption and signification, Falca's mouth performs a daily mystery of the reincarnation of power, both literal (power becoming the flesh of countless cows) and figurative (power creating a lack that only excess of loyalty and indebtedness to power can fill).

Like other apprentices, Falca transforms a secret pleasure into an outward attitude of resignation, but, unlike them, he lengthens his pleasure and savors it more intimately. His seemingly unlimited enjoyment disregards the official calendar according to which apprentices eat and study in order to become mandarins, the eternalized representatives of power or *caras pochas*, as Espinosa calls them. Here, *pocha* means "pale faced"—inexpressive and colorless—unconcerned for others, and indifferent to the existence of the world. The apprentices' "forgetting of the colors of fruits" speaks to their lack of exposure and sensitivity to the outside world, its variety and color. By learning to transform pleasure into resignation, the becarios practice becoming indifferent to the world, both human and nonhuman, and closed off to any exchange with it. The world exists to the extent to which it can be ingested into the self without residue.

While transforming pleasure into resignation, as the rest of the apprentices do, Falca actively consumes his pleasure, keeping his secret inside. The secrecy of his consumption becomes the guarantee of future enjoyment. That way, Falca repeatedly reenacts the mystery of the perpetuity of power and its serial reincarnation as flesh, be it a cow's, Falca's own, the flesh of mandarins—the regime's sacred cows—or the flesh of the apprentices: transitory substances that, as their rebellion proves, must remain submissive or be slaughtered.

I would argue that the secret that Falca's mouth keeps, the knowledge his tongue secretes while savoring the pleasure of keeping his enjoyment to himself, has to do with the unstable and bloody foundations of the power of Happy Governance. Established through the recurrence of stasis—the war against municipalists, the struggle for power among proconsuls, the destruction of the naked race—those foundations are secured through the consumption of the benefits that communing with power entails. The regime secures its grip on power by literally and figuratively feeding the existence of the castes. Among themselves, the castes appropriate and unequally apportion the totality of the human and divine universe. Each caste depends on the others to the extent to which it secures the division of the world into impermeable and impenetrable realities kept at a safe distance from the others. Not only the mediocrity of gods but also the weakness of human coexistence is a principle of security.

The rebellion and Falca's legend teach different but equally important lessons. The cruel punishment of the eight hundred thousand apprentices is an instruction for future generations not to rebel. However, the regime's decision to spare Falca contains another lesson. His example shows the strength of the desire to stay forever bound to the state that feeds him. As one of the characters puts it, the regime prefers those who are absent from a doctrinal part of the official ceremonies than those who are absent from the banquet that follows. In a word, gut is more important than brain, and as long as one thinks only about one's most basic necessities instead of doctrine, one can "swallow" any kind of doctrine. Privileging banquet over ideology shows a "gut" understanding of the fact that doctrine is secondary as long as one obeys the internal command mandating that the satisfaction of one's basic needs depends on the regime.[24]

We encounter here two different meanings of *gut*: intuitive or instinctive, feeling and belly. Happy Governance seeks to suppress any kind of natural gifts, spontaneity, or instinct, while valuing premeditation and conformity. In a sense, the regime subordinates gut to itself, or one meaning of gut to another: spontaneity and satisfaction-seeking desire are subordinated to the weakness and premeditation that originate in the fear of an empty belly. We are encountering here a form of bodily stasis in which one part of the body rebels and rules over another part (intestine over brain, belly as organ of fear and conformity over belly as site of pleasure).

In the aftermath of the rebellion, the regime proclaims the new "Law of Apprentices," a legal document aimed at preventing another rebellion by further regulating the status of the apprentices. The law and the ceremonial induction of a new generation of apprentices indicate that the regime cannot do without the only temporary caste because, simply put, without apprentices there are no mandarins. Apprentices are mandarins in the making, and mandarins are the interpreters of the regime's founding text, those who adapt the text to current events. They represent the regime's eternity but also its mutability and adaptability. As one of the mandarins states in the first version of the novel, the last thing a mandarin should do in the event of an internal conflict or civil war is hastily endorse a particular proconsul or faction. Instead, the mandarins should wait for the final outcome, always being on the side of the winner, whom they designate with the euphemism *ultimo suceso* (last/ultimate event).

The latter phrase is ambiguous. While encouraging the mandarins to side with the winner, it also affirms that the last event is not the one that counts as definite and uncontested but simply the most recent one. In other words, while standing on the beaten ground of a consummate victory, mandarins also anticipate future unrest, which will produce another victory, and so on, ad infinitum. ("The Scripture says," remarks one of the mandarins, "that one inexcusable event is replaced by the other, more inexcusable one" [186]). By always positioning themselves on the side of the winning faction, mandarins show that their power rests on a disregard for the collective nature of stasis as consecrated in Solon's law, which prohibits neutrality in a civil war. Mandarins thrive thanks to their cynical understanding of the ambiguous effects of stasis. They know that victory in stasis halts the movement only temporarily; it both suppresses unrest and foreshadows future disturbance.

Here, it is possible to identify one final implication of the rebellion of the apprentices relevant to Espinosa's critique of Happy Governance/Francoism. As mentioned before, the most dramatic outcome of the rebellion is the physical destruction of the sect during an orgy of violence carried out by the imperial armies with the soldier-theologian Abilio at their helm. But once the mission is accomplished, the mandarins, with their usual cynicism, start bemoaning the violence and referring to it as a savage, even cannibalistic ritual in which the regime devoured its own—*their* own—children. As cold ideologues, the mandarins aptly reframe the slaughter of the apprentices as a battle between two different factions or facets of the regime: the imperial armies representing the regime's fierce and dogmatic military-religious arm and the apprentices who are the dual personification of the brain's slow musing over future interpretations of the book and the stomach's slow digestion of conformity. After the guts of eight hundred thousand apprentices are spilled, the political and bodily hierarchy is reestablished. Describing the first generation of apprentices to begin their studies after the rebellion, Espinosa focuses on their hungry, emaciated bodies, their eyes full of fear and reverence, their stomachs caving in to meet the spine, and their spines bending down to meet the stomach.

However, the carnage that concludes with the reestablishment of the temporary caste does not bring stability, nor does it put an end to the regime's internal crises and bloody victories. With his persistent and cruel irony, which mimics and rivals the oppressive longevity of the polity that is his target, Espinosa reveals that the regime's bureaucrats—although not the mandarins—knew about the apprentices' secrets all along. They even helped them extend the state-sponsored diet by secretly feeding them donkey instead of cow meat. The institutionalized duplicity proves that in Happy Governance "la Ortodoxia cede ante la política, y ésta ante la economía" (Orthodoxy cedes to politics, and the latter to economy) (207). Falca's case, then, not only reveals the bond between orthodoxy, politics, and economics but also shows that corruption—identifying one's own well-being, and that of one's (political) family, with the regime's continuity—is the secret to regime's endurance. No one synthesizes this better than Braulio, a candidate for mandarin who, toward the end of the book, gives a speech entitled "Sobre la corrupción" (On corruption) and utters the following chilling warning: "El necio murmura: esto se halla corrupto, pronto caerá; más el sabio replica: esto va corrompiéndose, durará milenios" (The fool murmurs: this is corrupt, it will soon fall; but the wise one responds: this is prone to corruption, it will last for millennia) (563).

Espinosa's alternative to this corruption—the sacrifice of the intellect to the stomach and to the oppressive regime whose endurance is the key to one's material well-being—is protest. It is the nature of Eremita's protest to which I now turn.

Indignation and Movement of Protest

The will to protest is the foundation and root of Eremita's character. His protest against the regime of which he, an inhabitant of an ahistorical universe, had previously been unaware, emerges as a result of his encounter with three allegorical creatures, whom Espinosa, following Greek tradition—in this case, Socrates—calls "demiurges." The fragile and wounded bodies of the creatures, whose names are Enclenque, Homínido, and Lisiado, bear witness to their physical and moral hardship. They are personifications of vulnerability and defenselessness in the face of the injustice and oppression that they, and countless others, suffer. Both by their appearance and their words, the demiurges communicate to the protagonist the "terrible news" revealing the reason for their misfortune: the existence of Happy Governance. Together with giving the protagonist his fictional name, Eremita, the demiurges entrust him with the mission of protest. To that end, they awaken in him the properties and feelings that are necessary for him to carry out his mission: irritation, tenderness, and the capacity to feel shame.

Rather than a political activity geared toward the accomplishment of a specific goal, such as the toppling of an oppressive regime and the establishment of a more just one, the protagonist's mission of protest is more encompassing and more open ended, potentially endless. Eremita's protest is not circumscribed by a goal but instead constitutes a foundation of his way of being in the world. José López Martí, who for two decades was Espinosa's most constant interlocutor and appears in *Escuela* as a philosopher named Martino, establishes a connection between Eremita's lack of a proper name—his name is not "his" but is given to him by the demiurges—and the nature of his protest: "For Eremita, there is no name, nor can there be one, because the name situates, gives a determinate role, and indicates a continuity within a concrete order of things. But Eremita is, precisely, one who comes from the outside. His protest is not a reaction: His own being reveals itself as the opposition to the Hecho [another name of Happy Governance]. He is the absolute antagonist, antagonistic substance, so to speak."[25]

López Martí illuminates several crucial aspects pertaining to the nature of Eremita's protest. Among them is the fact that the protest does not emerge simply as a reaction to the unjust power: the origins of the character's antagonism reside in his very being. Eremita's protest is not grounded in an already existing set of ideas about politics, justice, or the nature of power, which would motivate his hatred of Happy Governance. Espinosa's fictional strategy of situating the character's childhood and youth in a peaceful and ahistorical world underscores the point that the outrage he experiences upon hearing about the existence of Happy Governance does not originate in a preconceived attitude or theoretical position. Rather, his reaction is depicted as spontaneous and uncontrollable. It manifests itself as an eminently physical experience: shaking and trembling, a bodily upheaval that, as the narrator puts it, feels like cataclysm: "La transmutación fue tan grande que mi cuerpo entró en cataclismo" (The transmutation was so great that my body went into a cataclysm) (71). This turbulent reaction engages and stirs up Eremita's entire being, taking it to the limit of pure unrest. His turmoil exemplifies a division at the core of his being, which can be seen as a form of what Simon Critchley denotes as "dividualism." Critchley's neologism describes a self that is shaped "in relation to the experience of an overwhelming, infinite demand that divides it from itself."[26]

The state of unrest that invades Eremita's being is a reflection of his proximity with the demiurges. His vehement rejection of the regime and the decision to devote his life to protest stem from the sense of outrage awoken by the moral and physical suffering of a fellow being. Espinosa's depiction of Eremita's outrage transforms into literature his namesake (Baruch) Spinoza's definition of indignation as "hatred toward someone who has injured someone else."[27] Eremita's corporeal cataclysm, a testimony to the relational nature of his being, is a compound of two concurrent states that oppose and inform each other: his visceral hatred of and opposition to Happy Governance and his affinity with those whom the regime oppresses and pushes to the margins: *gentecilla* (little people), dissidents, women. As a character defined by his mission of protest, Eremita comes into being through an unsettling exposure to an other, be it an other whose hardships he experiences in his own body or an other whose very existence is an attack against everything he considers real, worthy, and true.

The notion of stasis in the Greek sense—unrest generated by the encounter between opposing forces that come into conflict and thereby both inform and limit each other—stands at the origin of Eremita's protest. In that sense, López Martí's reference to the protagonist's "tranquil essence,"[28] which comes across in his calm demeanor and benevolent disposition toward others, overlooks the fact that Eremita's being also reflects the tension and coexistence of contrary feelings: his hatred of Happy Governance and love of Azenaia and the little people; his sense of the irresistible pull of the historical world (what he calls "libido de lo histórico" [libido of the historical]) and his desire to return to the ahistorical habitat of his childhood; and, finally, his philosophical disposition and lyrical, even mystical, sensibility. The experience of inner unrest is what propels his movement and sets him into motion, both in physical (the voyage) and existential terms (the series of encounters that give substance and meaning to his protest and strengthen the sense of his own being in the world).

Eremita's physical movement through Happy Governance starts, paradoxically, with his arrest, after he proclaims himself the enemy of the regime to the first village authorities he encounters. Given that neither the villagers nor the authorities are used to visits from those who overtly claim to be the enemies of the regime, they are unsure how to interpret his statement. Afraid that the protagonist is simply posing as an enemy of the regime in order to test their knowledge of proper legal procedures, they decide to send him to the capital.

The fact that the restriction on Eremita's freedom is a condition of his movement means that no one moves freely in the regime and that everyone, including enemies, occupies a fixed place assigned to them. In addition to showing the benevolent face of the regime that knows how to treat its enemies, the presence of those enemies also underscores the futility of protest. The dissidents' dedication to protest destines them to penury and marginality and serves as an indirect affirmation of the regime's stability and its triumph. Happy Governance grows on the soil of indifference to thought and to the world. Protected by their official status, the regime's members contemplate their reality with a sense of self-complacency and tedium, grounded in the belief that the regime, and with it their privileges, are eternal. They contemplate the possibility of the regime's ending only in relation to their own death, either civil (falling out of favor) or biological.[29]

In contrast to the tedium of the mandarins' lives, Eremita's movement connects him to the world that is inhabited not only by Happy Governance but by a myriad of other presences: animals, nature, little people, his beloved Azenaia—a fictional name Espinosa gives to Mercedes Rodríguez, to whom he dedicated the book—and, last but not least, his dissident friends, fellow enemies of the regime. Eremita and his fellow travelers, friends, and dissidents reveal themselves as beings in movement or transit. The random, unpredictable nature of these encounters and their equally unforeseen, although momentous, consequences shape Eremita's journey, which is inseparable from Espinosa's own life and that of the book.

The appearance in the novel's final version of the dissident figures absent from the first version reflects the history of Francoism as well as events from the author's biography. While the reorganization of the opposition was one of the main features of Francoism after 1956, the period of Espinosa's life that followed the completion of the first version, also in 1956, marked the beginning of his intense intellectual and personal relationship with the figures whose imprint on the novel's final version proved decisive: José López Martí (the novelistic character Martino), Takehiko Mitsukuri (Mitsukuri), Dionisio Sierra (Dionisio Kinós), and Mercedes Rodríguez (Azenaia). While Azenaia, like Don Quixote's Dulcinea, is absent from the novel, except for Eremita's continuous evocations of her, the theories attributed to the three male characters significantly influence Eremita and Espinosa's approach to their three respective areas of knowledge: philosophy and logic (Martino), ethics (Mitsukuri), and aesthetics (Kinós). Together with the impact of their theories, it is the fact of knowing them, of having met them and having been exposed to their presence that transforms these figures into expressions of different ways of being that, for Eremita/Espinosa, stand in opposition to everything Happy Governance represents.

While Eremita's encounters with hundreds of the regime's members produce a sense of desolation countered only by the trinity of emotions that the demiurges awaken in him (irritation, love, and shame), his encounters with the characters inspired by the author's friends generate something new. Eremita learns about the theories they develop in resistance to Happy Governance, which they view as a giant madhouse, a realm of nonbeing or, as Martino puts it, an "anti-utopia," something that is but should not be. The importance of Eremita's dissident friends for the book lies not just in the exchange of knowledge that takes place during their encounters but also in the theoretical importance of the notion of the encounter as at once a generator and result of their movement.

Espinosa's encounter, in 1964, with José López Martí added significantly to the philosophical component of the book's final version, where the character Martino appears as the epitome of a philosopher: a lover of wisdom and learning who remains outside the regime's intellectual circles but without quite subscribing to the ideology of the best-organized opposition group, named Sistemática Pugna (Systematic Battle). (Sistemática Pugna is in all probability code for the Communist Party.) From his appearance to his way of thinking, Martino, who conceals his philosophical inclinations behind the facade of the respectable, well-groomed individual with friends in high places, appears as the antipode of Eremita. Martino's speculative, systematic mind and his erotic proclivities, mentioned in a footnote, contrast with the spontaneity of Eremita's protest, which is devoid of conceptual sophistication, since it is rooted in his ethical outrage and his eternal love of Azenaia who—again, in Dulcinea-like fashion—appears as the ideal antidote to the distorted reality of Happy Governance.

Although the episode narrating their fictional encounter underscores the difference between Eremita's spontaneity and Martino's speculative disposition, a strong personal and intellectual affinity between the author and José López Martí makes Espinosa's literature inseparable from the points developed in López Martí's few, yet incisive, theoretical essays.[30] The importance of their friendship helps to contextualize one of the crucial aspects of the novel's final version: its theoretical dimension that goes hand in hand with the appearance of dissident characters in the novel. At the same time, López Martí's ideas about language significantly contribute to elucidating the philosophical, even ontological, underpinnings of Espinosa's notion of protest.

In the essay "El mundo como destrucción de la realidad" (The world as destruction of reality), undoubtedly his most significant statement on *Escuela de mandarines*, López Martí examines Espinosa's literary language differentiating between *world* and *reality*. The third notion appearing in the title, destruction, is unquestionably a nod to Heidegger's destruction (*Abbau*) of metaphysics. In fact, the difference between world and reality can—and perhaps should—be read in relation to the German philosopher's conception of the ontological difference between *Being* and *beings*. If, for López Martí, *reality* is defined as what is or what positively exists (*beings* in Heidegger's terminology), he reserves the term *world* for a reality that is not immediately accessible and that not only appears *in* language but manifests itself *as* language. This is to say, world is revealed in a language that does not merely name or describe what exists but instead carries out, enacts a destruction of reality as that which is given or simply exists.

How does that destruction of reality occur in Espinosa's novel? First of all, López Martí points to the way in which Espinosa subtracts the universe of Happy Governance from the parameters of what is realistically possible or even graspable. When Espinosa refers to a famous state that existed thousands of millennia ago, or when he mentions 680,000 speeches that someone named Sonsabio (*sonso sabio*, or "wise fool") composed and promptly forgot, he is not resorting to exaggeration and distortion in order to depict a certain reality. Instead, he uses nouns, names, and numbers—Sonsabio, 680,000 speeches, or the 600,000 cows Falca consumes—in order to provide access to that which cannot be captured as a reality but only as signification, that is, as language. "Objects and their signs," writes López Martí, "perform in *Escuela de mandarines* the function of mediators; 200,000 *quintales* of wheat that the stomach of Great Father Mandarin quietly cooks . . . do not remain in the text as a certain quantity of cereal, but, as meaning or signification, they help manifest that segment of the world that Great Father Mandarin is."[31] A segment or portion of the world manifests itself simultaneously with the appearance of the word that does not simply name the reality existing in the world. Instead, to the extent to which literary language makes that (of) which it speaks appear, it *is* world. "Literature . . . does not represent or render the world figuratively, but instead makes it explicit; in the last instance, it is the world itself."[32]

We have already seen this operation in place regarding Espinosa's usage of the term *batida* when referring to Civil War. Rather than simply designating or naming a particular event, the word *batida* makes its meaning appear. The meaning of the event surfaces together with the action the word names: leveling down the traces of an earlier rebellion, removing the ground under the defeated, destroying the feeble foundation on which they stand so as to prevent the memory of their rebellion from (re)appearing. The noun *batida* has an ontological function that consists in naming and thus preventing the disappearance of the naked race. Espinosa's usage of *batida* destroys—to use López Martí's terminology—the logic of the military operation the regime carries out in order to expel from the world those who were already expelled from language. In that sense, *batida* functions like *stasis*, which is not just a Greek name for civil war but a word that connects the action of standing or rising up to the emergence in the political realm of factions that stand in an oppositional relation to each other. The Greek *stasis* makes the word, the action, and its political meaning inseparable.

It is, again, Martino whom Espinosa quotes as the author of a theory about *objetos-nombre* (name- or word-objects), concerned with the objects that appear precisely when they are named. In one of his, in all probability apocryphal, books cited by Espinosa, Martino states, "We know of the existence of word-objects because of the existence of the word." However, the status of word-object is not abstract, ideal, or purely linguistic, given that the objects named do, indeed, exist in the world. At the same time, the word does not designate a known object in the same way in which the signifier *cat* designates a domesticated feline. Neither is the object identical to the word, nor does the word name an object existing independently of the instance in which it is named. Word-objects, concludes Martino, "surgen cuando aparece precisamente su nombre, y tienen, por tanto, un ser estético, no eidético" (appear precisely when their name appears and therefore have an aesthetic and not eidetic being) (294).[33]

Martino's theory of name-objects, whose being is inseparable from the act of being named, pertains to his broader ideas about the four *sentires*, or "knowledge-feelings"—logic, ethics, aesthetics, and memory. Martino's idea that "from the standpoint of aesthetics, memory or ethics nothing *is* or *is not*; it simply manifests itself" connects with the teachings of other dissident characters whose protest consists in creating an ethical or aesthetic "feeling" (*sentir*) or event (292).

Keep Going!

Following the tendency of Espinosa's book to bind different theories to the appearance of characters who not only expose but embody those theories, the centrality of ethics for Eremita's pursuit is associated with the appearance of Mitsukuri, a ghostwriter for a university professor named Climacio and in real life the author's friend and business partner in a Japanese-Spanish export-import firm. The relevance of Mitsukuri's teachings about ethics for Espinosa resonates strongly with the way in which Peter Hallward, in his introduction to Alain Badiou's *Ethics*, addresses the question "Why 'ethics'?," meaning, what is ethics and why does it matter for Badiou? Hallward writes: "Understood in terms of a philosophy of truth, 'ethical' should simply describe what helps to preserve or en-*courage* a subjective fidelity as such. The ethical prescription can be summarized by the single imperative: 'Keep going!' or 'Continue!' For a truth is clearly difficult by definition. . . . To keep going, then, presumes the ability to identify and resist the various forms of corruption or exhaustion that can beset a fidelity to truth."[34]

The corruption of truth, which for Badiou is another name for Evil, adopts three main forms, as outlined by Hallward: betrayal, which stands for "the renunciation of a difficult fidelity"; delusion, or "confusion of a mere 'simulacrum' of an event with a genuine event"; and terror, understood as "the effort to impose the total and unqualified power of a truth."[35] Each of the three forms of Evil is a perversion of one constitutive element of a fidelity to truth. Betrayal is a failing of subjective commitment; delusion undermines the universality of truth by finding its fulfillment in a particular community or people (this was the case with Nazism); and terror, whose example is Stalinism, grows from the desire to "objectify the truth," thereby obliterating the value of subjective fidelity. Hence, Badiou's conception of an "ethics of truth" is based on the following principles: "a sense of discernment (do not confuse the true and the false); courage and endurance (do not betray the true); moderation and restraint (resist the idea of total or 'substantial' truth)."[36]

The imperative to continue, to "keep going," expresses, in a nutshell, the thrust of the message Mitsukuri conveys to Eremita. To "keep going" here means several things: not abandoning the mission of protest, not allowing the existence of Happy Governance to engender discouragement and disillusionment in one's heart, and not being consumed by the sadness and despair resulting from contact with individuals who shamelessly display their selfish and passionate attachment to the regime. It also means maintaining one's commitment to protest, which Mitsukuri understands as a form of commitment to reality, to the real. He argues that, by repudiating reality and secluding themselves in the "estanco hierático y encrestado," the haughty hieratic domain of their official status, the mandarins have fallen prey to two fundamental temptations: "adorarse a sí mismos e inventar discriminaciones" (worship themselves and invent discriminations) (334).

If the nature of the mandarins' delusion manifests itself as the cult of the self and as an aloofness from the world, then the dissidents' commitment to the real requires that they take a different, higher road, avoiding the temptation of being in the world half-way, of looking askance at reality. "No . . . busquéis consuelos íntimos, que quedan donde nacen; no permitáis el deseo de estar y no estar a la vez en el mundo" (Do not . . . seek intimate consolations, which remain where they are born; do not permit the desire to at once be there and not be there in the world) (334). Mitsukuri's ethics teaches that, in order to continue their voyage through Happy Governance, Eremita and his dissident friends must endure and know how to cope with the contradictions that plague such a reality. As Mitsukuri puts it, in the world "existe la fealdad y la belleza, . . . y existe Molicio y Azenaia Parzenós. Tales contradicciones son el misterio, y del misterio nada puede concluirse. Por eso no parece lícito ser consecuentes" (ugliness and beauty exist, . . . and there exist Molicio [the owner of the honey-production empire] and Azenaia Parzenós. Such contradictions are a mystery, and of mystery nothing can be concluded. For this reason it does not seem acceptable to be consistent) (334). One of those fundamental contradictions that plague reality is the fact that Happy Governance exists. The regime is an embodiment of the unreal, which Espinosa defines as that which exists and yet *is not*. Secluded in their official residences and devoted to the enjoyment of their privileges, members of Happy Governance objectify the existence of Evil, which originates in delusion and lack of restraint. The delusion of these members consists in their proclaiming their world as *the* world because what is outside the regime does not count; their lack of restraint comes from their perception of their privileges and the regime as virtually endless.

If Espinosa's book identifies Evil with the existence of the unreal, then the *encounter* with Evil leads to a revelation of fundamental contradictions at the heart of reality. The purpose of Mitsukuri's warning about the coexistence of opposites is to remind Eremita and his dissident friends that intellect alone is not enough to grapple with such a contradiction. Something else is needed, and for Mitsukuri it is *will*, a faculty that he claims needs to be "más pura que la razón y su experiencia" (more pure than reason and its experience) (333). His conception of will as a defense against disenchantment or a temptation to withdraw from the world—perils that reason alone might not be able to surmount—culminates in Mitsukuri's final message to Eremita and his fellow travelers: "Nosotros seguiremos recorriendo el Imperio y tentando al mundo, donde nos espera la emoción, el pensamiento, el arte y la afección de todos los seres y cosas" (We will continue traveling through the empire and tempting the world, because it is there where emotion, thought, art, and the affection of all beings and things await us) (321). They will keep going because in the continuity of protest lies not just the possibility but, even more, a joyful promise of future encounters.

Through the appearance of dissidents in the novel and the exposition of their theories, Espinosa's book addresses nothing more and nothing less than the democratic potential of stasis. His ideas about the continuity of protest, about the philosophical, ethical, and aesthetical relevance of the encounter, and about being as "being with," all speak to the importance of stasis for democracy. Dimitris Vardoulakis's account of the relationship between stasis and democracy, exemplified first by Solon's law, prohibited neutrality during civic conflict. "Solon's law," Vardoulakis argues, "indicates that one ought to be active at the cost of losing their citizenship. Thus the law of stasis opens up a space where ontological, ethical and political concerns converge. Moreover, this convergence is possible because of the description of the individual as existing in an agonistic mode of being."[37] Solon's law does not promote violence as much as it asserts that passivity and neutrality are irreconcilable with democratic citizenship. The law of stasis treats civil strife as a limit situation that brings to the surface of political existence the constitutive role of "being with," being in tense proximity with others, for democratic politics. While it does not exclude conflict and competition, this tense proximity precludes treating the other as a simple obstacle or mere instrument for the achievement of certain material or spiritual goals. The foundational role of stasis in Athenian politics, and its lessons for contemporary democracy have to do with dismantling the vision of the other that exists in order to allow the self to "fulfill certain moral values independent of their encounter."[38]

Espinosa's work instructs us not to understand the term *encounter* lightly. Encounter—or better, the exponential proliferation of encounters—holds the key to the inexhaustible potential of Espinosa's book as a statement against Francoism and as a testimony to the ontological, ethical, literary, and political meaning of protest.

CHAPTER 4

Standstills of History

Nothingness, Tragedy, and Exile in María Zambrano's Thought

María Zambrano (1904–91) is, arguably, the most complex and original representative of Spanish post–Civil War thought. Her writings reflect some basic facts of her biography: her philosophical initiation as José Ortega y Gasset's disciple (albeit a highly unorthodox one), her loyalty to the cause of the Second Republic, and three long decades of exile—in Mexico, Puerto Rico, Cuba, Italy, and France—during which time she composed almost the entirety of her work. I focus here on several texts, both published and unpublished, written during the central phase in the development of Zambrano's philosophy, beginning in the early 1940s and culminating with the publication of *El hombre y lo divino* (1955), a book that represents in all probability her most significant theoretical contribution. Rather than inscribing itself strictly in the realm of philosophy, Zambrano's thought is situated at the intersection of several discourses, or *saberes*, namely, philosophy, religion, poetry (literature), and history. This liminal status can account for her uneasy, even contentious, relationship with the Western philosophical tradition, from the pre-Socratics to Nietzsche and, to a lesser extent, Heidegger. In addition, there is a certain confessional element in Zambrano's thought, related to her efforts to come to terms with the chain of violence and defeats that marks Spanish history, from empire to modernity and all the way to the 1939 Civil War and Franco's dictatorship.

In Zambrano's analysis of the religious and philosophical dimensions of the Western project of creating history she finds the guiding thread of

Western culture to be a vision of history as an autonomous human enterprise that brings to fruition the promise of human emancipation from external, nonhuman forces belonging to the sacred and divine realms. She argues that, albeit in different ways, both Western philosophy and Christianity contribute to the process of humanization—one could also say Westernization—of the world and its conflictive unfolding through the enterprise of creating history. The project of humanization—and the erasure of the trace of the divine "Other"—culminates in Nietzsche's proclamation of the death of God and the advent of the era of nihilism.

This chapter addresses three philosophical and existential tropes that Zambrano posits as forms of resistance to the unstoppable forward motion of history: Nothingness (*la nada*), tragedy, and exile. She locates these tropes at the conjuncture between movement and immobility, as forms of impasse that bring human life in history to a restless standstill of stasis.

In *El hombre y lo divino* (1955), Zambrano offers her vision of the history of the relationship between the human and the divine, humans and their gods. Contrary to what the title might suggest, the book is not the work of a theologian or of a historian of religion. Rather, it is a generically hybrid text composed of multiple, intricately linked threads that coalesce around two main lines of argument. On the one hand, Zambrano offers an account of the foundation of philosophy in ancient Greece and its subsequent constitution into the pillar of Western humanism, understood, in William Robert's words, as "a theory of human independence and self-sufficiency that frees humanity from reliance on divinity and positions it atop a hierarchical ordering of reality."[1] On the other hand, Zambrano's text reads like a novel whose thick plot centers on different versions—different reenactments—of the event that repeats itself throughout human history: the death of God or, rather, the successive deaths of different gods (not just the Christian one, but earlier Greek or Egyptian ones). For Zambrano the births of gods and their deaths stand out as two watershed moments in the ongoing quest for the humanization of the universe. If the emergence of gods, particularly in the pre-Christian era, could placate— even if temporarily—the terror and anguish of humans in the face of the external or internal forces (Nature and passions) acting upon their lives, then the waning and disappearance of gods have an equally important function: that of opening up more space for human life and allowing for a new configuration of the human-divine relationship.

Zambrano's book, then, follows the different twists and turns of a strange and conflictive human relationship with gods. This never-ending conflict also reveals a paradox about the divine role in history. That paradox resides in the fact that, without being human—while being *other* or *more* than human—different figures of gods decisively contributed to the Western project of creating human history unencumbered by divine presence. I would argue that Zambrano's account of the relationship between humans and their gods is built on the tension between the deaths and the death of God. The plural "deaths" refers to the role that the appearance and disappearance of different gods played in the historical process of the humanization of the world. The singular "death" refers not just to Christ's death as an ultimate act of sacrifice for humanity but also to the stage in Western history that sacrifice inaugurates. That stage, which stretches into the time of Zambrano's writing—and, arguably, into our own present— culminates in Nietzsche's proclamation of the death of God. The fact that Zambrano viewed Nietzsche's ideas about the Overman and the death of God as entirely congruent with the development of Western philosophy up to that moment did not, to her mind, make the predicament articulated in his thought any less dramatic, or even tragic. In the context in which conflicts with gods—and their deaths—were part and parcel of the changing human relationship with the world, Zambrano reads Nietzsche's thought not so much as an attack on God but as a violent reaction against the very Western legacy of the *bond* linking the human to the divine, and vice versa.

However, argues Zambrano, this kind of foundational relationship does not simply disappear when it is negated. Instead, the disappearance of one of the elements (in this case, God) obscures the entire relationship, rendering it incomprehensible, opaque. The obscured relationship with God—"la palabra casi impronunciable hoy" (today the almost unpronounceable word)—characterizes the historical present of Zambrano's writing. The unfathomable historical crimes committed in the decades prior to the publication of *El hombre y lo divino* brought to the fore the instability of limits establishing what or who is human and what makes for human relationship with the world and others within it. One could interpret Zambrano's assessment of the connection between the death of God and the enormity of twentieth-century crimes as a claim grounded in religious faith. She might, in fact, be saying that, without divinity to keep us in check, humanity's murderous—even suicidal—impulses inevitably run amok. Without denying the importance of Zambrano's religiosity for her thought, I sustain that a lack of engagement with her account of the human relationship with the divine—its ups and downs, highpoints and eclipses—would also limit our understanding of her unique perspective on the crisis of Western history and politics. Hence, it is important to indicate at the outset where the uniqueness of her perspective lies.

In a passage from *El hombre y lo divino*, Zambrano addresses a sense of instability and confusion at the historical moment in and *from* which she was writing. "The current moment," she says,

> se nos aparece el más mezclado y confuso por ser el que estamos viviendo (la vida es siempre confusión), y por la multiformidad del proceso, por la multitud de caras que presenta la situación frente a lo divino. Como si estuviésemos, en realidad, apurando al mismo tiempo todas las diversas situaciones que el hombre ha vivido en ese drama esencial frente a Dios o los dioses, y el hombre actual fuera el protagonista de toda la historia religiosa de la humanidad condensada.

> seems to us the most mixed and confused, both because it is the moment we are living (life is always confusing) and because of the . . . multifaceted character of our situation vis-à-vis the divine. It is as if we were experiencing all at once all the different situations that humans have gone through in that drama of their relationship with God or gods, and as if present-day humanity had to endure the entire religious history of humanity, but condensed.[2]

The peculiar historicity of Zambrano's present resides in its problematic—confused—relationship with the past. The present seems to be repeating or reliving the previous stages of human relationship with the divine. Moreover, it is reliving these presumably finished stages simultaneously, all at once. In light of Zambrano's text, we can see this condensation of the past in the present as a combination of two processes. On the one hand, the compressed form in which the past appears takes away the feature of its gradual unfolding through different epochs. The fact that all stages are present simultaneously means that they have lost their function as phases in an ongoing process that is moving somewhere. As we have already seen, the direction of the movement is the humanization of the world, the creation of human history. In other words, the past is present—*es* and *está presente*—but, in a static and unmovable way, it is emptied of its meaning as a process through which something is advanced, some conflict staged, some aspect of human condition revealed.

There is yet another consequence that this compression of different stages in human relationship with the divine has for Zambrano's understanding of the present. Condensation that assimilates, absorbs the past into the present, exemplifies a kind of forgetting or, at the very least, offers a testimony to an attempt to forget. What gets partially erased by leveling the ups and downs of the historical process of humanization is, on the one hand, the diversity of forms that human-divine relationship adopted at different points in time and, related to this, the nature of the conflicts and crimes that punctuated that relationship and moved it forward. To put it differently, the consummation of the death of God, which Nietzsche proclaimed but did not single-handedly carry out, does not only make the word/name *God* virtually unutterable, at least publicly. It also precludes asking the question about the deep, dark, and secret motivations guiding the process of humanization that, after being channeled through the successive births and deaths of many divinities, found its culmination in the human death of God that founded Christianity.

The inextricable connection between the human and divine destinies (in the West), which the death of Christ exposes and makes irrevocable, enters a new and final stage with Nietzsche's philosophical proclamation of the death of God. Nietzsche's gesture announces a completion of the long conquest of space and time in which human existence could advance undisturbed by divine presence. In the death of God, Zambrano sees the disappearance of the trace of divine resistance to the conquest of human autonomy and freedom. Once that resistance is conquered, nothing stands in the way of the human movement toward undisputed dominion over the world and history. But for Zambrano the story does not end there, if only because there is no end, no completion, to human history even after divine resistance disappears from the horizon and the darkness of oblivion envelops the shared human-divine past.

Zambrano's characterization of the confusion of her era relates to one of the central insights of *El hombre y lo divino*: once a philosophical proclamation of the death of God completes the project of human autonomy, what stands in the way, obscuring a path to the future, is nothing: Nothingness, or *la nada*. Zambrano's arguments about Nietzsche's Overman and Nothingness are among the most philosophically complex and poetically inspired portions of this work, and I address them more extensively below. Here I introduce just those aspects of her account of Nothingness that relate this notion to issues of movement and immobility. Zambrano's idea that Nothingness combines movement and immobility—it is inert and yet continually shifts places—points to the overall ambiguity that, in her view, characterizes this notion. Throughout the history of human relationship with the divine, references to Nothingness have had radically different connotations. Where God was posited as the ultimate expression of Being—truth and goodness—Nothingness was associated with Evil and non-Being. On the other hand, some mystical currents, such as the one represented by the seventeenth-century Spanish mystic Miguel de Molinos, thought of la nada as a path to union with God, a way of abandoning the self, dissolving it in the plenitude of divine presence. The meaning and place of Nothingness shift, depending on whether they impede or facilitate human connection with God.

In Zambrano's reading of Nietzsche, Nothingness refers to the impasse that arises when, through the invention of the figure of the Overman, the project of human sovereignty seems to have reached its apogee. Zambrano sees Nietzsche's thought as a double attack against philosophy and religion. His was a virulent reaction against two discourses that contributed the most to the Western project of humanization: philosophy, by articulating the notion of Being that facilitated human theoretical and practical capture of the universe, and religion, by offering God as a proxy that allowed humans to manage their fears and aspirations. Philosophy and religion, each in a different way, constructed a vision of humanity moored in transcendental notions—Appearance and Essence, Good and Evil, Truth and Lie—and divorced from life as a value in and of itself. In the figure of the Overman, argues Zambrano, Nietzsche's drive to destruction, represented by his rejection of the abstract divinity of philosophy and the suffering Christian God, intersects with his desire to release humanity from the tendency to devalue life, that is, to measure its value according to the "higher" standards of philosophy or religion. The Overman is, for Zambrano, a problematic—perhaps even a monstrous—figure, one of "extraño parto humano" (a strange human birth).[3] In contrast to the Christian God that showed its love for humanity by becoming human through Christ, the Overman is an entirely human creation that is also divine-like. It is a strange divinity engendered out of the depths of human despair over God's distance and a desire to annul that distance by abolishing the relationship altogether, that is, by announcing the death of God and the birth of the Overman.

The attempt to annihilate the human relationship with God exacerbates and takes to the extreme the ambiguity constitutive of the notion of Nothingness, which functions, as we have seen, in radically different ways: as a figure of human defiance and rebellion against divinity and as a path to mystical communion with the divine. The extreme ambiguity of the elusive notion of Nothingness also informs Zambrano's view of the historical juncture that frames her book. This juncture was marked, in the realm of thought, by the legacy of Nietzsche's project for overturning the Western philosophical and religious tradition and, in politics, by the crisis of European liberal democracy in the birth of fascism and a nearly uninterrupted succession of "hot" and "cold" wars (the Spanish Civil War, two World Wars, the Cold War, and so on). I encapsulated Zambrano's approach to this manifold crisis—philosophical, political, and cultural—in a statement that can now be recast in a more elaborate form. When, following the proclamation of the death of God, nothing seems to stand in the way of human divinization, what gets in the way of the continuing progressive movement of (Western) humanity is, precisely, Nothingness, la nada.

As stated before, the importance of the notion of Nothingness for Zambrano's philosophy, and her approach to individual as well as collective existence, resides in the way in which Nothingness inextricably combines movement and immobility, activity and passivity. Rather than defining Nothingness—likely an impossible task—Zambrano argues that its meaning shifts "según cambia el proyecto de ser del hombre; según que el hombre pretenda o no ser y según lo que pretenda ser y cómo" (according to the way in which the project of being human changes; according to whether a human being aspires to be or not to be, or what and how she/he aims to be.)[4] Both the historical conceptions of Nothingness and the ways of experiencing it—as, for example, in the states of nirvana or anxiety, both associated with the experience of Nothingness—change through history. This fluctuation of meanings and kinds of experience is, for Zambrano, an indication of the dynamic nature of Nothingness. As she puts it, "[la nada] es viviente" (Nothingness is alive/living).[5] Dynamism is not an inherent property of Nothingness, because having an inherent property would mean that Nothing is, in fact, something. Instead, the constant activity and restlessness that Zambrano attributes to Nothingness reflects negatively, like a shadow reflecting the contours of a body, the dynamism that is a basic property of human life.[6]

The quality Zambrano associates with Nothingness is neither immobility nor self-generated movement but instead that of offering resistance to movement (the movement of humanization). That resistance operates

in two basic ways: either by dissolving the movement—making it unnecessary, as if it had already exhausted itself or reached completion—or by
annulling the sense of distance that opens up the space for movement.
Because a human being is a project—and not an essence or a given—the
human conquest of Being moves by encountering resistance. "Cuando
el hombre se decide a ser, se siente ser y siente al par la resistencia que se
le opone" (When man decides to be, he feels himself being and he feels,
at the same time, the resistance that opposes him).[7] At different stages
in history that resistance came from different sources: notably God, the
sacred (understood in the specific sense Zambrano attributes to this
term), or from the inner depths of what she calls *entrañas*. Nothingness
is the last, that is, the most recent but also supreme form of resistance
that the project of humanization encounters. Why and how Nothingness
emerges as supreme resistance is an issue I will take up below. For now,
it is sufficient to establish that, insofar as it functions not only as the last
but also as the ultimate resistance, Nothingness instantiates, in the most
dramatic way, the historical impasse at which immobility and movement inform and oppose each other: "La nada es inercia. Invita a ser y
no lo tolera: es la suprema resistencia" (Nothingness is inertia. It invites
being and does not tolerate it: it is the supreme resistance).[8] Although
Zambrano identifies Nothingness with inertia, her description of it—as
an enticement or invitation to be that also impedes, disallows being—
resembles much more the junction between movement and immobility
characteristic of stasis.

For Zambrano, Nothingess is the notion that marks the last—most
recent but also, in a sense, final—stage in the development of Western
philosophy (history, religion, and so on). It also names a kind of subjective
experience, a sense of being enveloped by a dynamic, living void situated
both inside and outside the subject. The copresence of movement and
immobility is a feature of Nothingness as an ambiguous phenomenon: an
active challenge or invitation to be, and a passive resistance that engulfs
existence and threatens to dissolve its meaning. In the broader context of
Zambrano's thought, the overlapping of movement and immobility she

attributes to the elusive notion of Nothingness resurfaces in reference to exile: her own exile, that of the defeated Spanish Republic, and exile more generally.

Exile, Tragedy, and the Movement of Withdrawal

In a manuscript dated circa 1966 and classified under the heading "Antígona. La República. La Guerra Civil. La historia," Zambrano refers to an exile as someone who finds her- or himself "detenido sin reposar," "detained in restlessness," motionless but without finding calm.[9] This manuscript juxtaposes Zambrano's testimony on the status of Republican exiles in post–Civil War Spain with brief readings of figures like Sophocles's Antigone and the subject of Velázquez's painting *Niño de Vallecas*, which are treated more extensively in other texts.[10] Both the character of Antigone and Velázquez's paintings of village idiots and court fools—*bobos*—are poetic embodiments of her experience of exile. Village idiots and fools are liminal figures who cannot fully belong. Wanderers in perpetual motion, erring without origin or destination, they lack a home either in society or reason, whose light barely flickers in the eyes of Velázquez's models. Exiles resemble bobos in that both figures lack legitimate access not just to their historical *patria* but also to the human patria of *logos*, a term that means both "reason" and "word"—in particular, a word that is spoken truthfully. Both exiles and bobos have voices, although they remain unheard. Rather than making free use of language, they are its hostages, held captive to a word that goes unarticulated. They find themselves "al borde de la palabra, como si ellos mismos hubieran llegado a identificarse con ella de tal manera, que ya fueran ellos mismos una palabra" (on the brink of the word, as if they had come to identify with it in such a way that they themselves were already a word).[11] It is as if the exiles, personified by Velázquez's bobos and Antigone, identify with the word so strongly that, rather than *having* a voice or word, they *are* a word. Detained on the brink or border of the word, exiles testify to the word's power to set free both the one who utters it and the one who receives it. A word that sets one free is, to use Zambrano's own words, "una prenda," a pledge, token, or gift given freely. She crystalizes this idea in the essay "Un capítulo de la palabra: 'el idiota,'" referring to the word as "ese extraño ser que existe en tanto que se da" (that strange being that exists insofar as it is given).[12] The word is that strange being that exists when it is given without violence, without carrying the burden of excessive reasons, seething passions, or mandates, as is the case with Antigone's interlocutor, Creon.

Like the silence of Spanish exiles whose words, at the time of her writing, did not hold any interest for those Spaniards who were firmly installed in the present—"Ahora ya apenas al exiliado se le pregunta nada" (Now the exile is barely asked anything)—the faces of Velázquez's bobos testify to the absence or spectral presence of a word that remains unsaid, a word without a speaker or addressee.[13] In the essay "¿Cómo se lee una lengua muerta?," which examines the notions of utopia and exile in Zambrano's philosophy, Jorge Brioso recalls the thesis of Daniel Heller-Roazen's book *Echolalias*, according to which languages are born from the death of the infinite phonetic capacity characteristic of the prelinguistic phase of a child: "Entry to a specific language presupposes the death of that infinite capacity of articulation."[14] Lacking a stable access to language, Velázquez's bobos exist in the nonplace (*utopos*) where language has not been fully born out of the withdrawal, the death of its prelinguistic ground.

As personifications of exile, Antigone and the bobo, or "el idiota," exemplify a certain mode of being, namely, an existence that is detained in movement, halted in the transitional space of death (Antigone) or birth (el idiota). By their very nature, birth and death are instances of movement or passage that can be spoken *of* but not spoken *from*. One can speak of one's birth and death only in retrospective or prospective fashion, in relation to the movement of life they inaugurate or end. In the case of el idiota and Antigone, these two foundational moments in life expand and occupy the entire space of their existence. Their movement resembles immobility by virtue of being halted in transition. Zambrano sees the entire existence of el idiota as an interminable passage that expands the instance of birth and leaves it suspended: "Parece que el nacimiento sea todo en el idiota. Y como del nacimiento no hay razón, se queda así el idiota ante el sentir de la comunidad, suspendido entre cielo y tierra, como dejado, al retirarse, por un mar desaparecido para siempre" (It is as if birth were everything for the idiot. And since birth has no reason in it, the idiot thereby remains, in the face of community sentiment, suspended between sky and earth, as if left behind by a retreating sea that has forever disappeared).[15] El idiota is unmoored in place and time, permanently arriving and departing. The entirety of his existence is testimony to the event of birth of which no account can be given, and of which el idiota attests to only by virtue of his mere presence. Rather than inserting el idiota into the unstoppable, forward-moving current of time, birth leaves him abandoned on the shores of existence by a long-gone sea.

If the figure of el idiota seems to keep alive the trace of the immemorial event of being born, the curse of Antigone's birth—a result of the incestuous union of her parents, Oedipus and Jocasta—accompanies her all the way to the threshold of death. It would not be excessive to argue that Zambrano and Antigone share a common historical-poetic lineage. Both suffer the consequences of civil wars that leave them without "patria." That loss is compounded by the drama of their relation to siblings, their status as sisters. Sophocles's Antigone takes her own life after being punished for her decision to bury her brother Polynices in defiance of divine and state laws. In Zambrano's case, her departure into exile was aggravated by the difficulties endured by her mother and sister, Araceli, who remained in Nazi-occupied Paris, unable to leave, and, in Araceli's case, watched over and eventually tortured by the Gestapo.[16] It took the death of the mother and the deportation of Araceli's husband, who died in Franco's prisons, for the sisters to reunite and remain together on the long path of exile. Biographical as well as philosophical reasons compelled Zambrano to return to Antigone and even to write her own version of the tragedy, *La tumba de Antígona*, which differs from Sophocles's in that the protagonist does not commit suicide but instead remains in the in-between space that is neither life nor death.[17]

Rather than undertaking a reading of *La tumba de Antígona*, my goal here is to address certain points of intersection between Zambrano's interpretation of the universe of Greek tragedy, seen though the prism of Antigone's story, and her account of the historical tragedy of twentieth-century Europe and Spain. In Zambrano's view, Antigone in particular, and tragedy in general, perform a task that neither Greek philosophy nor religion could tackle: that of shedding light on the plight of a character who is suffering under the weight of an insoluble contradiction encapsulated in the tragic *aporia*. In a way analogous to the tomb in *La tumba de Antígona* functioning simultaneously as a space of birth and death, Zambrano's reading of tragedy searches for a space of mediation between two very different visions—or arguments—of human hope: on the one hand, philosophy's hope in reason, and on the other, Christianity's hope in the divine potential of human life. Zambrano's ideas about tragedy as mediation between Greek philosophy and Christianity provide the background for Andrew Bush's intricate reading of what he calls "the survival of Antigone." In this case, the term *survival* does not simply refer to the principal trait distinguishing Zambrano's version from Sophocles's, but functions instead as a trope that remits to what Bush calls Zambrano's "translation" of the Greek universe into the Christian era.[18] In a dialogue with Bush's account of different forms of passage (transit, transition, or translation) that structure his reading of Zambrano's version of Antigone, I wish to dwell here on the connections between tragedy and exile and, more specifically, the way in which Zambrano's views on exile relate to what she herself describes as a survival of tragedy in the Christian era.

The main element that connects Antigone to exile is her liminal status, noted by Zambrano and many authors before and after her, such as William Roberts, who sees Antigone as a foreigner, or Jacques Derrida, for whom she is "the system's vomit."[19] The entirety of Antigone's life and family history is condensed in the site of her entombment as she is awaiting death. In his reading of Antigone, Robert calls attention to the etymological proximity between the Greek words for tomb (*oikesis*) and home (*oikos*), a fruitful analogy for analyzing the trajectory of a young woman who transgresses the boundary between life and death.[20] She fulfills her duty to the family—first her blind father, Oedipus, and then her dead brother, Polynices—by contradicting the laws of the polis and family reproduction. Her loyalty to the dead outweighs her commitment to the living, including the man who was to become her husband (Creon's son, Hamon). In her 1966 manuscript, which overlaps with her work on *La tumba de Antígona*, published in 1967, Zambrano does not interpret Antigone's sacrifice as a sign of her obedience to the ancestral—read: conservative—mandates of the family, which is, in general lines, how Hegel read Sophocles's tragedy in *Phenomenology of Spirit*. Instead, she sees Antigone's sacrifice as an act that introduces a fissure in the edifice of Creon's law, opening the space for a new kind of relationship between the human and the divine, centered around the figure Zambrano calls "Dios desconocido" (the unknown God).

The standoff between Antigone and Creon is not just a conflict between two kinds of laws (state and family) but between two kinds of reason. Creon's decisions display what Zambrano calls "razón sin poros" (reason without pores).[21] His arguments, without being unjust, show a lack of piety that is, in her view, even worse than injustice. Zambrano wonders if Creon's defense of the victorious side in the civil war, and the blame for the war's misfortunes he lays at the feet of the vanquished, may not, in fact, be an attempt to purify himself of guilt for having won. In her account of stasis, Nicole Loraux notes that the Greeks used the same word, *nike*, to refer both to a victory achieved in war and as the result of a democratic voting procedure. It is, argues Loraux, as if there were something intrinsically bad in a victory that arises from internal division, even a peaceful one.[22] Zambrano herself says that "la victoria es siempre cosa de justificar" (victory is always something to be justified), a statement that seems to echo Loraux, while alluding not just to Creon's but also to Franco's victory.[23]

By closing himself off to Antigone's pleas and denying her the right to bury her slain brother, Creon also denies her the right to mix reason (logos) with speech acts like "conjuro, advertencia, llamada, invocación" (conjuration, warning, call, invocation) that are foreign to it.[24] Creon lacks what Zambrano calls "razón con poros" (reason with pores), a kind of reason that "permite justamente el diálogo, el intercambio con otra razón que provenga de otro lugar, de otro punto de vista, sea del corazón, sea de otra ley. El despiadado . . . sigue la lógica sin poros, no permite así el diálogo (allows dialogue and exchange with another reason that comes from elsewhere, from another point of view, whether one from the heart or from another law. One who is without mercy . . . follows the logic without pores, does not permit such dialogue).[25] "Reason with pores" is a catachresis—a rhetorical figure that misapplies a certain property to an object—which Zambrano coins to name the reason that opens itself to the limit at which we find ourselves exposed, touched, and moved by the Other.[26] It is that exposure to the uniqueness of the Other that Zambrano calls piety and that, elsewhere, she defines as "saber tratar con lo otro" (knowing how to treat/relate to the other).[27]

Creon's and Antigone's reasons cannot touch, because there is no common ground where they can meet. To hear Antigone's reasons, Creon would have to turn into someone else, someone other than who he is: a sovereign to whom belongs the decision to let live or make die. Similarly, for Antigone to obey Creon's orders—abandon Polynices's corpse, leave her prison/tomb, and return to the living—she would have to adopt his logic without pores, which leaves no options other than submission and obedience. This is where the tragic conflict occurs. In *Broken Hegemonies* Reiner Schürmann argues that "Antigone ends up broken, not exactly by disparate laws but . . . *singularized under one law, through a withdrawal toward the other.*"[28] In her singularity, Antigone is *not* One, a unified subject that can fully appear before—or be interpellated by—either the law of the family or of the polis. More than a conflict, tragedy stages an aporia, a situation with no way out other than death or divine punishment, neither of which can be seen as a solution to the concrete human predicament that generates tragic conflict.

Unlike Sophocles, Zambrano does not see Antigone's death by suicide as the only way out of the tragic aporia, a fatal blow that would cut the knot of her destiny. As noted before, in Zambrano's version of the tragedy, Antigone does not kill herself, but remains in the tomb, in conversation—dialogue—with the shadows of other characters whose presence she convokes. There are both poetic and philosophical reasons for letting Antigone linger in the passage, as she is moving away from the living and toward death, which does not arrive. That state of stillness in motion, of remaining caught in transit, allows Zambrano to dwell on the nature of the tragic impasse characteristic of Antigone's relationship to both humans and gods. For Zambrano, Greek tragedy in general, and Antigone in particular, reveal something fundamental about the human relationship to the divine that, at that juncture in history, neither philosophy nor religion could illuminate. Tragic conflict brings to light the figure of "dios desconocido" (unknown God), whose absence—absent presence—is revealed through the protagonist's suffering.[29]

In Zambrano's vision of tragedy, the existential movement from life to death is suspended either because a protagonist, as happens with Oedipus, is not fully born, or because, as in Antigone's case, death is withheld from her, even after she sacrificed her life. "Dios desconocido" is the name Zambrano gives to the resistance that stands in the way of the tragic protagonists' attempts to decipher the painful story that began at—or before—their birth, or to create their own version of the events leading to their death. In the universe of tragic aporia—a word that literally means "absence of paths"—those attempts face an insurmountable resistance: Zambrano's "unknown god," a dark presence that surrounds the protagonist immersed in her or his agony. One might expect, suggests Zambrano, that the advent of Christianity, and its revelation of a human god, would bring an end to this kind of impasse, that Christianity would transcend tragedy. But it is with, and moreover *because* of, Christianity that a new kind of resistance appears. This time, however, the resistance does not come from God but from history itself. Following the advent of Christianity, tragic impasse is not related to the protagonists' attempts to shed light on the conditions of their birth or death. Christianity, as Zambrano puts it, brings a new argument—new narrative—to humans grappling with their suffering and hope. That narrative is grounded in a certainty of being created in God's image, "[la] certidumbre de haber sido hecho a 'imagen y semejanza' de su Dios" (the certainty of having been made 'in the image and likeness' of their God).[30] One might think that this kind of fundamental certainty would undo the tragic knot of human despair and replace it with the newly found hope and sense of responsibility for creating human history. Things do not quite happen that way. Christianity, in Zambrano's view, not only does not do away with tragedy, but it instead transfers the tragic impasse from the realm of human relationship with the unknown God into the realm of history.

In his intricate analysis of *La tumba de Antígona*, Andrew Bush reads Zambrano's work as a simultaneously Christian and philosophical translation of Sophocles's tragedy. Bush writes: "Sophocles had led Antigone off, lamenting her solitude. Zambrano's Christian translation, on the other hand, offers an afterlife to his work of art, and redemption to Antigone herself in the form of the dawn of consciousness."[31] I would nuance Bush's approach to Zambrano's Christian translation of tragedy by pointing out that Zambrano viewed Western history as an expanded translation of tragedy. That translation does not happen at the textual level but at the level of action, through the endless process of the creation of history. Similar to the beginning of a tragedy, in which the crime has already been committed and the protagonist is left to suffer the consequences, the protagonist of the drama of Christianity is thrown, hurled into history to fulfill the promise of the Christian *argumento*: that of being a creator who carries out the Creator's work on earth. While in the universe of Greek tragedy the protagonist is placed before a law whose punishment she must endure, in Christianity one endures a similarly tragic sense of freedom and is forced to run against its limitations. In the Christian tragedy of history, it is the future that occupies the place of the unknown God, who makes himself known through absence.

As is the case with the unknown god of tragedy, the resistance that comes from history—from the future—throws (historical) movement into disarray. I referred earlier to Zambrano's assessment of her present as an era that condenses and renders simultaneous previous stages in the relationship between the human and the divine. It is possible to see this condensation as a simultaneous compression and retardation of history that does not seem to be moving forward or back but remains stuck in the state of restless confusion.

Zambrano's account of her exile following the defeat of the Republic in the Spanish Civil War, reflects the same experience of being suspended in a time that compresses earlier stages of Spanish history. The experience of exile is situated on the tragic threshold—"dintel trágico"—of Spanish history, marked by the recurrence of civil wars. "No es ésta, la última la que no debe de reproducirse sino ella misma, la guerra civil" (It is not just the latest [civil war] that should not be repeated, but civil war itself).[32] Those who were exiled following the 1936 Civil War found themselves left behind by what Zambrano, referring to Antigone's conflict with Creon, calls the "ciego presente," the present blinded by the future and closed to the reasons of those who cannot speak for themselves: the dead in the case of Antigone, and exiles in the Spanish case.[33] Like Creon, who demanded that Antigone abandon the subterranean realm of the dead and return to the living, many in 1960s Spain claimed that Republican exile had lost its purpose and that those who were still exiled were free to return if they so wished. Such claims, argues Zambrano, should not be interpreted as an invitation for the exiles to return. Rather, they articulated a demand that they—the exiles—leave their exile behind or, as Zambrano phrases it, that they de-exile themselves (*des-exiliarse*). She specifies that the word she employs "no es juego de palabras . . . no es lo mismo que si simplemente nos dijeran 'vuelvan' o 'vengan.' Y más todavía si nos llamaran por nuestro nombre" (is not a play on words . . . It is not the same as if they had simply told us 'come back,' or 'come.' And even more, if they had called us by our name).[34] Zambrano sees this refusal to come to terms with the persistence of exile as a symptom of a tragic impasse of Spanish history that manifests itself as an uncritical faith in the future and an unwillingness to look into the shadows of the past. Rather than allowing history to move, the lack of interest among Spaniards in those who remained in exile empties historical time of continuity, without which something called patria cannot exist. Without continuity patria turns into "un lugar ocupado por los que llegan, lleguen como lleguen, en virtud de la fuerza o en virtud de la fuerza de la edad" (a place occupied by those who arrive there, however they do so, whether by virtue of force or by virtue of the force of their age).[35]

Toward the end of his above-mentioned essay, Bush draws an important analogy between the tropes of transit and translation, and a broader historical context that Zambrano's treatment of Antigone indirectly invokes:

> Zambrano's concerns, highlighted existentially by her exile and her return, have their own historical context in the reconciliation of "the two Spains" (that is, the liberal and the traditionalist) and the project of "Spain" as one. The historicizing of Zambrano's Antigone . . . namely, the superimposition of Franco's subsequent tyranny on Creon's actual decree, touches directly on the relation between her theory of translation as *tránsito* of the weaver/translator and the post-Franco Transition, as it is still called, from dictatorship to democracy.[36]

My analysis of Zambrano's account of Antigone's tragedy in the context of her 1960s writings on exile reveals her lucid and uncomfortable anticipation of the problems inherent in the movement of transition. The sections of the 1966 manuscript that form part of "Carta sobre el exilio" portray exile as an aporia of Spanish history, a tragic impasse left unresolved. The exiled person is detained in an unending transit between the past that does not pass and the future suspended in anticipation. The static movement of exile is the flipside of the linear movement of history, whose conflicts are presumably put to rest by the success of the Transition. By contrasting *patria* and *lugar ocupado*, Zambrano calls attention to the fact that both the recent and remote history of Spain cast a long shadow of exile over those who are deprived of history so that those coming after could *occupy* the present. The purported historical victory of the democratic transition should not render us insensitive to the hostile overtones of the verb and the act of occupying the present.

Christianity and European Violence

Beginning in the 1940s and until the mid-1950s the problem of European violence emerges as one of the fundamental concerns for Zambrano. She was intellectually and affectively averse to interpreting that violence as one more symptom of the crisis or decadence of European (Western) civilization, a notion so frequently aired that, by the mid-twentieth century, it became a common opinion. There were too many factors at play in that crisis for her to be able to accept it simply as an indication that European cultural dominance had run its course and would inevitably be succeeded by another. Although in the early 1940s, when she began writing *La agonía de Europa*, Zambrano had not yet fully developed her ideas about tragedy, her approach to the historical drama unfolding before her eyes appealed to a kind of tragic vision. The "agony" in the book's title situated Europe at the threshold of a definite unraveling of a particular form of historical existence, thereby allowing a spectator—or, in her case, a witness—to cast one final look at the events that precipitated the end. In that sense Zambrano's title invoked what Schürmann calls tragedy's "nocturnal knowledge."[37] Zambrano's is a fleeting, rather than totalizing, vision of life or history that is approaching the point of no return, where it will either languish and stagnate under the pull of its own contradictions or invent a path leading to a more promising future. Zambrano hoped that the latter option, foreclosed in the tragic universe, might still exist in European history.

In *La agonía de Europa* Zambrano loosely defines culture as "un ensayo de ser," an "experiment at being."[38] The European crisis, whose most visible manifestation was the outbreak of new and more terrifying forms of violence, was therefore also a crisis of a specific experiment at being. For Zambrano the main feature of the European experiment is the idea that human life unfolds in and through history. However, it is her view that, from its beginnings, in the transition from the Greek to the Judeo-Christian era, European culture posited being as indissociable from violence. The roots of that violence were philosophical and religious, given that the conception of being disclosed through European history was a result of the encounter between Greek and Christian conceptions of human nature. Rather than enacting a harmonious synthesis between Greece and Christianity, philosophy and religion, European culture testifies to the effort at bridging the gap or, to use Zambrano's word, mediating between these two very different sets of paradigms. The task of European culture, and the key to its successes and failures, was to make them compatible.

As Zambrano sees it, the historical path of European cultural experiment, rooted in the conception of the human being that emerges from a combination of Greek and Christian models, was fraught with perils. One might go a step further, arguing that for Zambrano at the core of European belief is a vision of history as a perilous and yet inescapable undertaking. She associates the history-creating drive with the religious roots of European culture, established through the process of human identification with the most active God imaginable, one that creates the universe ex nihilo, "out of nothing." In the Greek cultural universe the problem of individual human existence didn't concern gods or philosophy, which was full of examples of lofty indifference toward matters of passing, rather than eternal and unchanging, nature. Unsympathetic to individual human tribulations, Greek philosophy extolled the virtue of ascetic self-control and sought to limit the excesses standing in the way of the pursuit of wisdom. In that context the revelation of a Christian god who adopts human form and partakes in human nature could have been seen as the ultimate divine gift, one able to appease the pervasive sense of uncertainty and distress that characterized the final stage of Hellenic culture. However, the gift of divine nature that humanity received through Christ's incarnation and sacrifice established the basis for what Zambrano calls the "terrible victoria [humana]" (terrible human victory).[39]

The consequences of that terrible victory determined the nature of European culture, particularly its focus on individual existence as a locus of unrelenting human struggle to live up to the responsibility humans received along with the gift of a shared human-divine nature. In an essay on the subject of European responsibility, Rodolph Gasché quotes Derrida's assertion that "the concept of responsibility has no sense at all outside of an experience of inheritance."[40] For Zambrano the inheritance of divine nature generates human responsibility for creating history, which she sees as a dominant feature of European culture through different stages in its development. However, the phenomenon of totalitarianism—Zambrano's most immediate concern at the time of writing *Agonía de Europa*—represents a new, sinister version of the European project.

In one sense, the advent of totalitarianism in the 1930s was compatible with that unstoppable drive to create history. In another sense, however, totalitarianism annihilates the tension between two worlds—passing and eternal, reality and utopia—without which that creative impetus grinds to a halt. In her critique of totalitarianism in *Agonía*, Zambrano condemns "la anulación totalitaria de la distancia, . . . falsificada mística que suplanta a la . . . consustancial utopia creadora" (the totalitarian annihilation of distance . . . falsified mysticism that supplants the . . . innate creative utopia).[41] Totalitarianism unravels two basic tenets of European culture: on the one hand, a need to introduce a distance between humans and gods, which was a guiding idea of Greek philosophy; on the other, the Christian legacy of inexhaustible human desire for surmounting that distance, for getting closer to God, not just in the other world but, even more important, in this one. While it functions prominently both in Greek and Christian conceptions of being, the notion of distance reveals a configuration of movement and rest that is different in each case. Greek philosophy neutralized the impact of capricious gods by establishing a notion of being that introduces reason, measure, and order—in a word, stability—in an otherwise turbulent world.[42] Within Christianity, the rootedness in a shared human-divine essence gives individuals the freedom to move but also to err and stray from the path leading to God. By emphasizing the importance of distance for the creative and inherently violent movement of European history, Zambrano's critique of "anulación totalitaria de la distancia" implies that totalitarianism not only introduces unprecedented violence into history but that it *violates the movement of history itself.*

In light of Zambrano's assessment of the violence inherent in the notion of creating history, it would be possible, even tempting, to read her critique of totalitarianism as a somewhat suspicious (Eurocentric) denunciation of an ideology that simply pushed to the limit the tensions and contradictions that informed European ideas about history. I would argue that, for Zambrano, totalitarianism is but one symptom of a danger that goes beyond the issue of finding the reasons for the waning of European domination and mitigating its consequences. It is not just the European crisis that preoccupies her but the exhaustion of the idea that human beings have the potential for imagining and creating their common historical world, built on an irreducible tension between the human and the divine, philosophy and religion, history and politics.[43] The disappearance of that tension, or its dissolution into what Jean Luc Nancy calls a "fascist temptation" that seeks the "*contraction* of politics and religion,"[44] amounts, for Zambrano, to the destruction or darkening of the horizon of human history. Somewhat paradoxically the exhaustion of the possibility for imagining and creating history emerges as a result of the excessive trust in human victory over any kind of resistance, whether it comes from nature, gods, or society itself.

European history, argues Zambrano, finds itself at a standstill, a point at which it encounters a new and particularly damaging form of resistance that does not come from the outside, from an Other, but from itself, from its own accumulated history. That standstill is a form of paralysis that results from two seemingly contrary attitudes: on the one hand, Europe's excessive trust in its capacity to surmount any obstacles to a continued historical progress, and on the other, its incapacity to respond to the dangers coming from within European society. In the early pages of *Agonía* Zambrano writes: "Todo conocimiento es lucha con algo extraño; ha habido en él un momento de peligro y urgencia" (All knowledge is struggle with something strange; there has been a moment of danger and urgency in it).[45] Based on her description of the manifestations of European crisis, it would seem that European culture has become desensitized to that element of strangeness and danger that mediates between thought and reality. Excessive trust in one's ability to tame the strangeness has as its flip side a paralyzing impotence before dangers that do emerge. And so, for Zambrano, writing about Europe means elucidating the historical impasse of a culture caught between the extremes of "terror y confianza" (terror and excessive trust)—both of which debilitate thought and render it powerless with respect to reality and the forces of history.[46] She sees a Europe that is besieged by the problems emerging from its own societies—principally, the economic and political inequalities of the interwar era—and whose historical primacy is becoming obsolete thanks to the triumph of a new quasi-religion that worships a divinity called Success.[47] Firmly set on the path of taming the external monster of Nature, whose "pavorosa realidad" (terrifying reality) gradually became reduced to "lo natural" as a synonym for the habitual and innocuous, European thought is at a loss when it comes to another, more dangerous monster: "Enigma y monstruo más pavoroso que el de la naturaleza: el monstruo de lo social" (enigma and monster more fearful than that of nature: the monster of the social).[48] Unlike Nature, which seems to have surrendered its terrifying powers, the monster of the social is endowed with the force of human life that is growing increasingly impatient before accumulated injustices. Driven by pressing needs, the oppressed strata of European societies do not tolerate waiting: "no espera[ban], no tolera[ban] la espera" (did not expect, did not tolerate, the wait).[49] The European intelligentsia, and particularly representatives of the venerable liberal tradition, stand mesmerized before the power of those unwilling to heed the siren song of progress and its promise of liberation. At the same time, out of the soil fertilized by the dissolution of European hopes grows a new religion whose guiding principles are resentment and a cult of success. The resentful animosity against Europe's diminishing prestige is, for Zambrano, a reaction characteristic of those who, in a moment of crisis, seek a new master. Success, the object of their worship, is "un señor que cambia, algo sin rostro, forma ni figura" (a master who changes, something that lacks face, form or figure) and, for that very reason, cannot engender enduring loyalty, but only passing devotion.[50] This combination of stagnation and agitation that marked the moment of European decline offers a framework for approaching or, rather, returning to Zambrano's vision of Nothingness as a last resistance to the notion of Being that unfolds in history, where it also reaches its limit.

Return of Nothingness

As a way of picking up on and furthering my earlier discussion of Nothingness, it is important to introduce here a crucial conceptual distinction between Nothingness and nihilism. As other scholars have noted, Zambrano's Nothingness is not the same as nihilism. In an important essay on the political dimensions of Zambrano's thought, Alberto Moreiras states that "in Zambrano, nothingness does not announce nihilism."[51] "On the contrary," he continues, "*la nada hace nacer*, 'nothingness brings into the world,' and what it brings is the *fondo sagrado*, 'sacred ground.'"[52] In an essay on nihilism and community that does not engage with Zambrano's thought, the Italian political theorist Roberto Esposito offers a somewhat elliptic definition of nihilism: "Certainly, nihilism has to do with the nothing, but precisely in the guise of its annihilation. Nihilism is not the nothing of the thing, but that of the thing's nothing."[53] Unpacking Esposito's characterization, we might say that nihilism negates Nothingness, understood as that inner lack or void that makes the thing—in his essay, community—possible. In other words, Nothingness impedes the closure or self-enclosure of the community, thereby keeping it from becoming an impenetrable, hermetic whole. For Esposito, it is the latter conception of community as wholeness without void that is, properly speaking, nihilist.

As noted before, for Zambrano, the main feature of Nothingness is its dynamism, its relentless resistance to any philosophical, religious, or political concept or doctrine that would expel whatever does not belong to the sphere of Being—defined as logos, God, or political sovereignty—into the desert of non-being, no-thing. As Zambrano poignantly observes in *El hombre y lo divino*: "Las cosas que no son nada, son algo cuando se padecen" (Things that are nothing are something when one suffers them).[54] This deceptively simple sentence situates Nothingness not within the realm of Being—that is, as the opposite of Being—but in the realm of human openness to the world, "la primera, originaria 'apertura' de la vida humana a las cosas que la rodean" (the first, originary "opening" of human life to the things surrounding it).[55] Rather than being a response elicited by something, a particular thing, suffering—in the sense in which Zambrano speaks of it—reveals that which, for us, *is not nothing*. The elusive nature of Nothingness, which, without being a thing, is also not (simply) nothing, brings us back to the ambiguity of la nada that combines activity and passivity, fullness and void, movement and immobility. In her account of the notion of Being as formulated in Greek philosophy, Zambrano argues that Nothingness emerges from las entrañas, the interior realm that remains foreign to logos and that makes itself known as "vibración solitaria y muda . . . pura palpitación en las tinieblas" (solitary and mute vibration . . . pure palpitation in the shadows).[56] Nothingness reveals the dimension of human existence that resists being reduced to logos, and it is through that resistance that we become exposed to the void residing in us and in the world.

Somewhat unexpectedly, in the midst of her discussion of Nothingness, Zambrano brings up the specter of civil war by evoking Cain's crime against Abel. What about Nothingness could elicit such a mention? For Zambrano, the experience of Nothingness reveals that we can never be absolutely alone. Next to us, there is always a shadow of an Other, whom she names simply *hermano*, a brother or a sister, whose absence invokes a memory of past fratricides and calls for a future in which such crimes will be impossible. "Más allá de 'el otro' se extiende el desierto de la ausencia de un alguien. A esa ausencia, hueco sin límites, llama el hombre de hoy la nada" (Beyond 'the other' extends the desert of the absence of a someone. Today's man calls that absence—a hole without limits—Nothingness).[57] Nothingness is the void created by the absence of an Other who, if she or he were there, would confirm to us that we are not alone, that one is never (just) One but is always surrounded by the trace of an absence that cannot be eliminated or forgotten. For Zambrano, the absent brother or sister takes the place of God, although a God whom we cannot kill. Just like Nothingness, the absence of a brother bears witness to a void that grows in us and together with us: "En el hombre, a medida que crece el ser crece la nada. Y entonces la nada funciona a manera de la posibilidad. La nada hace nacer" (In man, as being grows, Nothingness also grows. And then Nothingness functions in the manner of a possibility).[58] This deeply felt, almost maternal, Nothingness allows Zambrano to glimpse the possibility of history freed from the crime of a civil war and from exile as a form of punishment that preserves the trace of that crime in history.

Afterword

The analysis of the inherent instability and capacity for endurance of the Francoist regime undertaken in this book deepens our understanding of the genealogy of the current Spanish political system. Raúl Sánchez Cedillo synthesized that genealogy as follows: "The 'Glorious Crusade' of July 18, 1936, was the founding existential element of every norm Francoism created, including the current form of state and, to a significant extent, our present Constitution."[1] The 2007 collapse of the global financial markets and its pernicious effect on the fragile equilibrium of powers within the Spanish state and the EU underscored the continuities between Francoism and what Sánchez Cedillo calls the Rajoynato, the ruling political mentality of Mariano Rajoy's goverment (2011–18). The parallels between Francoism and the Rajoynato reflect the fact that both regimes were defined by their interim nature, their exceptionality. Despite the chronic provisionality of Francoism, its consolidation was a result of its adherence to three basic principles: anticommunism, limited or controlled pluralism, and the defense of capitalist development. For his part, Rajoy's leadership consisted in "administering and waiting," acting as if he were a broker calculating the maturity (*vencimiento*) of investments entrusted to him and guaranteeing stable revenues.[2] As Sánchez Cedillo aptly puts it, this *vencimiento*—a word that means not only "maturity" but also "date of expiration"—is the very form of the future for Rajoy: "La forma del futuro en Rajoy es la del vencimiento."[3]

Similar to Francoism, Rajoynato faced the task of administering its own exceptionality, all the while claiming to act as a guarantee of calm and stability in uncertain times. Despite the differences in their respective kinds of exceptionality—an authoritarian dictatorship and a democratic government whose policies increasingly depended on the calculus of external factors (the financial markets, the European Union, the Catalan independence movement)—both Francoism and the Rajoynato based their legitimacy on a defense of the continuity, however precarious, of the political system they represent. And in both cases, that continuity was endangered, whether by some version of liberal-communist-Masonic conspiracy, or by threats to Spain's post-1978 parliamentary constitutional monarchy from different types of "movements" (populism, separatism, or "los anti-sistema").

Throughout this book, I have deployed the ancient Greek term *stasis* as an interpretive tool in order to illuminate the tension between two contrary and yet inseparable facets of the Francoist regime: its endurance and its intrinsic impermanence. Recourse to stasis is a way of tapping into a rich field of reflection, both ancient and contemporary, on the Civil War (one of the meanings of stasis) not only as an event but as a form of internal division that brings into question—and can end up reasserting— political unity among citizens of the same state. On the one hand, the semantic field of stasis is irreducible to what we commonly refer to as civil war, since, as I have argued in this book, it refers to a multiplicity of contexts and situations in which movement and immobility coexist. On the other hand, different political usages of stasis allow the concept of civil war to be extended beyond the act of violent confrontation among members of the same polity. These different usages make the notions of stasis and/or civil war relevant for contemporary reflections about politics, from Foucault to Agamben, and from Dimitris Vardoulakis to the Tiqqun collective, a group of French authors and political activists who cofounded a philosophical journal, *Tiqqun,* and published several books. Tiqqun's *Introduction to Civil War* contains the following statement about the link between the modern state and stasis as civil war: "Etymologically the modern state stems from the Indo-European root *st-*, which refers to fixity, to unchangeable things to what *is*. . . . Today, when the state does nothing more than outlive itself, the opposite becomes clear: it is civil war—*stasis* in Greek—that is permanence, and the modern state will have been a mere *reaction process* to this permanence."[4] In its attempt to suppress stasis, the state disavows its own origins and purposefully misinterprets the foundational role of conflict in politics.

While the notion of stasis allows for thinking civil war beyond an actual event—in this case, the Spanish Civil War—it also helps problematize the ends (both goals and endings) of the regime that, however viciously and insidiously, claimed to have put an end to the political disorder of the Second Republic that had brought about the Civil War.[5] In focusing on the problem of the end of Francoism, this book seeks to contribute to a long debate about post-dictatorship and transition to democracy in Spain and Latin America. Both kinds of ends, the end of dictatorship and the end of transition, are fraught with difficulties. As I hope to have shown in chapter 1, the continuity of Francoism was inseparable from its obsession with its own end. However, the issue of the other kind of end, that of the process of democratic transition, which would conclude with the establishment of democratic "normalcy," is similarly laden with difficulties. In a recent book Luisa Elena Delgado offers a critique of the "phantasies of Spanish democratic normalcy," insofar as they are based on a defense of consensus and unity as the only mode of "being in common."[6] In *Ends of Literature* Brett Levinson points out the contradiction embedded in the notion of the "termination of transition."[7] If the very notion of transition depends on closure—anything called transition has to have an end—then the end of transition could signal what Levinson names "the end of the end."[8] The latter would amount either to something like a permanent transition, a transition without an end, or to a demise of transition signaling a return to "normalcy," in Delgado's words, or to "statist thinking," in Levinson's.[9] It is that paradoxical combination of movement and immobility embedded in the notion of transition of/from dictatorship that in this book receives the name of stasis.

NOTES

INTRODUCTION

1. Unamuno, *Vida de Don Quixote*, 176. English translation mine. All translations in this book are mine unless otherwise indicated.

2. Juan Carlos Monedero, "La parte que nos corresponde," *Público*, September 19, 2016, http://www.comiendotierra.es/2016/09/19/la-parte-de-culpa-que-nos-corresponde.

3. Errejón, "Regimen," 181, emphasis added.

4. Loraux, *Divided City*, 97.

5. Vardoulakis, "Stasis," 127.

6. Loraux, *Divided City*, 25.

7. Loraux, *Divided City*, 42.

8. Loraux, *Divided City*, 107.

9. Loraux, *Divided City*, 108.

10. Vardoulakis, "Stasis," 127.

11. Schmitt, *Concept of the Political*, 47, quoted in Vardoulakis, "Stasis," 134.

12. Schmitt, *Concept of the Political*, 47, quoted in Vardoulakis, "Stasis," 134.

13. Schmitt, *Political Theology II*, 75.

14. Vardoulakis, *Stasis before the State*, 69.

15. Vardoulakis, *Stasis before the State*, 63.

16. The term "hectic inertia" is inspired by the editorial statement of the journal *Stasis*: stasisjournal.net/index.php/journal/info.

17. Saz Campos, *Las caras del franquismo*, 36.

18. Linz, "Authoritarian Regime."

19. Linz, "Authoritarian Regime," 300.

20. Fraga, *El Nuevo anti-Maquiavelo*, quoted in Crumbaugh, *Destination Dictatorship*, 46.

1. LEGISLATING FRANCOISM

1. Fraga, *How Spain Is Governed*, 43.
2. Fraga, *Las transformaciones*, 11. Fraga might have been much more cautious about quoting Picavea had he known at the time that the Francoist legal system would create its own "seven deadly sins" in the form of seven fundamental laws.
3. Fraga, *Las transformaciones*, 65.
4. In fact, Franco never officially abolished the Republican Constitution. He did, however, institute a law that retrospectively proclaimed as criminals all those who did not collaborate with the uprising and who had fought on the side of the Republic. The Republic was overturned, outlawed, and retrospectively criminalized, all at the same time. To complement brutality with historical irony, the legal basis for penalizing the supporters of the Republican regime was the law of public order proclaimed by the Republic (Iglesias Selgas, *La vía española*, 24).
5. Fernando Carvajal, *La Constitución española*, quoted in Iglesias Selgas, *La vía española*, 26.
6. Ferrando Badia, *El régimen de Franco*, 10.
7. Sánchez Navarro, *La transición española*, 309.
8. The Movimiento Nacional, as its name indicates, was not a party in the strict sense of the term. It was a movement that gathered different factions existing within Francoism. It had political status but no political identity; it was an anti-party party. Purportedly, this limited pluralism was what differentiated Francoism from totalitarianism.
9. Arrese's first term as secretary general was 1941–45.
10. Arrese, *Una etapa constituyente*, 276.
11. Arrese, quoted in López and Rodríguez, "The Spanish Model," 6.
12. López and Rodríguez, "The Spanish Model," 6.
13. Arrese, *Una etapa constituyente*, 34.
14. As I discuss in the second chapter, 1956 was the year Dionisio Ridruejo was imprisoned for his participation in the university protests in Madrid. The incarceration was a culmination of his ideological journey from fascism to social democracy. That same year, Miguel Espinosa completed the first of three complete versions of what would eventually become *Escuela de mandarines*, published in 1974. As shown in the third chapter, both the form and the content of the final version of *Escuela* were commentary and critique of the regime's capacity for endurance.

15. Arrese attributes that confusion not to the Falange's power within the Movimiento but to the flawed nature of the 1937 Decree of Unification that "engendered the single party theory." Arrese, *Una etapa constituyente,* 150. This is a radical claim insofar as it implies that the political constitution of Francoism was already flawed at the moment of its inception.

16. Arrese, *Una etapa constituyente,* 94.

17. Arrese, *Obras Seleccionadas,* 1:1120.

18. Arrese, *Una etapa constituyente,* 154.

19. Linz, "An Authoritarian Regime," 38, emphasis added.

20. As Carl Schmitt remarks in the epilogue to the Spanish edition of his *Legality and Legitimacy,* the conception of politics that consists in emphasizing respect for law as a remedy against the arbitrariness of the rulers forgets Laberthonniére's warning that "directly behind every earthly law there are men who make use of it as a means for their power." Schmitt continues: "Father Laberthonniére goes quite far in his critique. *La maxime 'C'est la loi' ne différe en rien au fond de la maxime 'C'est la guerre'* [The maxim, 'It's the law' at core does not differ at all from the maxim, 'It's war.']. This connection between law and war is in fact surprising and sounds quite radical. The knowledge on which it is based can only be understood as the bitter fruit of experiences of civil war." Schmitt, *Legalidad y legitimidad,* 157–58.

21. Linz, "An Authoritarian Regime," 47.

22. Arrese, *Una etapa constituyente,* 214.

23. Arrese, *Una etapa constituyente,* 149.

24. Franco himself complained to Arrese about the difficulty of distributing positions of power among all those who claimed to deserve them. He even suggested that direct elections would be the most convenient system that would free him from the cumbersome task of having to select the best candidates for political positions.

25. This is how one of the foremost legal theorists of the "Falange," Luis Legaz y Lacambra, described the link between liberalism and the rule of law: "The rule of law is, in that sense, a juridical translation of the liberal democracy." *Introducción a la teoría,* 19.

26. Giuseppe de Vergottini defines the material constitution as the doctrine according to which "the original normative principle that justifies an ordering, that is, the constitution *par excellence,* consists in *the normative force of the political will.* . . . The material constitution presents itself as *the true source*

of the validity of a system." Bobbio, Matteucci, and Pasquino, *Diccionario de Política,* 378.

27. Fraga, *La crisis del estado,* 371.

28. Finer, *Theory and Practice of Modern Government,* 12, quoted in Fraga, *La crisis del estado,* 400n116.

29. Ruiz de Castillo, "Las entidades sociales," 385.

30. Fraga, "El articulado de la Ley Fundamental," 519.

31. Fraga, "El articulado de la Ley Fundamental," 517.

32. Fraga, "El articulado de la Ley Fundamental," 518.

33. Ruíz de Castillo, Fraga's senior colleague at the University of Santiago de Compostela, was a disciple of Hauriou and the translator of his works into Spanish.

34. Fraga's exhaustively documented book is not incidentally entitled *La crisis del estado.* The work was published in 1955, with a revised edition in 1958.

35. Nicola Matteucci's article on constitutionalism in *Diccionario de Política* relates the notion of constitutional government to the classical distinction between limited and mixed forms of government, where the former is based on the sovereignty of the law and the latter on the separation of powers. Matteucci argues that Charles Howard McIlwain's statement that "every constitutional government is by definition a limited government" applies primarily to limited, and not so much to mixed, governments. "Constitucionalismo," in Bobbio, Matteucci, and Pasquino, *Diccionario de política,* 397.

36. Fraga, *La crisis del estado,* 516.

37. See Gabriel Guillén Kalle's *Carl Schmitt en España.*

38. Schmitt, *Legality and Legitimacy,* 4.

39. Fueyo, *La época insegura,* 128.

40. Fueyo, *La época insegura,* 70.

41. According to Agamben, *auctoritas* "is the property of the *auctor,*" a term "that derives from the verb *augeo.* The *auctor* is *qui auget,* the one who augments, enhances or perfects another's action or juridical situation." Agamben, *State of Exception,* 85.

42. Kantorowitcz, *The King's Two Bodies.*

43. Agamben, *State of Exception,* 85. As an example, Agamben quotes Friedrich Karl von Savigny: "Law is nothing but life considered from a particular point of view" (85).

44. Fueyo, *La época insegura,* 71.

45. Fueyo, *La época insegura,* 419.

46. It would be possible to say that Christianity announced a revolution in the definition of authority, inflicting a final blow to the Roman conception of auctoritas. In *Roman Catholicism and Political Form*, Carl Schmitt analyzes the political dimensions of the transition between Roman Empire and Christianity, focusing that analysis on the concept of representation.

47. Fueyo, *Estudios de teoría política*, 72.

48. Fueyo, *La época insegura*, 214.

49. In order to hammer home his point about the importance of belief for politics, Ortega performs one of his usual gestures of calling on etymology to illuminate philosophy, and vice versa. While discussing the importance of two Roman political institutions, the *auspicia* and the Senate, he points out the etymological proximity between the terms associated with the activity of predicting (*auguria, auspicia*) and the property of *auctoritas*, which belonged to the Senate. The point is that "in Rome the notions of belief and state blend together [*se compenetran*]." Ortega, "Del imperio romano," 104.

50. Ortega, "Del imperio romano," 97.

51. Fueyo, *La época insegura*, 219.

52. Fueyo, *La época insegura*, 220.

53. Ortega, "Del imperio romano," 125.

54. Ortega, "Del imperio romano," 102.

55. Ortega, "Del imperio romano," 130.

56. Fueyo saw the same qualities in Schmitt. See his essay "Carl Schmitt y la dignidad del pensamiento politico," in *La época insegura*, 171–79.

57. Ortega, "Del imperio romano," 125.

58. Fueyo, *La época insegura*, 75.

59. On the issue of expansion of ideologies, see the essays "La autoridad del Estado y el Estado-máquina," "Doctrinarismo y atonía," "El partido cósmico," and "La democracia de acción directa," all in *La época insegura*.

60. Fueyo, *La época insegura*, 119–33.

2. THE MOVEMENT OF DIVERGENCE

1. Ridruejo, "Romance de la empresa vendida," *Materiales para una biografía*, 306. Page numbers for this poem are hereafter cited parenthetically in the text. All translations in this chapter are mine unless otherwise indicated.

2. Sontag, "Fascinating Fascism," 83.

3. Ridruejo, *Escrito en España*, 22.

4. Ridruejo, *Escrito en España*, 22.

5. Juliá, *Historias de las dos Españas*; Juliá, "¿Falange liberal o intelectuales fascistas?"

6. Gracia, *La resistencia silenciosa*, 250.

7. Badiou, *The Century*, 82. For Badiou, that overlapping of a focused search and aimless drifting, of "will and wandering," expressed by the notion of anabasis, makes the latter a suitable description for "a century that ceaselessly asks itself whether it is an end or a beginning" (83). The question of the beginning that is also an end, and vice versa, is brought up again in the course of this chapter.

8. Arendt, *Origins of Totalitarianism*, 463.

9. Giorgio Agamben associates the instrumental conception of political movement with stasis in the sense of civil war, which he views as an instance of the politicization and mobilization of the people for the purpose of the (re)establishment of state-power. See Giorgio Agamben, "Movement," generation-online.org, 2005, http://www.generation-online.org/p/fpagamben3.htm.

10. Gracia, *La resistencia silenciosa*.

11. Žižek, "Eastern European Liberalism and Its Discontents," 14.

12. While both Juliá and Morente focus on the trope of belated conversion, Gracia emphasizes the persistence of a liberal undercurrent that gradually dissolved an earlier totalitarian yearning. Gracia's *La vida rescatada de Dionisio Ridruejo* offers an expanded account of the biographical and emotional factors that contributed to his "desintoxicación ideologica" (93).

13. Halberstam, *Totalitarianism*, 3.

14. Arendt, *Origins of Totalitarianism*, vii, 459, quoted in Halberstam, *Totalitarianism*, 25.

15. Halberstam, *Totalitarianism*, 3. Halberstam's claim that liberalism produced a crisis of definition—that is, of meaning—of politics, to which totalitarianism responded by attempting to re-found the political on radically different grounds, echoes Arendt's observation that "liberalism . . . its name notwithstanding, has done its share to banish the notion of liberty from the political realm." Arendt, "What Is Freedom?," 155.

16. In the words of Charles Taylor: "Manipulability of the world . . . confirms the new self-defining identity, as it were: the proper relation of man to a meaningful order is to put himself in tune with it; by contrast nothing sets the seal more clearly on the rejection of this vision than successfully treating the world as object of control." Taylor, *Hegel*, 8, quoted in Halberstam, *Totalitarianism*, 18.

17. Halberstam, *Totalitarianism*, 15 and 46.

18. Halberstam, *Totalitarianism,* 47.

19. Halberstam, *Totalitarianism,* 46.

20. Arendt, "What Is Freedom?," 156.

21. The most perverse conclusion to come out of the linear conception of recent Spanish history is the revisionist thesis according to which Francoism prepared the ground for democracy, while the chaos of the Second Republic inevitably led to the Civil War. Ismael Saz Campos, the most engaging among the contemporary historians of Francoism, makes this point: "Whether we like it or not, there appears to endure in the imaginary of Spaniards an association between the Republic, Civil War, and Francoism, as a *concatenation of events in which the first leads to the second and the second is resolved with the imposition of the third; and under the third, furthermore, the great economic transformations take place that make possible the triumph of democracy in Spain.*" Saz Campos, *Fascismo y franquismo,* 13; emphasis added.

22. Ridruejo, *Materiales para una biografía,* 51.

23. Ridruejo, *Materiales para una biografía,* 245.

24. Ridruejo, *Materiales para una biografía,* 123.

25. In an article written after the formation of the Consejo Nacional, the governing body of the Movimiento Nacional whose function was to relay the decisions of the party to the institutions of the state and monitor their fulfillment, Ridruejo addressed the issue of the relationship between the state, the Movimiento, and society. He argued that, without the input and energy of the Movimiento, the state would inevitably turn into an impersonal creation, separated from society and insensitive to its demands. Given that a state divorced from society either perishes or turns into tyranny, the union between the new Spanish state and the Movimiento was to be celebrated as the "episodio nupcial" that averted the danger of the growing chasm between state and society. These nuptials did not mean that the two elements became one but confirmed that one could not exist without the other: the state without the revolutionary spirit of the "Movimiento," and the latter without channeling its energy through the mechanism of the state. Ridruejo, *Materiales para una biografía,* 47.

26. Ridruejo, *Materiales para una biografía,* 118.

27. Ridruejo, *Materiales para una biografía,* 118.

28. Ridruejo, *Materiales para una biografía,* 118.

29. Ridruejo, *Materiales para una biografía,* 121.

30. Cacciari, *Geo-filosofía de Europa,* 63.

31. Ridruejo, "Elegía ante la mar," *Hasta la fecha*, 462. Page numbers for citations from this poem are hereafter cited parenthetically in the text.

32. Rosales, "A Dionisio Ridruejo," 700. On the poetry of this generation, see Ferrán and Testa, *Spanish Writers of 1936*.

33. Badiou, *The Century*, 82.

34. Rosales, "A Dionisio Ridruejo," 700.

35. Rosales, "A Dionisio Ridruejo," 701.

36. Rosales, "A Dionisio Ridruejo," 701.

37. Arendt, *Life of the Mind*, 181.

38. Laín, *España como problema*, 418. Page numbers for this work are hereafter cited parenthetically in the text.

39. Villacañas, *Ramiro de Maeztu*, 434.

40. Julia, *Historias de las dos Españas*, 360

41. Machado, "Por tierras de España," cited in Laín, *España como problema*, 396.

42. Ridruejo, *Diario de una tregua*, 14. Page numbers for this work are hereafter provided parenthetically in the text.

43. This would explain Ridruejo's resistance to seeing urbanized, entrepreneurial Catalonia as the dominant part that might eventually engulf the rest. Rather than in industrial activity, the bases of the Catalan way of life are, for him, found in the interplay between the land and the sea, which conditions the nature of the region's landscape.

44. The only element of the scene that does not fit into the picture is a majestic oak tree that stands alone and evokes in the writer the sensation of "our real smallness" (112). Even in an episode that celebrates the beauty of the small, everyday world, Ridruejo leaves room for a fleeting yet admiring reference to the grandeur that surpasses all human measure.

45. Ridruejo, *Materiales para una biografía*, 120.

46. On this last point, Ridruejo distanced himself from José Ortega, for whom the problem of Spanish politics resided in the lack of minorities ready to lead the people, which meant that the main political force comprised people without leadership. In truth, argues Ridruejo, "in Spain there are only people and minorities too ready to impose themselves on the people using authoritarian methods." Ridruejo, *Hasta la fecha*, 42.

47. Arendt, "No Longer and Not Yet," 161.

48. Ridruejo, "Informe a Falange sobre febrero de 1956," in *Materiales para una biografía*, 285.

49. Ridruejo, "Informe a Falange sobre febrero de 1956," 285.

50. Ridruejo, *Hasta la fecha,* 93n1.

51. Ridruejo, *Materiales para una biografía,* 289.

52. Ridruejo, *Escrito en España,* 90.

53. Ridruejo, *Materiales para una biografía,* 262.

54. Ridruejo, "Informe a Falange sobre febrero de 1956," 285.

3. PARADOXES OF FRANCOIST STASIS

1. The first version, *Historia del eremita,* was published in 2012, and the second still remains unpublished.

2. Espinosa, "Carta a Jean Tena," 47. All translations in this chapter are mine.

3. Loraux, *Divided City,* 93.

4. Vardoulakis, *Stasis before the State,* 69.

5. Espinosa, *Escuela de mandarines,* 388. Page numbers for this novel are hereafter cited parenthetically in the text.

6. Bellón, *Miguel Espinosa.* The critical literature on Espinosa has focused predominantly on the two novels dealing with the context of Spain's transition to democracy, *La fea burguesía* and *Tríbada: Tractatus Theologiae.* With regard to *Escuela de mandarines,* the innovations in language and form attracted far more critical attention than the issue of Espinosa's treatment of Francoism. While Teresa Vilarós, who first introduced me to Espinosa's literature, rightly sees him as a liminal figure, suspended or trapped in the passage between Francoism and democracy, I wish to underscore the way in which *Escuela* anticipates Espinosa's criticism of the Transition. In that sense, I disagree with Fernando R. de la Flor's characterization of the Transition as "a border between incompatible worlds, between fabulously distant and strange eras that refract each other . . . [the] premodern world [Francoism] . . . and postmodernity." De la Flor, "Miguel Espinosa: La construcción de la disidencia," 151. For Vilarós's reading of *Escuela* in the context of the Transition, see her *El mono del desencanto,* 84–99. See also the essays by Sanz Villanueva, Fernández Prieto, and Vilarós in Polo García, *Miguel Espinosa: Congreso.*

7. Covarrubias, *Tesoro de la lengua castellana,* 201.

8. Among the compounds of *batir* are *abatir* ("to bring down" or, as Covarrubias puts it, "humillar y apocar") as well as *combatir* and *debatir.*

9. The term *municipalizantes* and the nature of their struggle resonates with the sixteenth-century Guerra de las Comunidades, an uprising of the local Castilian bourgeoisie against the Emperor Charles V, which ended in the rebels' defeat.

10. In his description of the consequences of the Batida, Espinosa tackles the issue of the regime's unstable foundations with a mixture of hyperbole and corrosive humor. Take, for example, Roxano, a hero of the Batida who perished far from the battlefield, devoured by a swarm of fleas so big that an army of three hundred servants, hired specifically for that purpose, could not protect him from the insects' vicious attack. As if such a gruesome death were not enough, once the fleas have devoured the flesh, they begin attacking each other with such fury that this civil war in the flea kingdom ends with the swarm consuming itself (305–6).

11. Agamben, *Stasis*, 14.

12. An episode from Juan Espinosa's biography of Miguel Espinosa, his father, illustrates the latter's deep distrust of those who refuse to take sides in a conflict, implicitly opting to side with the victor. The incident Juan Espinosa describes took place during his father's university days, when he engaged in a fistfight with a self-proclaimed leader of the gang of "fascists" who derided "los muchachos pálidos y estudiosos" (the pale, studious youth), referring to the future novelist and others like him. Years later, the erstwhile enemies became somewhat friendly, and the novelist took the opportunity to complain about the self-appointed arbiters: "Juan, do you remember those arbiters? . . . While you and I were thrashing each other, like the foot-soldiers of the two Spains, they stood calmly, observing the fight and immersed in the thoughts about their future. Look at them now: one, the president of the City Council and the other, Dean of Law School." Juan Espinosa, *Miguel Espinosa, mi padre*, 206. For Espinosa, as for Solon, neutrality during stasis was not an honorable option.

13. Vardoulakis, *Stasis before the State*, 1.

14. Agamben, *Stasis*, 51.

15. Heidegger, *Parmenides*, 41.

16. Artigues, *El Opus Dei en España*, 71.

17. Heidegger, "Question Concerning Technology," 17.

18. "Mi visión de aquella universidad me inspiró el libro *Escuela de mandarines*. Yo veía cómo se ponían la muceta, el birrete y tal; cómo se reunían allí en las inauguraciones de curso; . . . veía la sumisión . . . el gesto de los catedráticos: te acercabas a ellos para hablarles y no se paraban, seguían andando y tú ibas

detrás, y si te colabas al lado derecho, ellos miraban al izquierdo." García Martínez, ¿Quién es Miguel Espinosa?," 191.

19. Ramos Ruíz, *Profesores, alumnos y saberes,* 214.

20. Ramos Ruíz, *Profesores, alumnos y saberes,* 121.

21. I borrow the term "visceral register" from William Connolly's *Why I Am Not a Secularist,* 3, quoted in Critchley, *Faith of the Faithless,* 19.

22. This is another parallel between the legal status of apprentices and the Francoist regime's attempts to establish a stable legal structure, which I also examine in the chapter 1.

23. References to the starvation of peasants in the novel also underscore the connection between hunger and conformity, between eating and keeping one's mouth shut. During a banquet for a hero of the Batida at which the authorities consume copious amounts of food and libations, Eremita overhears a conversation between two servants who are recalling the era of hunger, when the poor ate only herbs and roots or the food they stole. Happy Governance's cynical solution to the problem of hunger is a law mandating that stolen food can be kept if it is stored inside the mouth. As one of the servants puts it: "Era truco llenar la boca y no abrir los labios, pese a la asfixia y los palos" (the trick was to fill one's mouth and not open one's lips, despite asphyxia and beatings) (300). The meaning of a legal injunction that dictates "respetar lo tragado" is ambiguous. Aside from the literal meaning (respect for what has been swallowed), it indicates that Happy Governance authorizes undue appropriation—the act of stealing—if it is carried out with the regime's approval. At the same time that it punishes the action of stealing food by beating and asphyxiating the perpetrators, the regime prescribes a specific *form* of carrying it out legally.

24. However, stomach can also be a locus of visceral hatred of Happy Governance and not just conformity. Espinosa quotes the case of a would-be enemy of the regime who, after eating dinner, began to ponder over the regime's existence and died shortly thereafter, overcome by sadness. A kind of anti-Falca, he found the existence of Happy Governance to be the truth he could not stomach.

25. Polo García, *Miguel Espinosa: Congreso,* 107.

26. Critchley, *Faith of the Faithless,* 6.

27. Douzinas, *Philosophy and Resistance in Crisis,* 160. As Douzinas points out, Spinoza's definition illuminates the decisive role of indignation in contemporary

protest movements such as the *indignados* in Spain, or *aganaktismenoi* in Greece, formed in opposition to the dire social consequences of neoliberal policies and austerity measures.

28. Polo García, *Miguel Espinosa: Congreso*, 107.

29. The regime's devotees view the event of their death and the end of Happy Governance with incredulity. After ruling for three hundred thousand years, the dictator Filadelfo—yet another dictatorial figure whose name starts with an F and who dies peacefully in his bed—utters the following phrase on his deathbed: "What a pity it is to die when Happy Governance has just begun" (196).

30. While excerpts of Martino's works—some of them clearly apocryphal, as they contain quotes from essays Espinosa wrote before 1964—appear in fragmentary form in the footnotes of *Escuela*, López Martí's published essays gloss different aspects of Espinosa's novel as a fulfillment of the philosophical potential of literary language represented by works of Espinosa as well as by Dante, Cervantes, Kafka, or Pessoa.

31. López Martí, "El mundo como destrucción de la realidad," n.p.

32. López Martí, "El mundo como destrucción de la realidad," n.p.

33. In a deliberately provocative and even distasteful way, Espinosa exemplifies the status of the word-object in a scene in which Martino watches his sister-in-law undress before him. Once she takes off the evening gown that symbolizes her status as wife of a regime official, Martino remains mesmerized in contemplation of her genitals. The crotch of Azenaia—the mythical name Martino's sister-in-law shares with Eremita's beloved—emerges as a name-object when the woman thrusts aside the attributes of her official status in order to reveal a hidden and clearly underappreciated dimension of her being to Martino, whose contemplative philosophical vocation reaches a whole new level of intensity in the act of admiring her. The word-object "Azenaia's crotch" refers to the ontological quality Martino/Espinosa ascribes to the part of Azenaia's anatomy that, by virtue of manifesting itself before Martino, ends up signifying the defeat of the mundane and conventional (she as a lavishly dressed wife of a regime member) and the appearance of the cosmic and necessary (the meaning her crotch acquires when it is unveiled before Martino). It is hardly necessary to underscore a phallocentric nature of this self-declared "philosophical" snippet.

34. Hallward, Translator's introduction, xi.

35. Hallward, Translator's introduction, xii.

36. Hallward, Translator's introduction, xii.

37. Vardoulakis, *Stasis before the State*, 69.

38. Vardoulakis, *Stasis before the State*, 73.

4. STANDSTILLS OF HISTORY

1. Robert, *Trials*, 37.

2. Zambrano, *El hombre y lo divino*, 182.

3. Zambrano, *El hombre y lo divino*, 205.

4. Zambrano, *El hombre y lo divino*, 213.

5. Zambrano, *El hombre y lo divino*, 213.

6. In *Persona y democracia*, Zambrano posits movement as a basic feature of human history. She critiques the idea that history has a purpose or finality that can become discernable by examining the past. The tendency to see the past as the foundation of the future is an "error" that she associates with "la dificultad que hasta ahora se ha experimentado de pensar en términos de movimiento. Y la historia lo es" (the difficulty that has been experienced up until now for thinking in terms of movement. And that is what history is.) (3:453).

7. Zambrano, *El hombre y lo divino*, 213.

8. Zambrano, *El hombre y lo divino*, 213.

9. Zambrano, "Antígona," 10. I am quoting from a manuscript held at the Fundación María Zambrano. On an unnumbered page of the same manuscript, she adds the following observation about an exile: "Su estar, por fijo que sea, es un moverse" (their being there, however fixed, is a movement).

10. Velázquez's *bobos* are a subject of another of Zambrano's texts, most notably her essay "Un capítulo de la palabra: 'el idiota' (Homenaje a Velázquez)," included in *España, sueño y verdad* and introduced by a stunning passage from García Lorca's poem "Pasaje de la multitud que orina (Nocturno de Battery Place)": "Será preciso viajar por los ojos de los idiotas / campos libres donde silban mansas cobras deslumbradas / paisajes llenos de sepulcros que producen fresquísimas manzanas" (One must travel through the eyes of idiots / open fields where tame, bedazzled cobras whistle / landscapes filled with tombs yielding the freshest of apples). Zambrano, "Un capítulo," 777. Jesús Moreno Sanz, the editor of *España, sueño y verdad* for Zambrano's *Obras completas*, points out that she misquoted Lorca's "mansas cobras de alambradas" as "mansas cobras deslumbradas." He rightly observes that this mistake makes complete sense, considering the way in which Zambrano's essay engages with

the motif of light as a metaphor for reason that remains hypnotized—tamed and powerless, like "mansas cobras"—in the idiot's gaze. As Moreno Sanz puts it, the idiot's "deslumbramiento" (bedazzlement) allows him to "mirar directamente al sol sin deslumbrarse" (look directly at the sin without being dazzled). Zambrano, *España, sueño y verdad*, 136n136.

11. Zambrano, "Antígona," 5.

12. Zambrano, "Un capítulo," 778.

13. Zambrano, "Antígona," 5.

14. Brioso, "¿Cómo se lee una lengua muerta?," 43.

15. Zambrano, "Un capítulo," 780.

16. Zambrano's father, Blas Zambrano, died in Barcelona in 1938, as the Civil War was drawing to a close.

17. See Zambrano, *La tumba de Antígona*.

18. Bush, "María Zambrano and the Survival of Antigone."

19. Derrida, *Aporias: Dying—Awaiting (One Another at) the "Limits of Truth,"* 8, quoted in Robert, *Trials*, 36.

20. Robert, *Trials*, 36.

21. Zambrano, "Antígona," 2.

22. Loraux, *Divided City*, 101.

23. Zambrano, "Antígona," 1.

24. Zambrano, "Antígona," 2.

25. Zambrano, "Antígona," 2.

26. Antigone speaks as if Creon listened to and could hear her words and reasons, as if what she was saying could appear or, as Zambrano puts it, "be seen through the pores of someone's eyes" (esos poros que son en principio los ojos). Zambrano, "Antígona," 2. Her mouth opens "la boca del infierno" (the mouth of hell) (2) and brings the netherworld into the light so as to illuminate the darkness that shrouds her family past and reduces the temporality of the polis to the realm of "el ciego presente" (the blind present) (3).

27. Zambrano, *El hombre y lo divino*, 227.

28. Schürmann, *Broken Hegemonies*, 3.

29. In fact, there is a specific Greek term, *pathei mathos*, which designates knowledge gained through suffering.

30. Zambrano, "Historia y tragedia," 5.

31. Bush, "María Zambrano and the Survival of Antigone," 100.

32. Zambrano, "Antígona," 10.

33. Zambrano, "Antígona," 10.

34. Zambrano, *La razón en la sombra*, 386.

35. Zambrano, *La razón en la sombra*, 387.

36. Bush, "María Zambrano and the Survival of Antigone," 107.

37. Schürmann, *Broken Hegemonies*, 4

38. Zambrano, *La agonía de Europa*, 362.

39. Zambrano, *La agonía de Europa*, 355.

40. Derrida, *The Other Heading: Reflections on Today's Europe*, quoted in Gasché, "European Memories," 293.

41. Zambrano, *La agonía de Europa*, 378.

42. Regarding the relationship between philosophy and religion, Zambrano notes that "el esfuerzo mayor de la filosofía ha sido siempre el de neutralizar los efectos de los dioses" (the great struggle of philosophy has always been that of neutralizing the effects of the gods). Greek philosophy and, later, Christianity opted for "tomar partido del hombre" (taking man's side) as a way of achieving a degree of equality in human relationship with gods. *La agonía de Europa*, 353.

43. As shown in chapter 3, Miguel Espinosa's scathing critique of the ideology of Opus Dei rejected the sect's vision of material prosperity as a path to achieving the benefits of eternal life, because it collapsed the difference between this world and the other.

44. Nancy, "Political and/or Politics," 6; emphasis added.

45. Zambrano, *La agonía de Europa*, 336.

46. Zambrano, *La agonía de Europa*, 337.

47. Zambrano's critique of ideology that elevates success into the parameter for measuring the value of individual and social existence strongly evokes the ruling mentality of our neoliberal era.

48. Zambrano, *La agonía de Europa*, 336.

49. Zambrano, *La agonía de Europa*, 336. It might be difficult to make the same assertion about the tamed monster of Nature in the era of climate change. Still, Zambrano was clearly aware that there remained an element of danger in Nature.

50. Zambrano, *La agonía de Europa*, 334.

51. Moreiras, "The Last God," 182.

52. Moreiras, "The Last God," 183.

53. Esposito, "Community and Nihilism," 28.

54. Zambrano, *El hombre y lo divino*, 218.

55. Zambrano, *El hombre y lo divino*, 218.

56. Zambrano, *El hombre y lo divino*, 211.

57. Zambrano, *El hombre y lo divino*, 214.

58. Zambrano, *El hombre y lo divino*, 213.

AFTERWORD

1. Raúl Sánchez Cedillo, "Rajoynato, municipalismos, sistema de contrapo-
deres," *Transversal*, September 2017, http://eipcp.net/transversal/0916
/sanchezcedillo/1505647019.

2. Sánchez Cedillo, "Rajoynato," n.p.

3. Sánchez Cedillo, "Rajoynato," n.p.

4. Tiqqun, *Introduction to Civil War*, 70. I am grateful to the anonymous reviewer
whose comments led me to revisit Tiqqun's text.

5. Here, also, I wish to thank the anonymous reviewer for bringing to my attention Sánchez León and Izquierdo Martín's *La guerra que nos han contado y
la que no.*

6. Delgado, *La nación singular.*

7. Levinson, *Ends of Literature*, 6.

8. Levinson, *Ends of Literature*, 7.

9. Levinson, *Ends of Literature*, 7.

BIBLIOGRAPHY

Agamben, Giorgio. *Stasis: Civil War as a Political Paradigm*. Translated by Nicholas Heron. Palo Alto CA: Stanford University Press, 2015.

———. *State of Exception*. Translated by Kevin Attell. Chicago: University of Chicago Press, 2005.

Arendt, Hannah. *The Life of the Mind*. San Diego CA: Harvest/Harcourt Brace Jovanovich, 1978.

———. "No Longer and Not Yet." In *Essays in Understanding, 1930–1954; Formation, Exile and Totalitarianism*, 158–62. New York: Harcourt, Brace, 1994.

———. "On the Nature of Totalitarianism: An Essay in Understanding." In *Essays in Understanding, 1930–1954; Formation, Exile and Totalitarianism*, 304–28. New York: Harcourt, Brace, 1994.

———. *The Origins of Totalitarianism*. London: Allen and Unwin, 1967.

———. "What Is Freedom?" In *Between Past and Future: Eight Exercises in Political Thought*, 143–71. New York: Viking, 1961.

Arrese, José Luis de. *Obras seleccionadas de José Luis de Arrese*. Vol. 1, *Treinta años de política*. Madrid: Editora Nacional, 1966.

———. *Una etapa constituyente: Un testimonio básico sobre la marginación definitiva de la Falange por parte de Franco*. Barcelona: Editorial Planeta, 1982.

Artigues, Daniel. *El Opus Dei en España*. Paris: Ruedo Ibérico, 1971.

Badiou, Alain. *The Century*. Translated by Alberto Toscano. Cambridge MA: Polity Press, 2007.

———. *Ethics: An Essay on the Understanding of Evil*. Translated by Peter Hallward. London: Verso, 2013.

Bellón Aguilera, José Luis. *Miguel Espinosa, el autor emboscado*. Granada, Spain: Comares, 2012.

Bobbio, Norberto, Nicola Matteucci, and Gianfranco Pasquino. *Diccionario de Política*. Madrid: Siglo XXI, 1982.

Brioso, Jorge. "¿Cómo se lee una lengua muerta?" *Lectora* 15 (2009): 43–60.

Bush, Andrew. "María Zambrano and the Survival of Antigone." *Diacritics* 34, no. 3–4 (2004): 90–111.

Cacciari, Massimo. *Geo-filosofía de Europa*. Translated by Diego Sánchez Meca. Colección Sileno, no. 13. Madrid: Alderabán Editores, 2000.

Connolly, William. *Why I Am Not a Secularist*. Minneapolis: University of Minnesota Press, 2000.

Covarrubias, Sebastián. *Tesoro de la lengua castellana o española*. Edited by Ignacio Arellano and Rafael Zafra. Madrid: Iberoamericana-Vervuert, 2006.

Critchley, Simon. *The Faith of the Faithless: Experiments in Political Theology*. New York: Verso, 2012.

Crumbaugh, Justin. *Destination Dictatorship: The Spectacle of Spain's Tourist Boom and the Reinvention of Difference*. Albany: State University of New York Press, 2009.

Delgado, Luisa Elena. *La nación singular: Fantasías de la normalidad democrática Española (1996–2011)*. Madrid: Siglo XXI de España Editores, 2014.

Derrida, Jacques. *Aporias: Dying—Awaiting (On Another at) the "Limits of Truth."* Translated by Thomas Dutoit. Stanford CA: Stanford University Press, 1993.

———. *The Other Heading: Reflections on Todays Europe*. Translated by Pascale-Anne Brault and Michael Naas. Bloomington: Indiana University Press, 1992.

———. *Specters of Marx: The State of the Debt, the Work of Mourning, and the New International*. Translated by Peggy Kamuf. New York: Routledge, 1994.

Douzinas, Costas. "Notes Towards an Analytic of Resistance." *New Formations* 18 (2014): 79–98.

———. *Philosophy and Resistance in Crisis: Greece and the Future of Europe*. Cambridge: Polity Press, 2013.

Errejón, Iñigo. "Régimen." In *Lugares comunes: Trece voces sobre la crisis*, edited by Pablo Bustinduy and Jorge Lago, 175–96. Madrid: Lengua de Trapo, 2013.

Escrivá Balaguer, Josemaría. *El camino*. Madrid: Editorial Rialp, 2002. Available at http://www.escrivaobras.org/book/camino-indice.htm, accessed December 14, 2017.

Espinosa, Juan. *Miguel Espinosa, mi padre*. Granada, Spain: Comares, 1996.

Espinosa, Miguel. "Carta a Jean Tena." *Postdata* 4 (1987): 47.

———. *Escuela de mandarines.* 1974. Reprint, Madrid: Ediciones de la Torre, 2002.

———. *La fea burguesía.* Madrid, Alfaguara, 2006.

———. *Historia del eremita.* Madrid: Alfaqueque, 2012.

———. *Tríbada: Theologiae Tractatus.* Textos de Alcance, no. 18. Murcia, Spain: Editora Regional de Murcia, 1986.

Esposito, Roberto. "Community and Nihilism." Translated by Lorenzo Chiesa. *Cosmos and History* 5, no. 1 (2009): 24–36.

Fernández Prieto, Celia. "*Escuela de mandarines*: La destrucción del discurso autoritario." In *Miguel Espinosa: Congreso,* edited by Victorino Polo García, 369–84. Murcia: Editora Regional de Murcia.

Fernando Carvajal, Rodrigo. *La Constitución española.* Madrid: Editora Nacional, 1969.

Ferrán, Jaime, and Daniel P. Testa, eds. *Spanish Writers of 1936: Crisis and Commitment in the Poetry of the Thirties and Forties.* London: Tamesis, 1973.

Ferrando Badia, Juan. *El régimen de Franco: Un enfoque politico-jurídico.* Madrid: Tecnos, 1984.

Finer, Samuel E. *Theory and Practice of Modern Government.* Westport CT: Greenwood Press, 1970.

Flor, Fernando R. de la. "Miguel Espinosa: La construcción de la disidencia." *Tropelías: Revista de Teoría de la Literatura y Literatura Comparada* 3, no. 7 (2012): 148–71.

Fraga, Manuel. "El articulado de la Ley Fundamental de 17 de Mayo de 1958." *Arbor* 40, no. 151–52 (July 1958): 515–22.

———. *La crisis del estado.* Madrid: Aguilar, 1958.

———. *How Spain Is Governed.* Madrid: Diplomatic Information Office, 1950.

———. *El nuevo anti-Maquiavelo.* Madrid: Instituto de Estudios Políticos, 1962.

———. *Las transformaciones de la sociedad española contemporanea.* Madrid: Ediciones Del Movimiento, 1959.

Fueyo Alvarez, Jesús. *La época insegura.* Madrid: Ediciones Europa, 1962.

———. *Estudios de teoría política.* Madrid: Instituto de Estudios Políticos, 1968.

García Martínez, José. "¿Quién es Miguel Espinosa?" *Barcarola* 26 (July 1986): 190–96.

Gasché, Rodolph. "European Memories: Jan Patočka and Jacques Derrida on Responsibility." *Critical Inquiry* 23 (2007): 291–311.

Gracia, Jordi. *La resistencia silenciosa: Fascismo y cultura en España.* Barcelona: Anagrama, 2004.

———. *La vida Rescatada de Dionisio Ridruejo*. Barcelona: Anagrama, 2008.

Guillén Kalle, Gabriel. *Carl Schmitt en España: La frontera entre lo político y lo jurídico*. Madrid: n.p., 1996.

Halberstam, Michael. *Totalitarianism and the Modern Conception of Politics*. New Haven CT: Yale University Press, 1999.

Hallward, Peter. Translator's introduction to Badiou, *Ethics*, vii–xxxv.

Heidegger, Martin. *Parmenides*. Translated by André Schuwer and Richard Rojcewicz. Bloomington: Indiana University Press, 2009.

———. "The Question Concerning Technology." In *Basic Writings*, edited by David Farrell Krell, 3–36. New York: Harper & Row, 1977.

Hobbes, Thomas. *Leviathan*. Edited by Noel Malcolm. Oxford: Oxford University Press, 2012.

Iglesias Selgas, Carlos. *La via española a la democracia*. Madrid: Ediciones del Movimiento, 1968.

Juliá, Santos. *Historias de las dos Españas*. Madrid: Taurus. 2004.

———. "¿Falange liberal o intelectuales fascistas?" *Claves de razón práctica* 121 (2002): 4–13.

Kantorowitcz, Ernst H. *The King's Two Bodies. A Study in Medieval Political Theology*. 1957. Reprint, Princeton NJ: Princeton University Press, 1997.

Laín Entralgo, Pedro. *La generación del 98 y el problema de España*. 1945. Reprint, Madrid: Espasa Calpe, 1997.

———. *España como problema*. 2 vols. Madrid: Galaxia Gutenberg, 2005.

Legaz y Lacambra, Luis. *Introducción a la teoría del estado nacionalsindicalista*. Barcelona: Bosch, 1940.

Levinson, Brett. *The Ends of Literature. The Latin American "Boom" in the Neoliberal Marketplace*. Cultural Memory in the Present. Stanford CA: Stanford University Press, 2001.

Linz, Juan José. "An Authoritarian Regime: The Case of Spain." In *Reader in Political Sociology*, edited by Frank Lindenfeld, 129–48. New York: Funk & Wagnalls, 1968.

———. *Totalitarian and Authoritarian Regimes*. Boulder CO: Lynne Rienner, 2000.

López Martí, José. "El mundo como destrucción de la realidad." *Postdata* 4 (1987): 69–74. Available at http://fdgfdfgdgfdgfdg.blogspot.com/2015/11/el-mundo-como-destruccion-de-la.html, accessed December 14, 2017.

López, Isidro, and Emmanuel Rodríguez. "The Spanish Model." Translated by Brian Anglo. *New Left Review* 69, no. 2 (2011): 5–28.

Loraux, Nicole. *The Divided City: On Memory and Forgetting in Ancient Athens.* Translated by Corinne Pache and Jeff Fort. New York: Zone, 2006.

Moreiras, Alberto. "The Last God: Zambrano's Life without Texture." In *A Leftist Ontology: Beyond Relativism and Identity Politics,* edited by Carsten Strathausen, 170–84. Minneapolis: University of Minnesota Press, 2009.

Morente, Francisco. *Dionisio Ridruejo: Del fascismo al antifranquismo.* Madrid: Síntesis, 2006.

Nancy, Jean Luc. "The Political and/or Politics." *Oxford Literary Review* 36, no. 1 (2007): 5–17.

Ortega y Gasset, José. "Del imperio romano." In *Obras Completas.* Vol. 6, *1941–1946,* 83–135. Madrid: Revista de Occidente, 1952.

Polo García, Victorino, ed. *Miguel Espinosa: Congreso.* Murcia: Editora Regional de Murcia, 1995.

Ramos Ruíz, Isabel. *Profesores, alumnos y saberes en la Universidad de Salamanca en el Rectorado de D. Antonio Tovar (1951–1956).* Salamanca, Spain: Ediciones Universidad de Salamanca, 2009.

Ridruejo, Dionisio. *Diario de una tregua.* Madrid: Destinolibro, 1972.

———. *Escrito en España.* Edited by Jordi García. Madrid: Centro de Estudios Políticos y Constitucionales, 1962.

———. *Hasta la fecha: Poesías completas 1934–1959.* Madrid: Aguilar, 1961.

———. *Materiales para una biografía* [Collected works]. Edited by Jordi Gracia. Colección Obra Fundamental. Madrid: Fundación Santander Central Hispano, 2005. Available at www.cervantesvirtual.com/descargaPdf/materiales -para-una-biografia—0/, accessed December 14, 2017.

Robert, William. *Trials: Of Antigone and Jesus.* New York: Fordham University Press, 2010.

Rosales, Luis. "A Dionisio Ridruejo, por su libro Elegías." In *Obras completas.* Vol. 4, *Ensayos de filosofía y literatura,* 700–701. Edited by Felix Grande, Antonio Hernández, and Guadalupe Grande. Madrid: Editorial Trotta, 1997.

Ruiz de Castillo, Carlos. "Las entidades sociales en el Estado Nacional." *Arbor* 151–52 (1958): 384–92.

Sánchez León, Pablo, and Jesús Izquierdo. *La guerra que nos han contado y la que no: memoria e historia de 1936 para el siglo XXI.* Madrid: Postmetrópolis Editorial, 2017.

Sánchez Navarro, Angel J. *La transición española en sus documentos.* Madrid: Boletín Oficial del Estado/Centro de Estudios Políticos y Constitucionales, 1998.

Sanz Villanueva, Santos. "Espinosa y el arte de la denuncia." In *Miguel Espinosa: Congreso*, edited by Victorino Polo García, 177–209. Murcia: Editora Regional de Murcia, 1995.

Saz Campos, Ismael. *Las caras del franquismo*. Granada: Editorial Comares, 2013.

———. *Fascismo y franquismo*. Valencia: Universitat de Valencia, 2004.

Schmitt, Carl. *The Concept of the Political*. Chicago: University of Chicago Press, 1996.

———. *Legalidad y legitimidad*. Translated by José Díaz García. Madrid: Aguilar, 1971.

———. *Legality and Legitimacy*. Translated by Jeffrey Seitzer. 1932. Reprint, Raleigh NC: Duke University Press, 2004.

———. *Political Theology: Four Chapters on the Concept of Sovereignty*. Translated by George D. Schwab. Cambridge MA: MIT Press, 1985.

———. *Political Theology II: The Myth of the Closure of Any Political Theology*. Translated and introduced by Michael Hoelzl and Graham Ward. Cambridge: Polity, 2008.

———. *Roman Catholicism and Political Form*. Translated by G. L. Ulmen. Westport CT: Greenwood Press, 1996.

Schürmann, Reiner. *Broken Hegemonies*. Translated by Reginald Lilly. Bloomington: Indiana University Press, 2003.

Sontag, Susan. "Fascinating Fascism." In *Under the Sign of Saturn: Essays*, 73–109. New York: Vintage, 1981.

Taylor, Charles. *Hegel*. Cambridge: Cambridge University Press, 1977.

Tiqqun. *Introduction to Civil War*. Translated by Alexander R. Galloway and Jason E. Smith. Los Angeles: Semiotext(e), 2010.

Unamuno, Miguel de. *Vida de Don Quijote y Sancho*. 1905. Reprint, Madrid: Ediciones Cátedra, 2005.

Vardoulakis, Dimitris. "Stasis: Beyond Political Theology?" *Cultural Critique* 73 (2009): 125–47.

———. *Stasis before the State: Nine Theses on Agnostic Democracy*. New York: Fordham University Press, 2018.

Vilarós, Teresa M. *El mono del desencanto: Una crítica cultural de la transición española 1973–1993*. Madrid: Siglo XXI, 1998.

———. "*La fea burguesía* de Miguel Espinosa: El pre- y el post- del desencanto español." In *Miguel Espinosa: Congreso*, edited by Victorino Polo García, 675–84. Murcia: Editora Regional de Murcia, 1995.

Villacañas, José Luis. *Ramiro de Maeztu y el ideal de la burguesía en España*. Madrid: Espasa-Calpe, 2000.

Zambrano, María. *La agonía de Europa*. In *Obras completas*. Vol. 2, 327–93. Edited by Jesús Moreno Sanz. Barcelona: Galaxia Gutenberg Círculo de Lectores, 2016.

———. "Antígona. La República. La Guerra Civil. La Historia." Manuscript M-517. Fundación María Zambrano, ca. 1966.

———. "Un capítulo de la palabra: 'el idiota' (homenaje a Velázquez)." In *España, sueño y verdad*. In *Obras completas*. Vol. 3, 610–825. Edited by Jesús Moreno Sanz. Barcelona: Galaxia Gutenberg Círculo de Lectores, 2011.

———. *España, sueño y verdad*. In *Obras completas*. Vol. 3. Edited by Jesús Moreno Sanz. Barcelona: Galaxia Gutenberg Círculo de Lectores, 2011.

———. "Historia y tragedia." Manuscript M-13. Fundación María Zambrano, n.d.

———. *El hombre y lo divino*. In *Obras completas*. Vol. 3, 99–359. Edited by Jesús Moreno Sanz. Barcelona: Galaxia Gutenberg Círculo de Lectores, 2011.

———. *Persona y democracia*. In *Obras completas*. Vol. 3, 363–501. Edited by Jesús Moreno Sanz. Barcelona: Galaxia Gutenberg Círculo de Lectores, 2011.

———. *La razón en la sombra: Antología crítica*. Edited by Jesús Moreno Sanz. Madrid: Siruela, 2004.

———. *La tumba de Antígone*. Madrid: Mondadori, 1989.

Žižek, Slavoj. "Eastern European Liberalism and Its Discontents." In *The Universal Exception*, 13–33. London: Continuum, 2007.

INDEX

*Hearing Voices: Aurality and New Spanish Sound
Culture in Sor Juana Inés de la Cruz*
By Sarah Finley

*Hercules and the King of Portugal: Icons of
Masculinity and Nation in Calderón's Spain*
By Dian Fox

*Paradoxes of Stasis: Literature, Politics,
and Thought in Francoist Spain*
By Tatjana Gajić

To order or obtain more information on these or other
University of Nebraska Press titles, visit nebraskapress.unl.edu.

CPSIA information can be obtained
at www.ICGtesting.com
Printed in the USA
LVHW091448051218
599363LV00005B/58/P